TRAVELLING ALONG WI

CW01024817

FOR

Joseph, Rachel and George

Travelling along with Methodism

A personal retrospect

Frank Garforth

One more step along the world I go,
One more step along the world I go;
From the old things to the new
Keep me travelling along with you.

Sydney Carter

Christygate
1990

© F. W. Garforth

First published in 1990 by Christygate Press, Arkangel, Westerdale, Whitby, North Yorkshire, YO21 2DT.

British Library Cataloguing in Publication Data
Garforth, F. W. (Francis William) *1917-*
    Travelling along with Methodism.
    1. Great Britain. Methodist churches. Biographies
    I. Title
    287.5092

    ISBN 0-948340-01-0

Printed by
William Sessions Ltd
The Ebor Press
York, England

Preface

THIS BOOK HAS A NUMBER OF INTERWOVEN THEMES. Embracing them all is my growing up within the ambience of Methodism; this is the justification for the title, and indeed for the book itself. I have tried to show what it has been like for me to be 'a child of the manse', to have been brought up, to have grown up and grown older within the embrace of Wesleyanism and, later, Methodism. It is a personal statement, not a historical documentary; this theme, therefore, is an undercurrent supporting the rest and not, I hope, unduly obtrusive.

A theme which occupies most of Part I is my formal education at school and university. Much of this Part is simple narrative and, I hope, pleasantly readable to anyone but of special interest to those who have shared with me the same educational institutions. Lighthearted at times it reflects something of the delights of being young, as well as suggesting what it was like to grow up, to be a child, a boy, an adolescent in those distant decades of the 1920s and 1930s. Obviously, because I am I *and* a child of the manse, this too is a personal statement; but it is not, I think, untypical of its time and situation.

But Part I is more than narrative. Because my life's work has been in education, I have written from the critical stance of an educationist surveying his own education and remarking on its virtues and defects (always, however, with gratitude for the positive good that it gave me). This is another theme. From it there should emerge an impression of what it was like to be at school in the 1920s and 1930s and how greatly educational thought and practice have changed in the past fifty years. There should also emerge some indication of my profound belief in the lasting effects of early environment. In chapters 1–7 this critical appraisal is incidental to the narrative. In chapter 8, however, I have attempted a summary assessment of my education; some readers may prefer to skip this and go straight on to Part II.

Travelling along with Methodism has been a lifelong process which is not yet over. Part II is concerned with my spiritual experience and spiritual growth (such as it has been) and pertains mostly to my later years. Chapter 11 attempts to summarise what have been for me the most influential and attractive aspects of Methodism.

From a very early age I have been aware, at first mainly through nature, of an element of mystery in life, of a pressure, intermittent but insistent, as of another dimension. There are hints of it in chapters 1–7, but it is given more explicit expression in Part II, whose title, 'Through a Glass Darkly', is explained in the introduction. Hence comes another important theme. I am a sceptic both by nature and by philosophical training; so it has not been easy to confine this sense of mystery within the limitations of doctrine. But in Jesus as Christ I find the most persuasive answer to my sceptical questioning. I have been a committed Christian for fifty years and a lay preacher for forty-five; Christianity, and Methodism in particular, have formulated for me that sense of a 'presence' which has 'disturbed' me all my life, and they have enabled its expression in credal form. This does not mean that all mystery is resolved, all questions answered; in fact the mystery deepens as I come nearer to the end of life. The Incarnation is itself the greatest mystery of all! But I am content to accept mystery as an essential ingredient of life, a haunting mark of interrogation which recedes elusively and inevitably before the advance of knowledge.

Readers or potential readers may well ask what is special about me that I should put myself into print and expect that anyone should be interested to read it. There is *nothing* special about *me*; but in many ways my experience is typical of those who have been brought up within the manse; typical too of the period of my education and early years in those two decades, a period now so long past that it is worth recalling for its contrast to the present time. So, although this is a personal statement, it is also representative of a kind of growing up, conditioned by time and circumstance, as much as descriptive of my own. It is as such that I offer it to the reader.

Finally, a word about the book's title. I had planned originally to call it 'Growing up with Methodism', taking 'growing up' in the sense of a lifelong process. However, it was pointed out to me that this might be interpreted to indicate a handbook of how to grow up a good Methodist. In the present title the words 'travelling along with' echo Sydney Carter's well known hymn (*Hymns and Psalms* no. 746) three of whose verses and the chorus end with the line 'Keep me travelling along with you' – the 'you' being God. In the title 'travelling' includes not only the notion of a lifelong pilgrimage, but also the suggestion of an itinerant ministry, the move from circuit to circuit (three-yearly in the 1920s and early '30s). This latter is an essential ingredient of Methodism and necessarily involved my father and his family.

The subtitle, I hope, explains itself without ambiguity.

Acknowledgements

MY GRATEFUL THANKS ARE DUE to the very many who have made possible the writing and publication of this book. I owe to my parents, to the Methodist Church and to my teachers and lecturers a debt which can never be fully appreciated or repaid. They gave me so much whose value I did not recognise at the time.

Francesca and our children have all read the manuscript in whole or part at various stages in its writing; so too has my brother, the Rev. J. L. Garforth, and my nephew, Richard Garforth, who is a chemistry teacher and Housemaster at Kingswood. The Kingswood chapters have been read by: Mr L. J. Campbell, Headmaster from 1970 to 1987; Mr G. M. Best, the present Headmaster; Mr J. W. Gardner, for many years Senior Classics and Second Master; Mr Michael Bishop, formerly Director of Studies and now Warden of the school's Wesley Centre; the Rev. Rupert E. Davies, the school's first Chaplain and later a President of the Methodist Conference. The last named has read the whole manuscript. Mr R. G. Vernon, who taught French at Magnus Grammar School throughout his professional career and for many years was Head of French, has read the Newark chapter. A number of friends have also read the manuscript in whole or part; these include Derrick Beacock and Jean and Eric Chicken. Mr Richard York of William Sessions Ltd., the Ebor Press, has given me valuable advice on many matters relating to the printing and publication of the book. There are others whom I should record, but unfortunately my memory does not suffice to recall them. To all these, named and unnamed, I am enormously indebted for correction, comment and advice. Needless to say, I alone am responsible for what is written in the following pages.

Once again Francesca has helped with reading the proofs and in many other ways.

The photograph of the Wesleyan School at Barnard Castle was supplied by George Holdsworth and Son, Scholastic Photo Specialists, Hartlepool. For the photograph of the Methodist church at Barny I am indebted to Mrs June Luckhurst, who has made a photographic record of all the Methodist churches in Teesdale. The photographs of Magnus Grammar School and of Newark were supplied by Queens Court Studios, Newark. I have not been able to trace the copyright owners of the aerial views of Kingswood, and I apologise herewith for any unintentional breach of copyright. The other photograph of Kingswood and that of Kelston Round Hill were taken by my nephew Richard. The photo of Mr W. I. Tidswell, my classics master in the first year sixth, was taken, unknown to him and by whom I cannot remember, through a hole in the back of a file. The print is well preserved after fifty-five years and was copied for reproduction here by Newland Studios of Hull. My son Michael took the photographs of Queens' College, Cambridge.

Permission to quote, on the title page, the first verse of Sydney Carter's hymn (*Hymns and Psalms* no. 746) was kindly granted by Stainer and Bell Ltd.

Contents

Illustrations

PART I

Child of the Manse

CHAPTER I

Early Years

I WAS BORN IN CEYLON (Sri Lanka if you prefer it) at a place called Jaffna in the north of the island. The date was July 3rd, 1917, when the so-called Great War was still deadlocked in the mud of Flanders. But that was another world whose bloody reverberations, despite the naval base at Trincomalee, scarcely ruffled the sunny palms of my birthplace.

My father was a Wesleyan minister whose 'call' was to serve on what was known as 'the mission field'. He was posted to Ceylon in 1905; my mother, an elementary school teacher, followed later and they were married in Colombo on August 25th, 1909. The bride (so reported a local newspaper of the area whence my father came) 'looked graceful and charming' in her 'Empire dress of cream grenadine', her wreath of orange blossom and bouquet of white carnations and maiden-hair. Alas that I never knew her in the prime of her beauty; there was little of it in the faded sepia of the wedding group that for years stood on our piano. Nor was it till long after their deaths that I thought of my parents as lovers and of my mother as a tender bride who sailed 5000 miles into the unknown to join her beloved. The reality first came home to me when I had to renew my passport in 1970.

1

A change in the law required me to produce not only my birth certificate but my parents' marriage certificate, and of this latter I could find no trace. So off I went to London, first to a sub-department of the Home Office, Dickensian in its dismal furniture and matchwood consultation booths (good enough, perhaps it was thought, for the immigrants who thronged it). I explained my position to a clerk in his kennel, who was evidently surprised at the colour of my skin, and showed him my birth certificate. 'At least,' he said, with an unexpected twitch of humour, 'you can see you're not a bastard !' But it was not enough to get me a passport. I went next to the Ceylon High Commission in Hyde Park. Here a charming Sinhalese lady listened patiently to my plight and gave me an address to write to in Colombo. This latter episode, so brief and delightful, was my nearest contact with the land of my birth in the fifty years since I left it.

Six weeks later the certificate arrived, impressively detailed in three languages. As I stared at it, the bold typescript flashed into novel significance: my parents too had loved, fondled, embraced and begotten children. Then for a moment the faded photograph was infused with colour, with tropical scents and sunshine, and I knew at last and too late that I shared with them in life and in death a common humanity.

In the early 1900s much of the world was coloured red. Empire, however, meant more than possession and trade ; it was an opportunity to evangelise. And an obligation too :

> Can we, whose souls are lighted
> With wisdom from on high,
> Can we to men benighted
> The lamp of life deny?

– thus the rendering of the Wesleyan and the Methodist hymn-books for a century or more and now at last excluded from the 1983 edition. For fifteen years my father carried the lamp devotedly until, in 1920, malaria and overwork compelled him to relinquish it for the more prosaic task of preaching to the converted back in Britain.

Of this period of his life and work I know little ; memory was too young to record (I was two and a half when he returned), and the snatches of reminiscence overheard from time to time never pieced themselves into a coherent picture. But I caught enough of names and words, of scene and incident, to make Ceylon a part of me. Beautiful names, like Trincomalee, Amradhapura, Batticaloa, have lent me their music through the years ; Kandy, Mannar and Point Pedro, taking substance from photograph and anecdote, were enlarged by childhood fantasy into a heaven of sunshine, blue seas and lush vegetation abounding in elephants, tortoises and other exotic creatures. Of these last there were constant reminders. Two elephants carved from a single round of coconut palm were my constant play-companions; a tortoise-shell, home of a family pet until its demise, stood for years on successive hearths as we moved from house to house. And there was innumerable brassware – cobras, lizards, more elephants, oriental gods perplexing my childish innocence by the full frontal display of their fecundities, magnificent brass trays laboriously beaten out by hammer and nail into incredible minutiae of pictorial detail (shall I ever forget the smell of Brasso as the shining metal emerged from its monthly polishing?). Words too of eastern (I think Tamil) origin were part of our daily discourse: talk of our *ayah*, so much loved and respected, recurred for years in table conversation; insects of any species were *poochees*; and *chicka* was the family name both for penis and for its use in urinating (I had no sisters!).

Of Ceylon itself I have no direct memory, though I like to believe that my early impressions, retained in the subconscious, have left some mark in range of sympathy and mental outlook. Dimly I seem to recollect being held in my father's arms at the ship's rail as it passed the volcano Stromboli en route for England *via* Naples; but this could well be fantasy or photograph instead of reality. My first undeniable memories belong to Sleights, a village near Whitby, and to the North Yorkshire Moors.

While in Ceylon my parents met and became close friends of a lady of independent means who was working there as an unpaid lay missionary. She owned a house on the edge of the moors at Glaisdale (two stations up the line from Sleights), an old stone-built farmhouse converted into a pleasant country residence. It was she who suggested that, for the year allowed my father to recover his health, she find us a house nearby. Which she duly did, a house in Sleights, white-painted with a balcony overlooking the village street. Dear Auntie Mabel, as we affectionately knew her, you gave me more than ever you could have guessed!

For it was here and in the fields and moors round about that I absorbed into my impressionable years that love of the sights, sounds and smells of the countryside which has been with me ever since. We had a maid for a time, a domestic help who took me for walks in the afternoon. Sometimes we would go down the hill to the River Esk and pick up sticks for kindling; here I remember vividly, as though still touching the nostrils, the damp smell of the vegetation; I remember still the sunlit, chattering water and the song of birds; and they come back to me not just as nostalgic memories but with a touch of mystery, of glimpses into an unknown. Sometimes we went up the hill, up Blue Bank (devoid of traffic then save for the occasional horse and cart), and on to the moors. Here there was space, wind and the sea in the distance – an enlarged perspective, different also from the riverside in its shapes, sounds and colours.

It was on one of these latter occasions, I remember, that the fact of death first touched my infant awareness. A funeral passed us as we walked up the village street towards the moors and inevitably I asked what was in the long box in front. Our maid, I am sure, did the best she could, but I was left with a savour of something more than mystery – a touch of fear, a sense of incompletion, an intimation of mortality.

Of my father's activities at this time I have no memory. Partly it was convalescence, partly what was called in Wesleyan circles 'deputation', that is being available to speak at Missionary Meetings and Anniversaries anywhere in that northern area. My mother's prime task was to unravel the knots of English shopping and catering, themselves barely recovering from the war, after ten years with servants and a cook. My brother, some years older, attended the village school, still standing in its solid, sturdy stone at the foot of Blue Bank. But there was time for picnics, especially for picking bilberries, which grew profusely on the moor, and their delicate flavour was a welcome addition to our straitened apple tart. Again, names have lent me their beauty – Littlebeck and Ruswarp, Iburndale and Ugglebarnby.

Most of all, however, I remember Auntie Mabel's house at Glaisdale. It was stone-built, of course, beyond the village, where the moor began; across the road was a pond for ducks, and beyond this a path across the open space where curlews wheeled and treeled and golden plovers camouflaged their elusive lament. Many were our visits there in the year we spent at Sleights, and later holidays reinforced my early impressions.

These are of scent and sound as much as of sight. Domestic water came from a shallow well in the front garden; a hand pump in the kitchen piped it to the main cistern, but for table use it was drawn direct by hand. With Bessie, Auntie Mabel's maid, I would go down the stone flags to the well and, as she held me, dip the jug, watch it slowly fill and lift it spilling on to the steps until her stronger hand took charge. Still there lingers in memory the cool, fresh scent of the water, infused with the dankness of moss and fern, and the sharp splish of the jug's drip reflected from the stone sides and the roof of the well. There was the kitchen too, spacious and stone-flagged and possessed of an indefinable fragrance which long years of baking and roasting, washing, ironing and scrubbing had subtly imparted to the fabric of wall and floor and furniture.

On stormy nights wind and rain swept straight off the moor, threshed through the trees and roared through the virginia creeper with imagined menace as I lay half-sleeping through its turbulence. Sometimes there was thunder, which the encircling valleys clasped to themselves in shattering reverberation until it burst protesting into the open heavens; and lightning too which struck zig-zag across the sky and gave to the moor for that instant of stunning brilliance a strange quality of lunar landscape. But there were quiet times, summer days of warmth and beauty, when the air was rich with the scent of heather, and when the bleating of sheep and the hoarse chuckle of grouse came drifting lazily over bent and bracken amid the steady background drone of bees.

It was one such day, years later when I was in my teens, that I set off for a day's walk, without map or compass, and lost myself in what seemed endless undecipherable miles of heather. There was no National Park then, no tarmac roads across the moor, and hikers were a rare phenomenon. Eventually, about teatime, I found my way to Goathland and thence by a road I knew to Glaisdale and a late supper.

It was an experience both frightening (at times at least), but also strangely enriching; for in a full day such as that, alone with the sights and sounds and scents of the moor, its changing shapes and colours as one slope emerges from another, its varied moods as morning yields to the full blaze of noon and this in turn to the contented peace of evening – in such a day one absorbs the moor into oneself, identifies with it, not just as a medley of sound, scent and colour, but as a living entity possessed of that 'something far more deeply interfused' that Wordsworth discovered in the Lakeland hills.

The early years, so Plato told us long ago and others have since reaffirmed, are the most receptive; it is then that children are most easily moulded 'and when any impression we choose to make leaves a permanent mark'. Not only those that are *chosen*, I hasten to add, but those too which come by chance circumstance. For it was not my parents' choice, no part of any deliberate educational programme, that for one of those early impressionable years I should grow up amid the moors and absorb their qualities. Not that I was aware of doing so, of course; and no doubt much of what I have claimed to remember of that year has been enlarged by imagination into an experience profounder than the reality. Yet perhaps not. For as we now know (and Plato did not – or not in Freudian terms) there are deeper levels of the mind, impenetrable to conscious memory, which hold and brood over perceptions and events to which at the time we give no more than fleeting notice; yet from these depths there issue forth, often in perplexing novelty, feelings, moods, ideas that shape us permanently and unpredictably.

So, I believe, it has been with me. For although there have been periods of many years when I have been unable to visit these Yorkshire moorlands, they have retained for me a fascination, a sense of mystery, of invitation, as if (like Odysseus and his Circe) to the bosom of an enchantress. Things have changed of course, both for me and for the moors. I have become familiar with other parts than Glaisdale and its vicinity – Fryup and Danby Dale, Westerdale, Rosedale, Bilsdale and Cropton Forest, each contributing from its own uniqueness to a broader total pattern. The lights of Teesside impose on the northern sky an artificial aurora which dims the true brilliance of the stars and warns of an encroaching urban civilisation of which my childhood was unaware. And there are other moorland areas which I have come to know and love: the mountain-girt solemnity of Rannoch, with its tangle of peat, burn and lochan; the vast acres of Sutherland held between the hills of Wester Ross and the blue waters of Moray; and those lonely uplands of the central Pennines from Middleton to Alston, whose natural pastures are heady in summer with the scent and bloom of innumerable flowers. Within this enlarged perspective the moors seem smaller, yet also (and perhaps because of this) more intimate; they have lost the restricted horizons of childhood, but the fascination remains.

If Plato is right, the moors have given me something else, though they are not, I think, the only source of it. I mean that love of nature which has been part of me for as long as I can remember. By 'love' I mean not just an interest in living things, a curiosity about natural laws and processes, nor simply the enjoyment of natural beauty or of activity in the open air. There is something deeper still which I find difficult to analyse into its components and harder still to express. Time and again, and not only among these moors, I have felt 'a presence that disturbs' – disturbs with a thrill of fear, of mystery, of incompletion, and at the same time soothes with an assurance that the mystery will be resolved, the incompletion in due time brought to fulfilment. With this has come a feeling of affinity with, of absorption into, the particular aspect of nature experienced at the time, whether large scale or small, of sight or of sound. And with it too has come the echo of a message, felt rather than heard, and only on the rarest of occasions expressible in words. 'Love' is not perhaps the best word for all this, but there is no other in English which expresses with even such partial adequacy the intensity of diverse emotions resolving from their climax into restful contentment.

On rare occasions the experience has crystallised, spontaneously and without conscious effort, in verbal form. The last occurrence was some twenty years ago when I was on holiday with my family in Northumberland. As we walked through trees and heather towards a nearby hill, we saw a lizard sunning itself on a rock by the side of the

track; and once again that strange mental alchemy distilled itself into
words:

> Spring-poised in taut anticipation,
> immobile on the impassive rock
> it hung,
> mothered, it seemed, from the same rich pregnancy
> that shaped the lichen-tinted sandstone
> whose borrowed colours
> merged the living with the dead
> in a deft artistry of concealment.
>
> Time also hung suspended;
> the fertile silence echoed
> with the images of monsters
> spawned from the fossil past's fantastic womb,
> drowned all in the abyss of mortality
> save for this little relic
> rescued from the wreck and wrack
> thus to seize my thoughts in wonder
> and fling them wide-eyed
> down evolution's enigmatic labyrinths.

The experiences have continued, but there has been no further flow of
words.

What the psychologists would make of it all I do not know – attribute it
perhaps to some Freudian complex, to a death-wish or a suppressed
desire to return to the womb. Maybe there are such psychological roots
for these experiences, so utterly possessing in their felt intensity and so
rarely caught in words, and for that deep relief I feel when I escape from
the city's claustrophobic pressure into the spacious, soothing solitude of
moor and mountain. I prefer to think of them as the choice fruit of that
distant year when the moors made their first impact on the dawning of
childhood consciousness.

I have come to know the moors far better since those early years and
in more intimate detail. Increasing knowledge has changed my response
to them; for I see them now, not simply as a manifestation of nature's
wildness and beauty, but also as a part of history. Imagination peoples
them with skin-clad tribesmen who lived on the tops and came down
through forested slopes (as they once were) to forage and maraud. I see
the moors too as part of a larger, cosmic process that has shaped them to
what they are, creating beneath their living surface a geological structure
which supports and feeds it. The moors themselves have come alive with
creatures of which my childhood knew nothing – woodcock and

greenshank, snowbunting, ringouzels and winter flocks of fieldfares and redwings. I have listened to the croak of frogs in moorland pools, watched the tiny scampering of shrews across the turf, the upthrust of soil from burrowing moles and the patient stoat in his bright russet deftly stalking his prey. One winter morning we woke to find eight feet of snow across the road outside and the moors transformed to a rare beauty tinged with the stark reality of isolation; and in that vast whiteness the cock pheasants strutted brilliant in the winter sun. And of course we have come to know the people, whose kindliness enhances the quality of life and whose rural skills and crafts are manifest in the routine of farming and the annual village shows.

To all this add the June evenings heavy with the lush fragrance of verdant growth, the December mornings when the moors are brilliant in reds and browns; add the smell of wood smoke and the delicious tang of burning peat; add the walks, the picnics, the village cricket, sunset and sunrise across the valleys and the ceaseless rhythm of growth and change – to be involved in this, to become part of it and thus in a sense immortalised! If only Auntie Mabel could have known how much she gave me!

She was small, plump and warm, with pink cheeks which were soft to the touch of my goodnight kiss; her hair was netted and her clothes demurely fashioned. She was a staunch Wesleyan devoted to her church, to which, I now know, she gave generously from independent means. I picture her fussing gently over the plants in her conservatory or over the splendid meals which must be precisely cooked and served. Her affectionate concern for our family I am content to have received gratefully without understanding the reasons; she was unmarried and when we knew her had no nephews or nieces. She lies now under the moorland turf in the graveyard at Glaisdale Head.

CHAPTER II

Cornwall

AT THE END OF HIS YEAR of convalescence and 'deputation' my father was appointed to a small Wesleyan 'circuit' (such is still, in what is now the Methodist Church, the official terminology) centred on Redruth in Cornwall. Whether he had any choice in the matter I do not know. The Wesleyan Church appointed clergy to its circuits through a system of invitations which were issued by circuit committees to particular men who, in one way or another, were regarded as specially suitable. If a man received no invitation, or none that he could accept, he was directed by a central committee to where a vacancy existed. Perhaps this happened to my father who, having spent the whole of his ministry so far in Ceylon, was virtually unknown in this country.

In the Methodist Church of today the same system prevails; when an invitation has been issued by the circuit committee and accepted by the chosen minister, the appointment must be sanctioned (as it usually is) by the central Stationing Committee. A small number of ministers have rejected the system, deeming it more consistent with Gospel teaching to go wherever their superiors might consider it appropriate to send them. My father was not among these, and when I was older I became uncomfortably aware from their talk at table of my parents' rising hopes, disappointments and tensions during the period when invitations were expected. Supposedly the system is more democratic and more sensitive to the match of a minister's peculiar qualities – preaching, pastoral, administrational or whatever – with local needs. But it lends itself, like all democratic institutions, to distortion by wire-pulling and the pressure of influence, self-assertion and popular repute.

However it may have been with my father, in September 1921 we found ourselves transported from one end of England to another, from the rigours of a northern climate to the more temperate air of the south west. In some ways the scene was not so different. There were moors

9

close by, though not the great expanses I had known in Yorkshire; the sea too was near, with cliffs and beaches and rocky bays not unlike the coast from Scarborough northwards. In other ways there was total contrast. Redruth as I remember it (unjustly perhaps) was a grey, dull little town, founded both economically and, alas, literally on tin mining. Red turgid liquid poured from mine sluices into streams whose pollution was further fouled by a variety of refuse.

It was by one of these streams that the fact of death again touched me with chilling perplexity. I was out for a walk with Gwen, our maid, when a man passed us carrying a sack. At the water's edge he stopped, pushed the sack below the surface and held it there. Curious, I asked him what was in it. It was a cat, he said, which was no longer wanted, and this was the easiest way of getting rid of it. Curiosity turned to a fascinated horror; I pictured the cat inside (we had one at home at the time) and tried to imagine the manner of its dying. The 'long box' at Sleights flashed through my memory and again there came that intimation of mortality with its disturbing sense of incompletion.

It came too when, as happened from time to time, a house partially collapsed into a mine shaft over which it had been unwittingly sited. For the whole area was riddled with such shafts which had never been mapped and whose existence, masked by an accumulation of debris, was now totally forgotten. Walls and roofs would cave in or totter crazily, exposing the intimate furniture of home life – a piano poised on the rim of a gaping hole, books, blankets and chamber-pots, the twisted wreckage of gas fittings. Here had been life, love, security, all of them shattered in a ruin as ruthless as it was unexpected.

There is not much else that I remember of Redruth and its environs. We lived in a terrace house in a street which sloped down towards a main road and looked beyond that to Carn Brea, a local picnic spot where there were huge granite boulders with marks on them like the impressions of giant fingers. Across the valley is a viaduct carrying the then Great Western line to Penzance; the trains always whistled as they crossed it – poo-woop, poo-woop – and then disappeared into the cutting beyond. This, of course, gave me a theme for games, and I would puff and whistle up and down the street, arms pistoning to and fro as I drove my imaginary trains from Redruth to the seaside beaches of Carbis Bay and St Ives. The modern diesels, alas, are no match for the beauty of those GWR engines, dark green and polished brass, whose bright steel rods and massive driving wheels displayed so dramatically the forces that powered them.

Of the surrounding countryside, apart from Carn Brea, I remember almost nothing. Beauty there must have been in the lush pastures and woods of the Cornish climate; and we had our family walks and picnics here as in Yorkshire; but, curiously, they have left no impression – ousted from memory, perhaps, by more vivid recollections of our summer holidays by the sea.

It was to St Ives we went each summer of our three years in Cornwall. We stayed in boarding-houses at the expense, I suspect, of one of my real aunts, my mother's sister, who had married money; for the cost of a fortnight for a family of four must surely have been beyond the means of my father's meagre stipend (another Wesleyan term which was part of our household vocabulary). The train journey was a delight both in anticipation and in actuality. We were taken to the station by pony and cart, and there in a jostle of excitement we waited for the first glimpse of the engine and its cream and brown coaches emerging from the tunnel. A whiff of smoke and oily steam, the flash of burnished handles and the fire blazing beneath them, and then we were in the carriage, scrambling for the corner seats as my father piled the luggage on the rack.

It was a short journey to St Erth, the junction for St Ives, and there was our train already waiting and the engine crew munching impassively at their Cornish pasties. From St Erth the line follows the margin of Hayle Sands, coming so close to the sea at Lelant that we could look straight down into the clear green water and marvel at the waving strands of seaweed and the occasional jellyfish. A mile or two on and the bay opened out to give us a view of the opposite coast and Godrevy lighthouse standing sentinel on its rocky outcrop washed by white-capped waves; then along the cliffs to Carbis Bay and finally, joy of joys, St Ives.

It was a glorious place then, with its golden sands, its rocky Island (so called), the cliffs of Clodgy, the great open bay, and always Godrevy at that far point where the coast curved north and east towards Portreath. At night the flash of the light came beaming through the bedroom window, slowly building up (as I remember it) to a sudden brilliance which briefly etched the patterns of the wallpaper and then extinguished them in total darkness. All night long it went on, that same persistent rhythm of illumination; but I was asleep long before I reached the 100 flashes I set myself to count.

The days were mostly spent on the beach. My brother and I dug 'rabbit holes' and built castles with spiral tracks to roll our 'sorbo' balls down; or else we made elaborate traps – deep holes covered with a criss-cross of sticks and a layer of sand and then left for the unwary to step into and plunge headlong (as indeed, to our merriment, they did!). Canvas beach tents, donkey-rides, ice-cream sandwiches and lemonade – these were all part of the familiar scene. Unforgettable is the smell of the sweaty leather on the patient donkeys and the flavour of moist wafers clutched in hot, sandy, salty hands. Unforgettable too the sticky, fizzy lemonade dispensed in pinch-necked bottles and sealed with glass marbles (this was long before the days of snap-open tins) which clicked and rattled as we jogged them back empty to the stall.

Sometimes we walked along the northern Porthmear beach to Clodgy Point and then on the cliff top towards Land's End (far beyond our reach, of course, but held out to us enticingly as a distant, end-of-the-world goal for 'when you are older'). It was beautiful there on a clear sunny day. The cliffs are not high compared with the enormous granite stacks around Cape Wrath or the sheer chalk of Flamborough; but to me they were impressive. I can picture still with unabated clarity the deep green of the sea washing on the rocky base below, feel still the freshness blowing cool from the Atlantic but touched already with summer warmth and scents as it brushed the grass and flowers at the cliff edge.

One day it was different. A mist blew up from the sea and caught us unawares, transforming warmth and colour into a chill grey uniformity. It was impossible to lose our way, for the sound of the sea and the slope of the land were themselves sufficient to guide us back. But my parents were troubled and afraid – I had never seen them so before; their fear infected me and I began to cry. This was my first conscious experience of fear whether in others or in myself. The loss of direction, the sun's extinction, the impalpable pressure of the imprisoning vapour, my parents' obvious alarm – it was new, disquieting, baffling, and hence the tears.

Our house at Redruth, the Wesleyan manse, was undistinguished – a simple terrace house like all the others in the row. There was a small back garden and beyond this, with a lane between, were the back gardens of the next street. In this lane, cinder-surfaced and untidy with weeds and the overflow from dustcarts, my brother and I played our simple games. Simple they had to be, for there was not then the superfluity of plastic toys (even if we could have afforded them) which youngsters now enjoy. Our one luxury, a present handed on from a cousin, was a tricycle; on this we charged endlessly up and down, swerving and braking and grazing our knees by the occasional tumble. This and the bouncing 'sorbo' balls (eagerly anticipated birthday presents) were our principal source of outdoor amusements. Briefly we entertained ourselves with catapults, manufactured from garter elastic and using pebbles from the garden path as ammunition. This diversion was quickly ended by the wrath of a neighbour whose windows we had chosen as a convenient target.

The back lane was the scene of a macabre incident which interrupted our games one day. There was a vigorous clucking as a man emerged from a garden gate holding a white hen under his arm. Intrigued we watched him put it between his knees and hold it firmly while he cut off its head with a penknife. The clucking ceased immediately, but then to our amazement he put the hen on the ground and it ran headless and spouting blood for several feet before collapsing. Oddly, I can remember no sense of revulsion or even fear at this grotesque spectacle, only a wondering fascination at the sight of the decapitated bird fleeing from, and apparently watched by, its own vacantly staring head.

Indoors our amusements were slightly more sophisticated. I had a Hornby clockwork train set, at first a single engine, a few trucks and a simple circle of rails. This was extended by successive birthdays and Christmases to include a second engine, a variety of rolling stock, a station, a tunnel, a level-crossing and enough rails and points to experiment with different layouts. How vividly it all comes back! – the smell of the oil in the clockwork motor, the push and pull of the brake and reversing rod in the engine cab (and my annoyance when the brass grips became unscrewed and lost themselves in the pile of the carpet), the contrived accidents as the engine crashed into an obstacle on the line or was urged too fast around a sudden curve. Our enthusiasm spilled over into the hours of sleep as we lay awake in our beds inventing 'engine tales' in which we impersonated engines, with realistic sound accompaniment, and played the parts of drivers, guards and crossing-keepers. It was too much for my parents who in desperation were forced to separate us; I was made to start the night in their bed and transferred to my own when both of us were asleep.

There were, of course, other sources of entertainment. Much of our time was given to collecting, swapping and arranging cigarette cards – a popular craze at that time and for long after. The only series I can recall was 'Cries of London', representing the various streetmongers who cried their wares in Victorian London. Some cards, whether by design of the manufacturers or by accident of distribution, were especially scarce; these were eagerly pursued and 'bought' from other collectors for the price of two, three or more of the commoner cards. Also in eager demand were clean cards straight from the packet and smelling deliciously of fresh tobacco.

There were books too, but as with toys they were few compared with today's abundance. I was learning to read by now, mainly from an illustrated story whose sub-title was 'The Tale of a Bold Bad Mouse'. What were the mouse's sins and their punishment, together with any cautionary moral they were intended to convey, I have now totally forgotten. At the time, however, the book was read to me so often that eventually I knew it by heart and could make the pretence of reading by turning the pages and reciting the corresponding text. This, I imagine, happens with most children. Another book I knew by heart was a children's version of *Swiss Family Robinson*, which held me with unremitting interest. There was also a book of Bible stories, bound in dark red cloth and illustrated with the pictorial sentimentality typical of the time; but the contents of this have left no impression on my memory. My efforts to read were given an unusual and unexpected impetus by the discovery in 1922 of the tomb of Tutankhamen and its wealth of gold. The newspapers were full of it and even my tender years could not escape the general excitement. I pored over the pages of photographs (not, alas, in colour) wishing I could understand the captions and begging my mother to help me read them.

It is difficult in our present push-button world of instant entertainment to imagine what life was like in the 1920s without radio, TV, recordplayers, cassettes and the various other instruments of diversion. All of us, children and adults alike, were thrown back on our own resources, compelled to exercise initiative and imagination in providing our own amusement. We invented games and pastimes (as children still do from their more copious resources) and created for ourselves pleasures which now come effortlessly from the machines of manufacturers. What we did not have we did not miss, and the potential of what we had was more fully explored. Life was simpler too; we expected less of it and were content with less. But the impact of things to come was not unfelt, for it was at Redruth that I first went to the cinema and saw Jackie Coogan in a film of which my only recollection is the flickering sepia of the well-worn celluloid.

For us life was simple partly because my parents were poor. My father's annual stipend could hardly have exceeded £200 (it was only £280 ten years later when we lived in Lincolnshire), though there was the house as well, free rent and maintenance, and an allowance for travelling and postage. My aunt's generosity gave us not only our summer holiday but also a maid (duly dressed in the uniform required by social conformity), who did the chores and took me for walks. There was also a Mrs Hendy who appeared on washdays and helped with the heavy manual effort indissociable then from the weekly wash. So that our poverty was not uncomfortable and my parents were, I think, exempt from much of the household routine of washing up and cleaning which their children and grandchildren have accepted as a matter of course!

My relationship with my parents was, I think, fairly normal for the time; on their side there was love and concern, and on mine affection and respect; but there was a certain distance between us, an absence of that open, familiar companionship which is common today. A clergy household is inevitably different from others. Much of my father's work was in the evenings – church committees and weeknight services in Redruth and the outlying villages. Mornings were spent at home in his study, a room apart which I rarely entered; in the afternoons he rested for an hour dozing in his armchair (and my mother too, in her bed – a habit they had both acquired during their years in Ceylon); then came the round of pastoral visits, on foot of course, to home and hospital. On Sundays there was worship to conduct, morning and evening and sometimes in the afternoon too, making the day (in Wesleyan jargon) a 'three-decker'. My mother too was involved in the church and other good works which often took her out in the afternoon and evening. Consequently I was left a good deal to myself or to Gwen, the maid, who took me out for walks. By day my games were mostly solitary, for my brother was at school and in any case had his own group of friends. There was, however, a little girl across the street with whom I occasionally played and who insisted on calling me 'Peter'. She provided my only contact (metaphorically) with coevals of the other sex during the two years before I started school.

A more literal contact arose from the habit of sharing my parents' bed while they drank their early morning cup of tea. My mother's loose nightdress would now and again expose a breast. I was fascinated by its size and by the way it shaped itself so smoothly to her movements as she stretched for her tea. Especially I wondered at the large brown nipple which contrasted so markedly with my own insignificant pimple. Its purpose, however, escaped me at the time and for long afterwards.

Relations within the family were sometimes strained. I remember standing on a table stamping wildly and shouting at the top of my voice, 'Damn you! Damn you!' The cause of the outburst I have forgotten, as also the source of my vocabulary which shocked my parents, while my brother and Gwen looked on with mild and mirthful surprise. Once I was scolded – again for reasons now forgotten – and in a fit of resentment rushed out through the kitchen door and off to school dinnerless. A few days later I succumbed to a feverish cold which prolonged itself into suspected TB, though it was more likely the beginning of tonsillitis. I was ordered to stay in bed until my temperature had been normal for three days. My parents, touched perhaps with some remorse at the possible, but unlikely, connection between my illness and the *contretemps* which preceded it, were especially troubled. Their love and patience must have been sorely tried in the three months that followed, and I can remember their visible relief, and my own no less intensely felt, when at last the thermometer released me from captivity and I tottered out of bed.

There was another incident which briefly strained relations and also brought me to the first dim awareness of the stirrings of conscience. I had been sent down the street to the corner shop to buy potatoes. They must have been a round variety, for as I brought them back up the hill they seemed ideal for rolling down the slope. Half a dozen of them I despatched thus, delighting as I watched them jump, jostle and overtake each other in their erratic progress along the gutter. So absorbed was I in this novel entertainment that I neither noticed the diminishing weight of the bag nor imagined that my mother might herself detect the loss of contents. She was indeed suspicious when I arrived home with the survivors, but I insisted stoutly that none were missing and she took my word. I knew then that I had told a lie; I was sorry and troubled, though I could not have put the name of conscience to my inquietude. Moreover, I suspected that my mother knew it, and this suspicion thrust out from me an uneasy defensive screen which temporarily estranged us.

Inevitably the Wesleyan Methodist Church was an integral part of our lives. The house we lived in and all its furnishings were the property of the local church. Its vocabulary was the commonplace of my parents' table conversation; we listened, my brother and I, to talk of circuits and stipends, of Leaders' Meetings, Class Meetings and Quarterly Meetings, of Chapel Stewards and Circuit Stewards (these last of great importance, for on them depended the repair and furnishing of the manse), of Foreign Missions, Home Missions and Chapel Anniversaries. Nearby, some-where along the Falmouth road, lived 'the super', the superintendent minister who had overall charge of the circuit and with whom my father made the quarterly plan of preaching appointments for the various chapels in the circuit – a complex task this, requiring the services of a number of lay or 'local' preachers on whom the church was, and still is, heavily dependent. Most of this nonconformist vocabulary was meaning-less to me at the time, but through constant repetition.I absorbed it into myself, and significance dawned as the years passed. (For the benefit of the uninitiated perhaps I should explain that there was then also a Primitive Methodist and a United Methodist Church, each an indepen-dent and to some extent, regrettably, competitive organisation, with different traditions and different hymn-books, though their forms of worship were not basically different from the Wesleyan. In 1932 the three Churches were united, save for a few dissenting congregations, under the single title of Methodist. A reminder of that divided Methodism can still be seen here and there built into the brickwork of chapels still in use.)

Of my father's work I have little recollection – mainly the pleasure of accompanying him occasionally on his visits to country chapels at Illogan and Portreath. His conveyance was pony and trap, for cars were few and public transport, save for the railway, non-existent. We jogged along enjoyably in the fresh morning air, he no doubt meditating on his forthcoming sermon, and I delighting in the motion, the steady rhythm of hooves, and eyeing curiously the dung which emerged from time to time, sharp-smelling and fresh-brown, from under the pony's tail.

Every Sunday morning, except for these occasional country excursions, I was taken to the large Wesleyan chapel in the centre of Redruth. It was unique among Methodist chapels, so far as I know, in being built over or adjacent to a railway tunnel which runs beneath the town. In front was a grating through which came smoke and steam as the trains passed under. This phenomenon I awaited with eager anticipation, associating it in my innocence, not so much with the GWR, as with the imaginary fires of hell into which the wicked might be conveniently cast from the very steps which supposedly led to heaven. In other respects the chapel, as I remember it, was conspicuously Methodist in structure and furnishing – a raised central pulpit, behind it the choir stalls, and in front the rows of characteristic pitch-pine pews. Each had its felt strip covering the seat; underneath were hassocks, intended for the knees in prayer but more commonly serving as foot-rests (for Methodists, unlike their Anglican brethren and sisters, prefer to sit and bow their heads instead of kneeling).

The service normally included a 'children's address' – stories of Christian heroes or of daily life with suitable exhortation appended – and a children's hymn. To these I was expected to attend and, when I could read, to join in the singing. The rest of the service I spent crayoning or turning over the pages of my picture books, the book resting on the seat of the pew and I facing it with my knees on the floor. One Sunday, when I discovered too late that I had forgotten my crayons, a kindly worshipper leaned over from the pew behind and dropped a pencil in front of me. It was one of those indelibles, superseded now by the ubiquitous biro, that ran a reddish purple when licked; I amused myself for the duration by drawing lurid sunsets. On another occasion, surfeited with pictorial activity, I resorted to other means of diversion. In those days the exposition of the Gospel was often accompanied by rhetorical flourishes which included a generous use of arms, body and facial expression to impress the message. Fascinated by the display of one especially dramatic preacher, I sought to imitate his gesticulations, flinging my arms around and distorting my face in what must have seemed to the immediate onlookers a shameful parody of the occupant of the pulpit. Inevitably my histrionics were shortlived.

On Sunday afternoons my mother conducted a private Sunday School for the benefit of my brother and myself. This consisted of hymns, Bible stories (from the dark red book already mentioned) and prayers. The hymns were mostly of the action type, to be accompanied by suitable movement and gesture. One of our favourites was:

> Jesus bids us shine with a pure, clear light,
> Like a little candle burning in the night:
> In the world is darkness, so we must shine;
> You in your small corner and I in mine.

The two of us stood in opposite corners of the room, each holding a lighted candle and pointing first at each other and then at ourselves as the words required. Another was:

> Hear the pennies dropping,
> Listen while they fall;
> Every one for Jesus –
> He shall have them all.

And then the chorus:

> *Dropping, dropping, dropping, dropping,*
> *Hear the pennies fall;*
> *Every one for Jesus –*
> *He shall have them all.*

As we sang, we passed a missionary collecting box to and fro between us, dropping in our pennies and shaking vigorously to magnify the rattle of the coins. There was another hymn of which we sang alternate verses as solos and the chorus together:

> If I were a beautiful, twinkling star,
> I'd shine on the darkest night;
> I'd seek where the dreariest pathways are,
> And light them with all my might.

> *Though sun or moon I cannot be,*
> *To make the whole world bright,*
> *I'd find some little cheerless spot*
> *And shine with all my might.*

(Appropriately, one of the authors of this was Grace Gleam.) There were many others, all of them in the old Wesleyan Sunday School hymn-book but most of them excluded from the current Methodist version as unsuited to modern taste or religious sentiment. Strangely, when I looked up these three hymns in order to quote them, I could remember only the first line of each; yet the tunes of verse and chorus sprang into memory as clear as when I sang them nearly seventy years ago. And who knows how these forgotten tunes, forgotten yet retained to echo in subconscious caverns and issue forth over half a century later, may have influenced choice and outlook through those intervening years?

Two other features of my Wesleyan upbringing are worth a mention. A major source of the chapel's income was the autumn bazaar which was held in the adjoining schoolroom and involved many weeks of fervent preparation. There were stalls for home-made cakes and sweets, stalls for jam and garden produce, stalls for second-hand books, for toys and clothes and jumble, a 'white elephant' stall, a bottle stall (anything in bottles except alcohol, of course), and various other devices for extracting money. The bazaar itself was a great occasion; I loved the bustle and colour and smell of it as I scurried from stall to stall in the crowded schoolroom, fascinated by the growing piles of coins, and peering anxiously from time to time through the press of bodies to make sure that my mother was still near.

In the summer came the Sunday School Treat, an outdoor party for all the scholars and many of their parents somewhere in the surrounding countryside. Lannar was the site of one of them; another was Gwennap Pit, a natural auditorium where John Wesley preached during his evangelising tours of Cornwall. Though I was not myself a scholar, and my brother had ceased to be, we were allowed to attend as a concession to the manse. I have no recollection of the means of transport – was it horse-carriage or charabanc? – and little of the occasions themselves, except for the saffron buns which were doled out, one apiece, from enormous baskets. I had no great liking for them, but there was nothing else to eat; they tasted of hair-oil, and I have never understood why the Cornish like them (if they still do).

It was at Redruth, some time in the last two years of our stay there, that I began my formal education. I was sent to an elementary school whose headmistress, a staunch Cornish Wesleyan, was a friend of the family. My parents were spared the twice-daily chore of taking me to and from the school; motor traffic was virtually nil and there was little danger for a child of five or six walking unescorted the half mile each way. I remember it as a red brick building surrounded by the standard asphalt playground; its classrooms were typical of the time – long wooden desks, folding partitions, and windows high in the wall to prevent distraction. At morning assembly we sang hymns (already learnt by heart and practised), sat fidgeting through Bible reading and prayers, and then burst out in a babble of infant chatter to our various destinations.

The instruction, also typical, was geared to talk, chalk and rote learning; its aims were limited, a grounding in the three R's and the elements of good behaviour. There was some concession to the arts in the form of singing; the tunes, I remember, were printed in tonic sol-fa, and on the classroom wall was a large poster of the octave in doh, ray, me, etc. There was an element of competition in the 'medals' awarded for good work; and though it was a matter of pride to win one, I cannot recollect any resentment at failure.

I had learnt to read and tell the time before I entered the school; when I left it at the age of seven, I could read easily and write competently, if not wholly legibly. I knew my tables up to 12 × 12 and could perform correctly simple calculations of a kind that apparently defeat many of today's 15-year-olds. Of course, there was much missing that is taken for granted in modern infant schools – play, paints, pets, structural toys, dance, group activities, outdoor games; but the instruction, despite its curricular limitations, was kindly and efficient – a reflection of the headmistress – and I never felt it as oppressive. My one source of distress was the tunic in which I was sent to school. It was a brown imitation-velvet material edged with a wavy cream strip; underneath I wore short knickerbockers, and the total effect, in my view, was hopelessly girlish. In a mixed school (and though I had little awareness of sexual differences) it made me one of the girls and I hated it.

CHAPTER III

Barnard Castle

IN 1924, AFTER THREE YEARS IN REDRUTH, we moved from one end of England to the other. Very likely we spent a night somewhere en route, perhaps with my mother's relatives in Walsall; but I can remember nothing of the journey north.

Barnard Castle is a small country town on the Durham bank of the Tees, about half way between the river's polluted mouth and its source in the wild, peaty moorlands of the upper Pennines. It has a large cobbled market-place and a spacious open main street, wide enough for two separate roads and a line of trees between. The street slopes down towards the castle and the river, beyond which is the road to Bowes, rising steeply through the pastures on the Yorkshire bank. Below the castle is a 16th century stone bridge, beautiful in its structure and solidity of purpose, but dangerous now for the congestion of modern traffic. Once the town was a market centre for the surrounding countryside; there is a reminder of this in the ancient Butter Market, an octagonal stone building at the eastern end of the marketplace.

Another distinctive feature of the town is the Bowes Museum. It was built to house collections of the Bowes family and was opened in 1892. Its chateau-esque style either appals or impresses by the sheer effrontery of its alien intrusion into the English scene. For me its contents, especially the Natural History section, were a never-failing source of interest.

Barny, as we learnt to call it, still retains much of the charm we knew in the 1920s – and this despite the litter of cars that cram the marketplace and spill over into the broad spaces of its main street. Away from the crowds one can lose oneself in the mediaeval past of the Balliols who built the castle and founded the Oxford college, or in the old town by the river where inspiration came to Dickens for his *Master Humphrey's Clock*, or in the Museum's hoarded treasures of other times and places. There is still peace, no less now than fifty years ago, in the riverside woodlands

21

above the town and along the meadow path that leads to Abbey Bridge a mile or two below. And nothing can take from Barny its key position at the entrance to upper Teesdale, an enchanting landscape of lush watermeadows, whitewashed farms and cottages, gaunt stone-walled hill pastures, and brown streams that chatter down from the high windswept haunts of peewit, curlew and golden plover.

Our manse was in Galgate, near the top of the double main street; it was stone-faced but brick at the side. There were steps from the front door down through the garden to the flagged pavement, and then, as one turned towards the town, there was that view down the street between the trees to the Bowes road – which from here looked almost vertical up the opposite hillside. Behind were outhouses and a long walled garden, around one side and the back of which ran a cinder-covered lane not unlike that at Redruth. There was a path right round the garden, wide enough for the tricycle, which still survived; and some thoughtful predecessor had provided a swing and with it endless hours of healthy amusement. At the bottom were a raspberry patch, gooseberry and currant bushes and space for vegetables; along the inner side, away from the lane, was a row of standard fruit trees. Altogether we were well supplied with fruit – in fact I cannot conceive what we did with it all after satisfying our own fairly modest needs in jam and preserves.

The house was large, with two front rooms downstairs and my father's study at the back overlooking the garden. There was plenty of room for my indoor childhood games, especially the Hornby train set, now building up to substantial size, and – a new delight this – for my Meccano constructions which too became more elaborate as the sets were steadily enlarged. It was in the manse at Barny that I first became aware of my father's study and of the books that lined its walls. The study had a pervading atmosphere, both literal and metaphorical, an air of its own redolent of pen, paper and the printed word, of application to reading and writing. My father was no scholar; he had been a builder's apprentice and assistant before acceptance into the ministry and his years at theological college. But he genuinely loved books; he read and reread them, marking them, annotating them and drawing from them material for his sermons. He was encouraged in this by Auntie Mabel, who too was a great reader, and something of their enthusiasm infected me even at that early age. It was his ambition that I should have a better education than he, above all that I should go to university; that he succeeded in this was due, I believe, in no small measure to the subtle impact on my early years of that book-lined room apart.

Another memorable room, for different reasons, was the kitchen. It was a working kitchen with a scrubbed deal table and an old-fashioned,

Barnard Castle: the castle and the River Tees

Barnard Castle: the Bowes Museum

cast iron, black-leaded hearth. This latter had an oven on one side and a water tank on the other; it would be a valuable antique if it still existed. The tank, no longer watertight, was used for drying kindling; occasionally the sticks overheated and filled the room with the fragrance of scorching wood. My mother baked most of our bread and all our cakes and puddings; the actual baking was done in a gas oven as black and antiquated as its coal counterpart; but the dough was left to rise on the hob, and here too the ingredients of the cakes were warmed and softened, all of them contributing peculiarly and deliciously to the general accumulation of savours.

Because my father's work took him out most evenings, lunch was our principal meal; tea was bread and butter, jam and cake. There were no school meals in those days; during term I walked the mile and a quarter each way to eat at home. In the holidays it was different; then I shared both the meal and the cooking which preceded it, claiming as my right the licking of all sugary spoons and basins and, on baking days, a taste of the kneaded dough. (My brother was by this time at Kingswood, the boarding school where I was later to follow.)

I am not sure that my mother enjoyed her baking, though she took a pride in her cakes, which were excellent; but it was cheaper than buying. Money was short, or so I was given to believe. One day I spilt some sugar on the floor and received from her an unexpectedly abrupt reprimand: 'If only you knew how poor we are!', she said. On another occasion, being at a loss for amusement, I asked for 6d. to buy a ball; this was firmly refused. We had a maid nevertheless, or a succession of them, for they were hard to keep at the price we could afford to pay; but for this, as for our holidays, we were still indebted to Auntie Kate's generosity.

One effect of our poverty, actual or supposed, was to drive me to subterfuge in securing entry to neighbouring and less straitened homes. In one was a boy of my own age called Stephen; his father was a local coal merchant who generously allowed us our fuel at less than normal retail price. Their teas were more plentiful and more substantial than ours; they included a cooked course and a range of cakes beyond anything that appeared on our table. I would go round to their house and ask if Stephen could play, hoping with reasonable confidence that I would be invited in and asked to stay for tea. Sometimes my approach was accompanied by a roughly made toy – a paper windmill or a boat to sail on the lily pond. 'Look,' I would say when the door was opened to my knock, 'I have made this for Stephen.' These clumsy advances, at which I now look back with some feeling of shame, can scarcely have deceived his parents; but their kindness overlooked my childish contriving and I was thus allowed access to a home environment more normal, as well as more ample, than that of the Wesley manse.

Another house which I occasionally visited was that of an elderly lady who lived in a whitewashed cottage a few hundred yards below the manse and who amused her retirement by keeping cats. Here I could go only by unsolicited invitation which, though infrequent, was always welcome. For there was something in the oddity of the menage which amused and attracted me even at that age; besides, I liked cats and even more her cakes, and I was happy enough stroking the former and eating the latter while listening absently to her persistent prattle.

My friendship with Stephen ended tragically. On the last day of our stay in Barny, when our possessions, cleared from the manse, were on their way to Newark on Trent, we were all invited to his house for lunch. This was to facilitate our departure by an early afternoon train to Darlington and thence on the main line to Newark. An hour or two before the meal my brother and I went to play (he with an older brother and sister). In the course of our games Stephen climbed on to the roof of a shed to retrieve a ball; he slipped and fell off, and a stick he was holding penetrated his skin just below an eye. It was a nasty gash; he was rushed to the doctor, but at the time there seemed no cause for special alarm. However, this was long before the time of antibiotics; the wound turned septic and Stephen lost the sight first of one eye and then the other. I do not think I was to blame, though I was a participant in the game and may well have encouraged him on to the roof. Yet the incident remains vivid in memory to this day; it was a theme of nightmares until well into middle age, and for years it raised perplexities in my mind as to the integrity of a God who could reward the kindness of parents with such horrific consequences to their child.

Another experience which gave me nightmares, but without religious implications, was a visit to a hospital in Darlington for the removal of my tonsils. For the two years previous I had had frequent short illnesses with high temperature and rusty throat. Tonsillectomy was not then the routine it has since become and our doctor was reluctant to submit me to it. Each morning for months my father patiently painted the back of my throat with a sweet-tasting iodine concoction, using an angled brush which was bought specially for the purpose. When neither this nor repeated gargling had any effect, the word was given and one August evening I found myself in a ward with a dozen other boys awaiting next morning's execution. There have been great advances in anaesthetics since then, but in those days it was chloroform: firm hands held one to the operating table while a gauze was placed over one's nose, and then, resisting violently, one inhaled the sickly vapour until oblivion came. It is all so vivid still – the choking pressure of suffocation, the nauseating cloud of thickening darkness, the struggle to escape. And then to wake up kneeling in bed crying and spewing blood into an enamel dish while twelve other boys added their howls to a cacophony of babel! Unforgettable too is the relief when my mother came later that day to remove me.

Family walks and picnics were part of our life in Barny as they had been in Redruth. The sea was farther away here, but the countryside was on our doorstep, and a greater variety (the sea apart) than in Cornwall. Close at hand were pastural walks through hayfields rich in summer with clover, sorrel and buttercup; a few hundred yards took us to the River Tees and the woodland paths along its Durham bank; Flatts Woods was another expanse of woodland bordering a tributary which runs from the golf course to join the Tees a short way above the castle.

On the Yorkshire bank was a beautiful wild area of woodland, lush in early summer with bluebells and, in the marshy ground of the valley bottom, with kingcup and campion. This was Deepdale; it stretched from the river almost to the open moors near Bowes, and it was notable, in addition to its natural beauty, for the curving railway bridge of tubular steel which carried across it the line from Darlington to Kirkby Stephen. During the war it was occupied by the army and used for military training – with what result I have never dared to see.

Further afield were the moors between Bowes and Cotherstone – a favourite walk this, from one village to the other – and further still the bare fells of the upper Pennines, with High Force and Cauldron Snout the obvious points of attraction. Cars were few in the 1920s, and my parents never owned one; but buses and trains offered a wide range of excursions, and the very mode of travel, infrequent as it was for us, was an adventure in itself. (There are no trains now; Catcastle Bridge has gone from Deepdale, and so too has the slender stone and steel bridge across the Tees.) Once or twice a year Auntie Kate and Uncle Jack would visit us in their Armstrong-Siddeley (later a succession of Daimlers); then we could explore the more distant reaches of the Pennines as far as Alston, and beyond that to the Lakes or southwards to the Yorkshire Dales. It was an enchanting world that surrounded us – bewilderingly so to me now in its recollected and revisited loveliness and tinged, as inevitably it is, by the regretful glance of nostalgia. Its beauty was not lost on my childhood, but the main impact was unconscious, absorbed into and confirming in me that 'disturbing' love of nature already implanted by the Yorkshire Moors.

A favourite picnic place was Abbey Bridge, a mile and a half down the river from Barny and a few hundred yards below the picturesque ruin of

Egglestone Abbey; behind, towards the town, the Bowes Museum towers out of its trees. We would walk the couple of miles from the manse, most of it through fields, my parents in turn carrying the picnic basket while I picked flowers, chased my ball, pursued despairingly the occasional rabbit, or threw sticks and stones into the river.

The bridge is a narrow, crenellated stone structure which spans the Tees where its dark brown waters rush through a rocky gorge. It was a toll bridge then; I forget the toll, or even whether there was one for pedestrians; but there was, I seem to remember, a board (amusing to me) with details of charges for various classes of livestock and vehicles, including handcarts and gipsy caravans. There was also a tollkeeper's house, demolished now, which supplied enamel jugs of hot water for picnic teas. This was our first place of call, to order the hot water; then we found a picnic place a short way upstream, for the river is too dangerous at the bridge for children to play. Further up it opens out into small coves with an abundance of stones to throw, trees to climb and banks to slide down. Behind were the fields where I could kick my ball and scamper energetically in pursuit of it.

Another favourite picnic place was at Cotherstone, a straggling village of no particular charm situated a few miles up river from Barny. What drew us here was a wooded stream chattering through mossy boulders and the ruins of an old mill. A further attraction was the train ride which took us clanking over the bridge high above the Tees, then through woods and meadows and along embankments gay with primroses, bluebells, wild rose or vetch according to season. The joy of it! To stand at the open window of the carriage (the old up-and-down, notched leather-strap window), the rails clickety clocking beneath us, the smoke from the engine drifting deliciously into our noses and grittily into unwary eyes, and the panorama of countryside unfolding for a brief four miles its exciting variety of interest!

It was a place of peaceful beauty, in springtime sprinkled with primroses, violets and anemones, in summer full of a languorous moistness and the lazy drone of flies. Here too there were stones to throw, trees to climb, rabbits to chase and grassy slopes to slide down ('But mind the cowpats, dear!'). Unlike Abbey Bridge it was safe here to paddle, stand knee-deep in the cool water, fish for tiddlers, overturn stones to pry beneath. For tea we lit a fire and boiled water from the stream; the smell of the wood smoke lingers still in my nostrils, as does the sight of it, weaving blue into the dark summer foliage of the alders. Along the road above the stream was a row of houses, in one of which lived a genteel and kindly couple whom we always visited on these occasions. I remember them for two things: a musical box from which, miraculously, there popped out a small brightly coloured bird, its beak quivering to the melody from within; and the half-crown invariably pressed into my hand as we left.

Occasionally, when Uncle Jack and Auntie Kate were staying with us, we picnicked further up Teesdale at Langdon Beck, a mile or two beyond High Force. This latter we visited on the way; for it was a pleasant walk through the fragrant half-light of the pines among which the path winds down to the river; and for me there was the added fascination of freshly-fallen pine-cones and elusive squirrels. Then there was the spectacle of the fall itself, impressive even to a child as it plunged to the dark, turbulent, unapproachable depths at its base; but it was no place for picnics. Langdon Beck is different. Here, where the beck is crossed by the road to St John's Chapel, the land is wild and open, the flow of water gentle and caressing; and there is space to play. Here too I sensed that disturbing presence which speaks inexpressibly from the moorland texture of wide skies and solitude, wind-blown grass, bird-cry and wild flower. It has been the same whenever I have returned.

Picnics apart, there were seasonal excursions to gather crab-apples and blackberries, which provided free ingredients for our home-made jams and jellies. There were also regular shorter walks in the surrounding countryside. For my father loved walking, and as his working hours were mainly morning and evening, he would often refresh himself with an hour's stroll in the afternoon, myself trotting at his side for company. I count it a great blessing that my childhood years in Barny had such a ready access to country sights and sounds, to rural beauty so easily and freely available – and as yet unspoilt by the paraphernalia of affluence. I was now increasingly and consciously aware of an intimacy with nature which hitherto had been realised but dimly, if at all. Moreover, I was at an age now to experience more actively, to remember more vividly; thus were my earlier, more passive impressions reinforced to establish an enduring structure.

One excursion deserves particular mention for its unusual, or even unique character, since for me the experience is almost certainly unrepeatable. There was a total eclipse of the sun visible in northern England on June 29th, 1927. My brother was away at school, but the rest of us and hundreds of other families rose before dawn and were driven by car or charabanc to various vantage points throughout the county. Ours was east of Barny, on grassy ground near Greta Bridge. The sun rose clear and unimpeded as we waited in the open field; the air was filled with the sound of birds and bees, with the scent of clover and fresh-cut hay; around us was all the manifold activity of a summer day just newly born. As the sun moved closer to its eclipse, the clouds covered it and we were denied the full glory of the corona; at Richmond, a few miles away, they saw it all from start to finish. But I remember as though it were yesterday how the day dwindled to twilight, then to full darkness, and with this a growing hush of suspended animation which shrank to empty, unearthly silence, as though life itself had been extinguished. Then the process reversed; the world was reborn and repossessed; we had breakfast and went home. The next occasion will be on August 11th, 1999!

Of our holidays during these three years I remember little. One summer we were able, by exchanging houses, to spend a week at Roker, a seaside resort on the Durham coast and a poor substitute for the cliffs of Cornwall. This was during the general strike of 1926 when the railways were obliged to use low quality imported coal. From the carriage window I watched entranced as the engine scattered showers of sparks among the heaps of ungathered hay (it had rained for much of the previous month). Of Roker itself I remember only the pool in the park where my brother and I sailed our newly acquired and greatly treasured toy yacht – and our grief when it sank beyond our reach!

There was also a week at Ambleside; it was my first introduction to the hills, but of this too I can recall only one incident. My mother and I had walked to the top of one of the lesser fells, perhaps 1000 feet or more. While she rested and enjoyed the views, I pursued the new-found pleasure of scrambling among the rocks. When I turned to look for her, she had gone! I remember the sudden sense of deprivation, the hollow pull of fear at the stomach – not the same infection of fear that brought me to tears on the cliffs of Clodgy, but something deeper, more elemental, inexpressible. Of course we were soon reunited, for she was looking for me as I for her, and my panic was shortlived. But here again, perhaps, in different setting, circumstances and manifestation was the touch of that *mysterium fascinans* which at the same time allures, disturbs and strangely satisfies, and which in later years has drawn me irresistibly to moors and mountain-tops.

The Wesleyan Church and its work in my father's wide country circuit continued to provide much of the daily context of our lives. There was the usual talk at table of circuit affairs, of bazaars and missionary meetings, Wesley Guild, Girls' League and other activities and institutions, some of them now defunct with the passage of years or the merging of what were then three separate Churches into the one Methodist. Most of this meant little to me; but I was expected as 'the minister's boy' and as part of my religious education to share as I could in the life of the local chapel. The building itself, at the bottom of the wide main street, is among the pleasanter specimens of Methodist architecture – stone-built, with a small, graceful spire, and fitting acceptably into the general style of the town. Inside were the varnished pine pews and the raised central pulpit which were characteristic of the period; they survive still in hundreds of Methodist chapels throughout Britain. (I have mentioned earlier that the Methodist Church makes great use of lay or 'local' preachers. For a typical circuit might consist of a dozen or more scattered chapels, and to serve these there would be only two or three ordained ministers – clearly too few alone to provide Sunday worship for so many congregations. My father was never, therefore, the one incumbent of a single chapel nor even its regular preacher.)

Every Sunday morning my mother and I (and my brother when at home) walked the half mile or so to church. Of the worship I remember almost nothing apart from its outward form, which was the traditional Methodist structure of five hymns sandwiching prayers, Bible readings and sermon. The 'children's address' was a regular feature; in this, as I have explained earlier, the preacher attempted by means of stories, biographical episodes and modern parables to provide for the children a modicum of spiritual edification suited to their understanding. It was also intended to make them feel themselves a part of the worshipping congregation, sharing in its fellowship. The intention was good, but the attempts were not always successful. Indeed it is a difficult task, requiring an understanding of immature minds and considerable dramatic skill, to hold the interest of children of widely different ages scattered throughout an adult congregation. It became the custom in later years to bunch them at the front so that the preacher could address a more homogeneous audience; then, after the singing of the children's hymn from a rather limited selection in the Methodist hymn-book, they would be allowed to leave. More recently they have begun to be segregated for their own worship and instruction, and the 'children's address' has fallen out of fashion. Again, I recall little of the scores I must have listened to (my father gave a series on *Pilgrim's Progress*); but I remember that some were good and that I looked forward to this light relief from the tedium of an act of worship which to me was mostly incomprehensible. I was thought too old now to draw or to read my own books during the service; hence, 'Don't fidget, dear' became an oft-whispered bidding during the sermon.

I was also required to attend Sunday School. This was at two o'clock and meant hurrying through Sunday lunch, which was always roast joint and two veg. – the best meal of the week, for it was my father's hardest day and he needed it, so my mother argued. We had individual cards to register our attendance; they were stamped with a purple star as we entered and if we collected the requisite number of stars, we were awarded a prize at the end of the year. I never achieved this honour.

Whether for temperamental reasons or because I had a surfeit of religion at home, I found it difficult to take Sunday School seriously. I interrupted the teacher, giggled, pinched the girls' bottoms and generally made a nuisance of myself until one Sunday afternoon I was sent out. Instead of going straight home I wandered through the woods for what seemed an appropriate time and then presented myself at home as if nothing untoward had happened. But the truth emerged during the course of the week; my parents confronted me with aggrieved disapproval; I was in disgrace. However, I never returned to Sunday School.

Morning prayers were a regular feature of our lives both at Redruth and at Barny and for long after that. After a brief Bible reading we would all swivel on to our knees and bow our heads into the chairs we had been sitting on (I can still feel the texture of the upholstery on my forehead). I remember turning round to see my father 'performing' as he composed extempore prayer for divine forgiveness, protection and guidance. His eyes shut, the sunlight glinting on his greying hair and the gold of his watch chain, he himself had a certain air of distant divinity, as if belonging to a world quite alien to my own. His petitions made and the Lord's Prayer repeated together, we turned to the more important concern (for me) of breakfasting and dashing off to school.

At bedtime I recited, under my mother's supervision, a set formula of prayer whose main concern seems to have been the well-being of myself and the nearest members of our family. After reciting the verse

> Gentle Jesus, meek and mild,
> Look upon a little child;
> Pity my simplicity;
> Suffer me to come to Thee,

I proceeded to 'Please bless Mummy and Daddy, Lawson away at school, Uncle Jack, Auntie Kate and Auntie Mabel', and sometimes extended my petition to include Felix our cat. I cannot recall that my horizons were ever extended to include my unfortunate fellow-children of God in less prosperous parts of the Empire, though as an ex-missionary's wife my mother can hardly have been unaware of them.

For a time and while my brother was at home we continued with our Sunday afternoon 'school' at home – save that it now took place after tea when my father was on his way to conduct evening service and safely out of ear's reach (for he was very sensitive to noise, especially when preparing his sermons). But as my brother was now away at school for most of the year, a class of one was hardly viable, and this part of my religious education soon lapsed. However, as I grew older and could stay up later, I was expected to accompany my mother to evening service at our own chapel. What I chiefly remember of these evenings is the enclosing warmth (literal and metaphorical) of the chapel, which seemed to wrap me round in a protective cocoon; this and the hearty singing of an evening congregation as yet undiminished by the rival attraction of radio and television and, among the elderly, by the fear of mugging. For the Methodist hymn-book (Wesleyan in those days) includes many hymns of powerful rhythmic and melodic content; and Methodist congregations, Wesleyan, Primitive and United, have always been notable for their singing.

Bazaars and concerts were part of the normal routine of church life, and in these too I shared. One concert included a series of tableaux from the novels of Charles Dickens: various scenes were presented on the stage, in character and costume but motionless, frozen at the peak of dramatic significance. (It is a genre little practised at the present time.) I was chosen for Oliver Twist asking for more – no doubt because I had an air of undernourishment, not through underfeeding however, though school milk, had it been available, might have made a difference. Even so I had to suck in my cheeks in order to enhance the effect. Thus I found myself a very frightened little boy, dressed in rags and holding out my enamel bowl to the burly grocer who was wielding a large soup ladle. For some reason the audience thought it good and clapped us into several encores. I have had a horror of acting ever since!

There was one church activity which I especially enjoyed. It was customary just before Christmas for the ministers to go round the circuit collecting money from missionary boxes, which in those days could be found in almost every Methodist household. I often accompanied my father, walking sometimes several miles to outlying farms. Why just at this time of year I never understood, but it had one great advantage. For it was also customary, particularly among the farming community, to have Christmas cake and ginger wine available for visitors; and of course we always had our share. The wine was non-alcoholic, otherwise my father would not have accepted it, for he was strictly teetotal, following the firm tradition of the Methodist Churches.

Christmas itself was becoming more of a reality during these years at Barny – not, alas, for any theological significance, but because it was a time of good fare, presents and parties. The Christmas hymns which we sang with gusto acquired a nostalgic sentimentality which obscured their theology (as well as wintry associations quite foreign to their historical origin). As Christmas approached each year, I began to hum to myself the tunes of 'Once in royal David's city' and 'O little town of Bethlehem' while trotting to and from school or holly-picking with my parents. At the same time I imagined the presents I might receive (after duly posting my requests up the chimney).

Stockings, of course, were hung at the end of the bed and found filled next morning with the usual titbits of sugar mice and tuppenny puzzles and an apple and an orange for make-weight – all wonderfully exciting in our straitened circumstances! Presents were distributed by my father after breakfast on Christmas Day. They had been laid out on the couch (we never had a Christmas tree nor the wealth of coloured wrapping paper that abounds today); from here they were ceremoniously taken one by one, announced, and placed in eager hands. The time of distribution ensured that we would wear our new gloves for church; equally it ensured that for most of the service our minds were occupied with additions to our Hornby and Meccano sets.

Another well-remembered feature of Christmas is the parties in our own house and among other families. All that I can remember of their detail is a game of 'rewards and forfeits'. I have forgotten how it was played, but the rewards were kisses and the forfeits were bumps on the bottom with a knee. One little girl with plain, straight, mousey hair and no overt attractiveness was especially fond of applying these to me. I remember the odd sensations which I experienced on these occasions, recognised now as perhaps my first sexual awareness. One year we had a 'white Christmas'. We took a toboggan (another present from Auntie Kate) to the Deer Bolt, the pasture sloping down to the river on the Yorkshire side. The swift thrill down the run and the hard, crisp, crunching snow remain for ever associated in my mind with Christmas.

I have often wondered what my parents thought was the effect on me of growing up in a Wesleyan household. Certainly it made little conscious impact at the time – except for one thing: I developed a morbid fear of hell, which became for me a vivid reality of eternal punishment and scorching flames. For a time I totted up every occasion that I uttered a 'swear-word' (nothing more substantial than 'damn', 'blast' and 'hell' itself – the richer, more familiar expletives of today were unknown to me in Barny). Would 100 qualify for hell, I wondered? Or would a minister's son have a lesser dispensation? I soon exceeded the 100 and gradually ceased counting; my later school experience at Newark on Trent cured me of any sensitivity in this respect. Why this fear I cannot understand. It was not obtruded on me at home, nor was it conspicuous in the doctrines of the Wesleyan Church. More deeply rooted and enduring was the 'atmosphere' of the local chapel, and of the whole circuit in so far as I had contact with it. The bazaars and social evenings, the warmth of winter evening chapel, the hearty singing of tuneful hymns, the general air of geniality – all these and no doubt much else now long since forgotten have contributed a foundation of propensity, indeed of affection, towards the Wesleyan Church of my upbringing.

It was at Barny that full-time education became for me an established feature of childhood, taken for granted except in the intervals of tonsillitis. I attended the old Wesleyan School (1839) at the bottom of the hill by the river. From the old town one approached it by a narrow alley which had the playground wall for one side. At the front there was grassland known as the Demesnes (why not pronounced Dee-mez-nez, I wondered childlike? – and some of the children did!). This gave us scope for play, both flat and slope; and along one side ran the Tees. In those days the river was liable to sudden floods or spates, less so now that the reservoirs are built higher up Teesdale; we would stand on the bank at playtime and watch the flood waters racing past with trees and timbers and an occasional dead sheep (that savour of death again thrusting disquiet into a child's glee). It was from the Demesnes that I first saw an aeroplane – the first anyone had seen except perhaps the headmaster. A boy told him of it late during afternoon school; out we all trooped, and there it was, just audible, a speck against the sky. We watched spellbound until it was out of sight; we then went home. That headmaster was more human than I realised at the time!

The school was a single-storey stone building erected as a Wesleyan contribution to voluntary grant-aided elementary education, presumably under the Royal Lancastrian Society. I remember it as two main blocks of classroom space, within each of which separate classes competed for room and quiet; strangely, I cannot remember being distracted (except when a child was caned); discipline was rugged and we knew we had to learn. Behind was the asphalt playground and there, disjunct from the main building, were the toilets, boys' and girls' back to back and smelling of stale urine. Up the hill by the church was the Anglican National School, proclaiming its identity in bold brick lettering; this had belonged (to give it its full title) to the National Society for Promoting the Education of the Poor in the Principles of the Established Church. Presumably it was now, like ours, administered under the aegis of the Durham County Council; for us it had a certain musty air of sanctity; it was also feared for its bullying and we tried to avoid the path that ran past it to the town and home. The Wesleyan School is now demolished and the space it occupied has been grassed over into a play-park.

Compared with the splendid buildings and equipment of today our school was a dump; but it gave us open space and a sense of freedom; and we learnt in it. The headmaster I remember as an austere gentleman whose regime was firm and efficient; I felt a contrast with my Redruth school. He took us one day for arithmetic while our class-teacher was

The Methodist Church at Barny

The Wesleyan School at Barny

absent. The subject of the lesson I have forgotten, but it involved drawing a straight line freehand; I disobeyed instructions and used the edge of a book. He suspected what I had done, but when questioned I denied it. He then held the paper horizontal to his eye, fore-shortening the line to gauge its straightness. I still denied it. 'I don't believe you,' he murmured and moved on. I learnt two useful lessons from this incident: one was his test of straightness; the other was to lie with greater circumspection.

There were no play methods in that school; our business was to learn the three R's, and on the whole we did. Every morning we recited our tables, individually and in unison, adding each new one as acquired; and I rehearsed them to myself as I trotted between home and school. (Why were 7 × 8 and 7 × 9 so especially elusive, then and now?) Of the other two R's I remember almost nothing; yet the teaching must have been effective, for I was at no disadvantage when I entered the grammar school at Newark. For scripture, in this denominational school, we read verse by verse round the class; absence of explanation left us uncomprehending.

The clatter of slates was a normal part of our daily routine, *and* the shivering screech of the pencils; paper was scarce and reserved for special tasks and exercises. We were required to bring a pencil to school; morning and afternoon we filed in past one of the masters, holding up our pencils for inspection; those who had none were punished. This encouraged us in subterfuge: it was possible to show one's pencil and then, with care, to pass it to a boy who had none; alternatively (and this was my favourite ruse) one could find a piece of stick, sharpen the end on the stone of the wall, blacken it, and conceal all but the point in one's clenched fingers while slipping past the inspecting eye.

We were a wide social mix, from the very poorest to the sons and daughters of well-off shopkeepers and business men. The poor were dressed in patched rags and clacked along in clogs. I wondered at their noses dripping yellow snot and their hands ugly with warts and calloused finger nails; they smelled and we avoided sitting next to them.

It was during these years at Barny that there first dawned on me an awareness of sex; with it came the inevitable curiosity about anatomy and reproduction. That boys and girls dressed differently I had recognised at Redruth – hence my resentment at the tunics I was forced to wear. I now began to wonder what lay beneath the skirts of my female associates and why they sat to urinate. (Since at that age they were all flat-chested, I did not have the further problem of incipient breasts.) I had absolutely no idea. I was conscious too of a certain attraction towards girls, and I had my favourites among them. There was Jane, straight-haired and plain but lively and affectionate; she especially enjoyed the party game of bumps and kisses. Betsy, with her dark tossing curls, was pretty but aloof. These two I saw at chapel; they were regular attenders at morning service and I relieved the tedium of the sermon by trying to attract their gaze and then retreating in giggles behind the pew as our eyes met. It was Joyce whom I chiefly admired; she lived nearby and we played together in the back lane such simple games as a boy and girl could share. Curiously, I have forgotten what she looked like, but not her attractiveness and my desire to be liked and noticed by her. My childish imagination invented incidents of heroic rescue in which I saved her from perils of flood, fire, and shipwreck.

These friendships were wholly innocent; they brought no nearer the satisfaction of my sexual curiosity. Of course I asked my mother the obvious question, 'Where do babies come from?' I was told 'You mustn't ask, dear,' and left in ignorance.

It may be that on one occasion she did indeed attempt to enlighten my darkness, but in a manner which more or less guaranteed lack of success. We were staying with Auntie Kate, whose daughter was a year or two older than myself. It was decided one evening that Joan and I should share the bathroom for our daily bath. For five minutes we were left alone together, she in the bath and I drying myself outside it. 'Come and look at me,' she said as she lay on her back in the water. But I was so conditioned to regard what lies between the legs as 'rude', that I rejected the offer. She then turned over and repeated it. 'Well,' I thought to myself, 'it can't be wrong to look at a girl's bottom,' and peered cautiously over the edge of the bath. What I saw told me nothing; my ignorance of the female genital apparatus remained as total as ever.

The first break in the darkness came in my last year at the Wesleyan School. A girl of nine or ten had been found in possession of a note which suggested that she had been a partner in sexual intercourse with some of the boys. Although this was highly improbable and no more than a piece of childish bravado, the note caused consternation among the staff, ripples of which were felt among the pupils. To me it was all meaningless; surprised at the fuss therefore, I asked one of my male friends to explain. He did so very simply, using both manual gesture and certain crude anatomical terms current among boys at that time but as yet unknown to me. In my innocence I asked again why anyone should want to do this. 'That,' he said, 'is how you get babies.' Strange, is it not, that information so fundamental should come by means so fortuitous and unexpected! To me the revelation was abrupt, startling to the point almost of incredulity. However, I accepted it in good faith and thus gained a partial, tantalising foothold in forbidden territory as well as adding to my vocabulary several new words which I must leave to the reader's imagination to supply.

School did not, of course, occupy the whole of my time; beyond its walls the abundant energy of childhood found outlet in a variety of activities. And activities they were; for leisure was *doing*, a constant exercise in inventiveness. It could not be otherwise, since there was no radio, no television, no switching into ready-made entertainment to fill out a temporary vacancy between tea and bedtime. For winter evenings I had my Hornby trains and Meccano set. For the former there was no permanent location; the track had always to be dismantled after use and relaid on the next occasion. New layouts had to be devised, new journeys imagined through different landscapes, new tunnels, bridges and embankments improvised from books, boxes and a variety of household paraphernalia. Over it all hung the sallow light and persistent susurration of the gas mantles; many years were to pass before we enjoyed the benefits of electricity.

I cannot recall that I was much given to reading. Books there were in plenty about the house; my father's study was full of them, and my mother too was a regular reader of lighter literature. The only reading I can remember from this period of childhood is *Tiger Tim's Annual* and its associated weekly comic. No doubt there were other books, but they made no permanent impact. At some time I became enthralled by the adventure stories of R. M. Ballantyne, *The Young Fur Traders, The Gorilla Hunters*, and many others; but I suspect this came a year or two later, after our move to Newark.

In summer I enjoyed much extended horizons. Apart from the garden, the back lane, the walks with my father and the occasional family picnics, I had the run of the town and the local countryside. Once school was over, and within the bounds of meals and bedtime, I was free to come and go as I pleased. Traffic was no hazard; nor was there any fear of attack or molestation. This freedom to wander at will I count as one of the greatest blessings of my childhood – lost now to the majority of children in the urbanised, transport-dominated England of today. Yet looking back I feel some surprise that my parents allowed me to be so venturesome. For the banks of the Tees are precipitous in places and the river itself is deep and fastflowing. In fact I came to no harm beyond the occasional cut and bruise. Perhaps, with a wisdom of which I was ignorant at the time and have since underestimated, they weighed the physical risk against the advantages of freedom and deliberately chose the latter. If so, I am sure they were right.

Much of my time was spent in the Flatts Woods which stretch from the golf course to the Tees; it was then a small piece of mature forest with majestic pines and oaks, but it has since been demolished and replanted. Sometimes I would trip and trot along the ups and downs of the red cinder paths, careless of time and conscious only of an exuberance of energy which a mere walking pace could not contain. Sometimes I would leave the paths to wander among the pines whose great columns, gummy with exuding resin, tapered through a tangle of dead branches into the over-roofing darkness. One special delight was a game of sticks and stones, played along the banks of the stream which flowed through the woods. I would throw a piece of stick into the water and follow its course downstream. When it stuck against the numerous stones and boulders or was stranded in a backwater, I would try to dislodge it by throwing stones, precisely aimed to left, right or behind as the situation required. With two or three players the game became a race whose purpose was not only to dislodge one's own stick but to impede those of one's competitors. Many were the absorbing hours thus spent.

The woods along the Tees were different; the trees were deciduous, mostly oak, and there was light and space for growth beneath them. Here according to season were anemones, primroses and bluebells; later came garlic and dog mercury; among them grew ferns and feathery grasses. Where the woods ended, beyond the railway bridge, was a mass of blackberry and willow-herb. Further than this I never ventured, and only rarely so far; at one point the path narrowed between two rocks, locally known as 'the wishing stones' (if one could pass through them without touching, one was allowed to wish); this was normally the limit of my excursions. From below the path, through the trees and flowers, came glimpses of dark water and the glint of sunlight; occasionally a train crossed the bridge and by great good luck, combined with hard running, one might just be beneath it as it clattered over. From these expeditions I always brought flowers home to my mother, tightly clutched and wilting bunches of as many varieties as I could find in the woods and bordering fields. Later I began collecting and pressing them; their musty smell and faded colours remain vividly in memory. A growing interest in the natural world led me further to tadpoles and tiddlers, which I kept in a large metal washtub in the back garden; their life was always disappointingly short. For long it was my ambition to find and keep some newts, but these eluded my search.

In these wanderings through the woods and fields round Barny I was beginning to recognise and consciously to acknowledge something deeper, more significant, than a child's simple delight in physical activity and exploration of the natural world. I was aware, in a manner which I could neither make explicit to myself nor explain to others (even had I wished), of an affinity with the growth around me. But more than affinity; for it was not just that I felt involved with the trees and flowers, with the wind sifting through the pines, with the water tumbling and sparkling over the stones – as if I were part of them and they of me. They carried also with them a message and a fascination. They spoke of a presence, disturbing yet exhilarating, of a mystery tenuously felt but deeply, patiently insistent, permitting no escape; they drew me to themselves. Here once again the sceptical reader may accuse me of exaggeration, or distortion, of imposing on childhood the nostalgic ruminations of adolescent and later years. Yet although the words I have used are inevitably those of maturity, to the best of my belief they genuinely describe what I actually felt and experienced at the time. And after all (if the parallel is not too presumptuous) the poet Wordsworth had much the same experiences but more intensely

> among the fields both day and night
> And by the waters all the summer long

– unless of course he too was guilty of nostalgic distortion!

Although content to be alone I was never lonely; nor was I without friends. There was Dick (he it was who unveiled to me the mysteries of sex). Since he lived in the marketplace a mile or so from the manse, we could not easily arrange to play. (Telephones were a rarity then, and my father went through to the end of his ministry without one.) So our friendship was mostly one of schooldays; his father's shop was on my shortest route to school; here we would meet and part on our journeyings to and fro. Ginger was another and more frequent companion. His father was a drayman for the LNER, whose goods depot was close to the top of Galgate; their house was near enough for casual calling. Often Ginger was out, helping on delivery rounds; occasionally I caught him on the point of departure and was allowed a seat beside him on the dray. This was a treat indeed! Magnificent were those great horses, with their huge shaggy hooves and jingling, shining brasses! And how their muscles bulged and rippled as they responded to the driver's curses (unsparing of our tender ears) and strained to set their load in motion! Ginger's garden had a large beech tree; it was well endowed with branches which gave us ready and various access to the top. Here we would squat for half an hour at a time, swaying deliciously with the wind and peering out over trees and roofs to the distant hills and moors. From that time climbing trees was among the chief delights of my boyhood.

However, the scene was soon to change. My father's three-year period at Barny was due to end in August 1927, an event presaged for months beforehand by talk of stipend and manse and grammar school. It was somewhere in the Midlands, a place called Newark on a big river with boats and barges and on the main line from London to Scotland. I could not visualise it, for my world was closely circumscribed and my scant knowledge of geography entirely unsupported by pictorial aids. But I had a vague sense of apprehension, of a door closing behind me, and beyond it . . . ? Well, that would reveal itself in good time; childhood does not concern itself overmuch about the future.

Meanwhile there was all the ritual of packing to be gone through. When preparing to leave Ceylon my father had acquired a number of large wooden cases (tea chests I think they were) for despatching the family possessions back to England. Thenceforth they accompanied our every move, from Sleights to Redruth to Barny to Newark and later to Ilkeston, Horncastle, Portessie (on the Moray Firth) and finally to Padiham in Lancashire. Between each occasion of use they were stored in attic or outhouse, and although their appearances were infrequent, they became a familiar part of our household equipment. Throughout their thirty years of use they were packed with the same bright yellow sneezy straw, fastened with the same rusty screws, and to the end still bore the label of the Union Castle Line which had originally conveyed them from Colombo. These were now retrieved from their three-year exile and lined up in the hall and study to await their turn.

Packing, if I remember rightly, took about two months – why so long I could never understand. Essential furniture was provided by the circuit and we had few pieces of our own. Our possessions consisted mainly of books, brasses, pictures, china, clothes and various personal articles like the Hornby trains and my mother's sewing machine. Nowadays the work would be left to professional removers and finished in a couple of days or less; but my father did it all himself, wrapping each item with meticulous care, spacing it precisely from its neighbour in the box and stuffing the interval with straw. At last the lids were all screwed down; what could not be boxed was stacked in the hall; the house, stripped to its essentials, assumed a disquieting impersonality, as if it neither belonged to us nor we to it – as indeed was the case. Then came the day of departure, the lunch with our neighbours (and the tragic accident to Stephen) and finally the train to Darlington where we caught the connection south.

CHAPTER IV

Newark on Trent

WE WERE MET AT THE STATION by the circuit stewards, officials of the church whose duty is to supervise the appointment, departure and arrival of ministers; thence we were conveyed the few hundred yards down Appletongate to the manse.

For me, our first arrival at a manse was always an exciting adventure. Here was a new geography of house and garden to explore, a host of exciting opportunities for my accustomed boyhood pursuits and the invention of others. Up and down the stairs I raced from room to room, hopefully claiming this one or that one for my own, and quick to spot the obvious differences between our new manse and the previous.

The manses were indeed all different. Some were terraced, some detached; some were of brick, some of stone; at Newark we had attics, at Ilkeston a cellar. All had gardens, small or large but enough for at least a modest vegetable plot. Best of all in nostalgic retrospect was the manse at Portessie on the Moray Firth, where my father was posted in 1938. I was at Cambridge then, and my pleasure in it was necessarily different from that of boyhood. It stood on the edge of a rise which fell steeply down to the sea. On this side the garden wall looked north over a widening angle of water, blue or grey as the weather determined, to the hills of Caithness and Sutherland softly rounded by distance. At night we watched the streamers of the aurora weaving to and fro like searchlights on the far horizon. When war brought a total blackout, the stars shone with piercing brilliance in a velvet sky. The sunsets were magnificent. For me it was a place of enchantment; it gave me comfort, assurance and profound spiritual enrichment; it spoke with the voice of God.

My parents' interest in a new manse was essentially different from mine. My father looked for a quiet study with a desk and shelves for his many books. My mother hoped for a serviceable kitchen and a cooker not overburdened by age; she hoped too for a provision of furniture which would be at least adequate for our comfort and would not shame our visitors. (At that time the furnishing of the manse was the responsibility of the circuit stewards; it surprises me, looking back, that some of them could accept in the manse standards of furnishing and decor which they would not have tolerated in their own homes. My mother's tears are a sad testimony to this.)

The boon of electricity we did not enjoy until the mid-1930s, half way through our stay in Horncastle; I well remember my delight in this novelty as well as my interest in its installation. Until then lighting as well as cooking had been by gas, save at bedtime when we lit our way by candle. It is difficult now to imagine those gas-lit years; there was no summoning of light at the touch of a switch; instead was the fiddling process of turning on the gas, hastily lighting a match and reaching up to the mantle, taking good care not to touch its fragile fabric. Incredible too it now seems that through every house where gas was available there ran a maze of little lead pipes filled with a highly toxic and explosive substance; yet we never gave a thought to the dangers! Among my most persistent memories of that era are the soft, susurrous purring of the lit gas, and the acrid smell of a new mantle as it burned off its stiffening coat of wax.

The manse at Newark was a large, detached, redbrick house with attics at the top and garden on four sides. The attics were a valuable asset: they provided storage for the empty packing chests and also for our annual crop of cooking apples; to me they gave a permanent layout for my Hornby trains and space beyond that for playing with bat and ball against the ceiling.

The apples were a particular source of malicious pleasure. They were laid out in rows on top of the boxes; many of them went bad, transmuted in the process from green to a soft spongy brown. Thrown from the attic window they smacked the path below with a mushy scattering of rotten pulp which was a delight to both ear and eye. To the pedestrians before whose unsuspecting feet they exploded they were a source of astonishment and anger. The gate into the front garden was arched by a single hoop of iron; our maid was precisely beneath this one day on her way home when a well aimed apple hit the peak of the arch and caught her in a shower of putrescence. Too startled for anger at the time, she later complained to my mother and put a temporary stop to this sport.

The garden was as large as that at Barny, but a different shape; at the front and sides there was room only for trees and shrubs, but in the main garden there was space for vegetables and fruit bushes as well as apple trees; there was a lawn too, and a variety of sheds which gave me opportunity for play. Among my vivid recollections of the garden are the tall balsam plants with their pink flowers (a special favourite of my mother) and of the tortoiseshell butterflies which haunted them in late summer. On one of the sheds, which had a metal lattice along its side, grew nasturtiums; these were favoured by cabbage butterflies whose green and black caterpillars swarmed over them, gouging holes in their circular leaves. Never forgotten are the sight and smell of these caterpillars and their repulsive green excrement. A side street bounded the garden on its west side, separated from it by a heavily creosoted wooden fence which I used, like the attic wall and ceiling, for playing bat and ball; the hot summer smell of the creosoted wood is another unforgettable item from this package of boyhood.

At the far end of the side street was a senior school (boys and girls aged eight to fourteen years). These children, in terms of the family slang, were 'purds'; that is, they were poorly dressed and belonged to the working class; and although some of them might appear in grammar or high school, this was not their proper milieu. They were to be looked down on and sometimes feared.

Newark is a manufacturing town of moderate size surrounded by agriculture; eastwards are the broad fields and skies of Lincolnshire; south is the beautiful and fertile Vale of Belvoir. As befits such a setting, it has a large market-place which in our time was regularly filled with stalls on Saturdays. Important among its industries are the breweries; for these, we were told, it is indebted to the gypsum in the local water. The white 'sails' of the great brick malting houses are familiar to all who know the town, and no less familiar the boozy smell that drifts along its streets. To me and my playmates their high brick walls offered abundant opportunity for various games of ball which occupied the vacant hours of summer evenings when homework was done.

Entertainment of a different kind was provided when one of them caught fire. It was in November after dark, but the bright glow in the west was visible even through the drawn curtains and the gaslight. Although it was my bedtime, I was allowed out with my friends to watch the spectacle – which indeed it was, for although the building was on the riverside and there was no lack of water, it was completely gutted. Neither poetry nor the artist's brush could ever match what memory still holds of the awesome splendour of that scene. It was like a page from Dante's Inferno or Virgil's underworld or Pliny's account of Pompeii's devastation – all of them as yet unknown to me. But thoughts of hell did cross my mind as I stood transfixed on the bank of the Trent, my senses assaulted by the hiss and roar and stench, the crash of blazing timbers, the cyclonic upswirl of brilliant flame, the constant rain of sparks and hot ash, all of it magnified and multiplied by echo and reflection and the hot, rancid, flurrying

Newark: the spire of the parish church

Newark Castle and the River Trent

breeze. At last the flames subsided; in the encroaching darkness the walls glowed red hot; jets from the fire engines burst explosively into surging steam against their bulging brickwork. The best of the spectacle was over; it was 11 o'clock and time to go home.

Curiosity drew me to the scene again next day; but now, even to my childhood years, the contrast was stark, depressing. Instead of the previous night's magnificence I found only the scorched shell of the building; the black ash was sullenly steaming, and pouring into the river was an obscene flow of yellow liquid like the effluent from some grotesque sewage plant.

Another odorous industry which then afflicted Newark was a bone-meal factory which stood half a mile to the north by the side of the main railway line. Here open truck loads of raw bones waited in sidings for treatment; a useful by-product at this stage of the process was the mass of maggots which were shaken into trays and sold in penny bags to the local fishermen. I bought many a bag myself during my addiction to this hobby. The trays of white maggots, writhing and heaving in a kind of perpetual fermentation roused in me a strange mixture of fascination and nausea. To the population of Newark the bones themselves and their conversion to fertiliser brought occasional discomfort. For when the wind was in the north-east, a heavy stench of decay seeped pervasively through streets and houses, displacing the cheerful effluvia of malt and beer, and forcing us to close doors and windows even in the height of summer.

It was at Newark at the age of ten that I began my secondary schooling. I was sent to Magnus Grammar School situated on the western outskirts of the town. It was then a school of about 250 boys, mostly day, but there were still a few boarders perpetuating a tradition which reached back to the 16th century. It was named after Thomas Magnus, a 16th-century politician and administrator, who was a native of Newark and in 1529 had founded there a free school from which the Grammar School traced its descent. It had a simple coat of arms with the legend *sicut Deus vult* (as God will), and a bright red and green school cap but no formal school uniform; prefects were distinguished by the addition to their caps of a conspicuous white tassel. There was, I believe, a school blazer, but such refinement was far beyond my parents' means; I cannot remember that I ever felt deprived for lack of it. (My clothes were bought at Foster Brothers in Nottingham, for my Uncle Jack was a director of the firm and allowed us to charge them to his account.)

The school was red brick, save for the hut which housed the first year. At the back it faced pleasantly westwards over spacious playing fields; within these the First XV pitch was sacrosanct, forbidden under threat of

Magnus Grammar School: the front entrance

The school from the rear

punishment to all but the chosen feet. It was built, according to the best educational wisdom of the time, for formal instruction at desks and benches. There was no dining accommodation, for there were no lunches – schools then were for teaching not welfare! It had the normal school hall which, since it was used for physical training as well as assembly, was lined with parallel bars and had no seating. Of morning prayers I have no recollection whatever except for the occasion when special petition was made on behalf of a boy who was injured when cycling across the A1. Classrooms lined the hall and also the corridors which stemmed T-like from the dais end of it; the air of the corridors was always unmistakably tainted by gaseous emissions from the laboratories. The fees were £3 a term, paid immediately on arrival on the first day; the unlucky boys whose parents forgot were sent home. The headmaster in my years was a clergyman; he moved noiselessly about the school on rubber soled shoes and was rumoured to swing a good cane.

It was a bright September morning when I first set off for the school, my cheque in my pocket, my bright new cap perched proudly on my head and my satchel flapping empty at my side. As yet I had no bicycle of my own, but across the road was another boy, also starting at Magnus, who would take me on his. It was not illegal then to ride two on a single bicycle, and it was common practice for one boy to carry another sitting on his crossbar – dangerous, of course, and spillages were frequent but injury rare. Some cycles had a small step attached to the left of the back axle; on such a machine one could carry a pair of passengers, and this too was not uncommon.[1] However, it was not long before I had my own bicycle, second-hand and single-speed, but a treasured possession which brought me happiness over many years.

As there were no school lunches, I had to cycle twice daily the one and a half miles each way. It was a pleasant exercise, enlivened by the company of friends and fraught with little inherent hazard once the A1 was safely crossed. We created hazard by racing three abreast or three on a bicycle down the one significant slope towards home or by attaching reins of string to our handlebars and pretending to be jockeys. Sometimes we dared each other to ride with eyes shut from one lamp-post to the next or the next again. Providentially we came to no harm from such pranks, but the catch of fear still comes to my stomach when I think of them; in the traffic-choked streets of today they would be unthinkably foolish.

[1] The purpose of the step was to enable a rather clumsy method of getting on: gripping the handlebars one straddled the back wheel, put one's left foot on the step and pushed off with the right; when the cycle was moving, one eased forward into the saddle and brought both feet on to the pedals.

What I should find when I arrived at the school I had no idea. Previously I had known only the red brick building at Redruth and the squat stone structure at Barny, each with its cramped ration of asphalt play-space (blessedly supplemented at Barny by the riverside Demesnes and the open country beyond). Magnus would be different, but how different I could not imagine. It belonged, had I been aware of it, to the Renaissance and Public School tradition with roots in the classical past, in moral discipline and compulsory games. This was reflected in the simple (but not unpleasing) formality of the architecture, which matched its plain directness of purpose, and in the ample games field neatly laid out in a hierarchy of rugby pitches. On that September morning, redolent with autumn's mellowness of scent and colour, first impressions were favourable. The early sunshine gave to the building, the field and its encircling trees a welcoming warmth which augured well. On the rose bushes which edged the inner boundary fence was a mass of bright squashy hips; we swooped on these and, satchels flying and caps tumbling, we hurled them at one another in joyous exuberance of combat until the whistle summoned us to pay our fees and submit to medical examination. This done we were shown to our hut; here a hustling, chattering scrabble of thirty-five excited boys, we waited for our form master to unlock the door.

Inside were four rows of lidded desks, a table and chair for the teacher, and a blackboard with its easel; these were the basic furniture for the prevalent conception of efficient teaching; the walls were bare. Textbooks were issued subject by subject during the first week. I well remember our delight if the set was new or if, from a pile of battered copies, the odd new one came our way. Remembered too is the pride and sense of possession with which in that first week we wrote our names on the labels within and thus claimed them, albeit temporarily, as our own. And of course we were allowed and expected to take them home as might be necessary. The rows of desks were closely packed, leaving us little room for movement unless summoned to the master's table or the call of nature – the latter often simulated for the sake of a different relief. For how our young limbs itched and fidgeted under pressure of that imperious energy which, interminably it seemed to us, clamoured vainly for release!

Such was the scene for the start of our secondary schooling. Here for the first time I encountered Latin, French, rugby football and compulsory homework; here for the first time found myself in a class consisting only of boys taught only by men – an environment exclusively male save for the school secretary and the headmaster's wife and, I have been reminded, one female member of the staff by whom I was never taught. For myself I scarcely noticed the absence of girls. Despite my interest in them at Barny and a continuing curiosity about the female anatomy, they were little more to me than boys differently dressed. Moreover I was coming to the age when mutual interest between the sexes is at its lowest ebb and segregation therefore least noticeable to them. This with all the rest of it I took for granted, as did my fellow pupils. We knew of no alternative; and it was all so fresh, so exhilarating in its novelty, its sudden expansion of experience. The usefulness of what we were taught I never thought to question. I buckled down to *amo, amas, amat* and *je parle, tu parles, il parle* as if it were the most natural thing in the world and even a kind of game – which in a sense it was, for all our work was tied competitively to marks and monthly lists. And it was a game I was good at; for I found the work easy and I was usually at or near the top.

I have little memory of routine lessons in that first year. We were taught the basic subjects of the curriculum – English, mathematics, history, geography – together with the minima of religious instruction, physical training and art; French and botany were also part of our fare; and for the A class, to which I belonged, there was Latin too. Streaming was well nigh universal in the grammar schools of that time, and Magnus was no exception; mixed ability and group teaching were as yet unheard of outside the few 'progressive' schools, whose practices were slow to filter into the wider field of public education. Teaching was instruction by chalk, talk and textbook, directed at pupils in desks and classes. For the brighter few it was supported by the incentives of form orders and prizes, for the rest by the negative inducement of avoiding censure and punishment. Learning by discovery, by guided use of resources in a structured environment had not yet penetrated the pedagogics of secondary schooling.

I was good at languages (except my own); Latin and French I picked up easily, slotting smoothly into memory the grammatical forms and parroting them on demand; the syntactical rules I likewise learnt and applied with mechanical readiness. Hillard and Botting and Kennedy's Shorter Primer were our Latin textbooks, both devoid of illustration except for those illicitly doodled in the absentmindedness of tedium. Throughout this first year we plodded through exercise after exercise, up to fifty sentences a week, translating into Latin unlikely propositions about the Romans and their generals (among whom Labienus was especially prominent), their enemies, their captives, slaves, wives and children. The purpose of it all, in accordance with centuries of tradition, was to establish in our resistant brains a solid edifice of grammar and syntax to enable us, at some presumed later stage, to read what the Romans themselves actually wrote. Who the Romans were, where and when they lived, and what the nature of their achievement we had little idea, and as little was done to enlighten us. Their daily life and culture remained a closed book – partly, it might be said in excuse, because there were indeed no textbooks to portray them. Few if any of us were aware that they had conquered Britain and covered it with the best system of roads it had enjoyed until the 19th century. *Romani Britannos superaverunt* was not for us a statement of fact but the solution (or alternatively the start) of a grammatical puzzle.

French was not much different; we learnt and applied the rules, read short passages of continuous prose and translated innumerable sentences from English into French and *vice versa*. Of the French people themselves we had little impression; but at least our textbooks were illustrated, and from these drawings (to which we added our own decorative and sometimes obscene appendages) we learnt that their style of life, dress and food was different from our own. There was a small amount of oral work, but tapes, cassettes and language laboratories were still in the future; the idea of French as a means of communication scarcely entered our heads.

The master who taught us botany sometimes brought a bag of specimens – leaves, grasses, berries, rose-hips and the seed 'wings' of lime and sycamore. One day he arrived with a supply of brussel sprouts which he carefully distributed desk by desk throughout the class. Then, after telling us to peel off two or three of the outer leaves, he turned to the board to write on it the botanical terms relevant to a complete dissection. But dissection was not to be. No sooner was his back to us than we brushed the dirt from our sprouts and with uncanny unanimity put them in our mouths and munched and swallowed them. When he turned again to resume the lesson, the sprouts had disappeared. My memory still retains the hot taste of the raw vegetable and the expression of mingled astonishment, exasperation and wrath on our teacher's face; but I cannot remember what penalty, if any, he imposed on us or how the lesson proceeded.

A prank which I intended for him misfired and erupted into a French lesson. I had the idea of collecting a number of bluebottles (the large blue flies that boom and buzz through drowsy summer afternoons) and releasing them *en masse* in the classroom. After a hasty lunch I spent half an hour in the garden capturing about twenty of them and packing them into a matchbox – a task which required care, persistence and nimble fingers, for these flies are vigorous and keenly resist restraint. Back at school and bored with grammatical explanation I took the box from my pocket to ensure the security of its occupants. Alas, it came open and from it exploded an angry troop of bluebottles which streamed like raiding commandos to the nearest window. Momentarily grammar was drowned by the detonation of buzzing; for a split second the master's mouth hung open, frozen in mid-sentence by the shock; then, wisely choosing to ignore the interruption, he resumed explanation; the class quickly returned to its passivity and the bluebottles disappeared through the window.

Next September we moved up into the main building. Here I spent the remaining two years of my time at Magnus, one of them (perhaps both) in a classroom opening off the main hall. I find it difficult to differentiate the one year from the other; nor is there much to be said of them, for not much is remembered. Instruction in the basic subjects, including Latin for our A class, continued as before. The content of our history and geography lessons is lost beyond all recall – which is perhaps a measure of their impact on me. My memories of English lessons are almost as void. Here a special point of interest, eagerly awaited and noted with communal delight, was the behaviour of the master who, in his more dramatic moments would gesticulate wildly and froth at the corners of his mouth. Inevitably Shakespeare was part of our syllabus. We read *A Midsummer Night's Dream* and *Julius Caesar* round the class, enduring rather than enjoying the experience, and were made to learn substantial passages by heart. This latter I did not resent, for I found memorisation easy and was not wholly insensitive, even at that age, to the nobility of the language. But the teaching did little to advance my competence in calligraphy and composition, both of which were poor and remained so for years.

From all the religious instruction to which we were exposed (time-tabled as 'Divinity') a single incident remains. One of our teachers, for reasons as obscure to me now as then, required us to know by heart the full roll of the kings of Israel and Judah. When it came to the summer examinations, one of our class attempted to compensate either for idleness or for shortness of memory by writing their names on his desk. Alas, his deception was discovered! He was dismissed from the classroom and assigned a nil mark for the Divinity paper.

For a time art and singing were part of our diet; I had no propensity for either and no interest in them. Again a single incident escapes oblivion. During one week of the year – I forget precisely when – the school organised an egg collection on behalf of the local hospital. The fate of the eggs, whether they were sold, employed in some gigantic culinary adventure, or simply fed to the unfortunate patients – this we were not told. Our task was to solicit eggs from parents and friends and bring them intact to school. This was in the days before the household refrigerator; inevitably, therefore, some of our donors, whether by accident or intent, offloaded on to us eggs of doubtful condition. It was also before the invention of the plastic egg container; most of us carried our eggs to school in paper bags. Art was time-tabled for first period on the day of collection at school, and an empty desk in the corner of the room was an obvious recipient for eggs broken or malodorous which we thought would be unwelcome. Moreover, since the master's name was Hammond, what more appropriate than to offer him a supply of eggs for breakfast! It was our delight in subsequent weeks to sniff the air on entering the art room and comment on Mr Hammond's menu. Later, at a convenient moment in the lesson, the more adventurous among us would gingerly raise the lid of the desk and, with a variety of histrionics, pretend to suffocation and collapse. It was a month or two before the removal of the eggs deprived us of this source of light relief.

Latin I continued to enjoy, but chiefly as a mechanical exercise which I could perform with ease and accuracy; to most of my classmates it was, I am sure, a dreary and mindless activity whose only obvious purpose was to avoid rebuke or punishment. Geometry too I enjoyed; its logical procedures give it some resemblance to Latin grammar and syntax, and I could perform its simpler exercises with the same facility as those of North and Hillard. Arithmetic had little appeal. Our textbooks were stolid, dull and unrelieved by diagram or illustration; they consisted, so it seemed, of endless questions on ratio, proportion, percentage, speed, cost, quantity, area, volume – all of them hopelessly remote from the practical needs of boyhood and the unsophisticated economics of 3d. a week pocket money. But there was a difference; it lay in the master who taught us. For he was more than a teacher; I remember him also as a scholar, an educator and a gentleman. He was quiet, mild, tolerant – qualities which we were quick to take advantage of; we fooled him unmercifully, and yet we respected him; and we learnt from him. When chaos was deepest, he would stand at his desk, surveying us with a calm, incredulous reproach which eventually brought silence, attention and a resumption of work. Moreover he was willing to digress, and on occasion (after some initial prompting) would launch out into such topics as the fourth dimension and the speed of light. These are all that I can remember; of far greater importance were the digressions themselves, for it was thus, by his willingness to depart from instructional routine, that I obtained my first glimpses of an intellectual world wider than the classroom.

Physics and chemistry were added to our curriculum at the start of my second year. Hitherto our study of the sciences had been confined to botany; this had been presented within our own classroom to reluctant recipients, for fruits and flowers had little obvious interest for boys of eleven. But now for the first time we entered the unknown territory of the science laboratory. How vividly I remember the excitement of it! Here was a chattering bunch of youngsters jostling into this strange domain of balances and bunsen burners, its shelves lined with bottles of every rainbow hue, pervaded by the smell of gas and chemicals, and furnished with benches instead of the familiar hinged seats and lids of the classroom desks.

It was an extension not only of knowledge and activity but also, inevitably, of vocabulary. Gas jars and test-tubes, pipettes and spatulas, calories and coefficients of expansion, concave and convex, litmus and phenolphthalein, as well as the limited number of chemicals permitted for our use – all these came tripping off our tongues with the delight as of some new game. It was an extension too of sensory experience; for here in the laboratory were *real things*; not symbols merely on the printed page to be juggled endlessly by pen and brain into our exercise books, but actual objects – prisms, lenses, crystals, thermometers – which we could feel and hold and handle.

I found both subjects congenial from the beginning, chemistry more than physics; experiments, both watching and doing, were a particular pleasure. No doubt we were fortunate in our masters, both of whom were brisk, businesslike, efficient, and exercised a firm but kindly discipline. Our chemistry master was an athletic Welshman with a sly tinge of humour. When a boy let slip a winchester from a shelf high up towards the ceiling, he leapt from his bench, caught it like a rugby ball and shouted 'Mark!' (Rugger was his game, and he was a formidable opponent in the annual Staff Match.) The physics master I remember chiefly for his demonstrations of expansion, optics and magnetism performed on the bench in the tiered physics room. We watched fascinated as 'Pepper's ghost' emerged mysteriously into the darkened room, iron filings patterned themselves on the paper over the magnet, and metal bars proved their expansive properties on the improvised pointer-scale.

Little detailed knowledge remains from those two years introduction to physics and chemistry – my only period of regular formal instruction in the sciences. I can recall a few chemical symbols like Fe and Pb, H_2SO_4 and $KMnO_4$, some simple facts about the elements, about acids and alkalis, the properties of matter, light and heat. Even this little is not insignificant in a society increasingly orientated towards science and practical do-it-yourself. Far more important, however, was the foothold these years gave me in a new world sharply contrasted, in language, concepts, outlook, activity and the furniture of instruction, with the rest of my book-and-language dominated studies.

An immediate consequence of this was a sense of unsatisfied questioning, of vast areas of interest inviting exploration, which led to an eager reading of whatever elementary books on science were available; among these was a magazine series called *Our Wonderful World* (later bound into four volumes) to which my parents subscribed on my behalf. A more distant consequence has been an attitude of accepting science, of seeing it as part of the normality of things. It is perhaps because of this that, though trained in classics, I have never felt oppressed by the 'two cultures', arts v sciences, dualism, but have acknowledged both as complementary and equally enriching constituents of the same universe of experience. Nor is it fanciful to attribute to these two years the first stirrings in me of that sense of intellectual mystery, of final inexplicability, which is the source of metaphysical questioning and the parent of philosophy. Fanciful or not, most of this was far in the future and impossible to recognise at the time; but it points to the wisdom of those who devised our curriculum and ensured that our impressionable years were exposed to this vital broadening of intellectual horizons.

With few exceptions our masters were kindly and conscientious; those whom we could not positively like (and dare not fool) we tolerated – having no alternative – and performed our due tasks with resigned obedience. Their teaching was efficient but formal. There was little deliberate appeal to interest, for the doctrine of 'child-centredness' had scarcely penetrated the pedagogy of grammar schools. Success, it was thought, lay in systematic instruction backed by constant practice in and out of class, by competitive form lists, the threat of punishment and the fear of failure in public examinations. Magnus was not, of course, unique in this! Looking back I am impressed by the patience of our teachers. We were a restless, exuberant group of youngsters – not malicious, but bubbling with the effervescent energies of boyhood and inclined to any kind of experimental naughtiness which circumstances and our lively imaginations might suggest.

Sweets were a favourite form of diversion. Popular among us was a coconut butterscotch, pleasantly rough to the tongue; when sucked it gradually released the desiccated nut, which could then be separately chewed and savoured. And there were aniseed balls; these were dark brown and about half an inch in diameter; within they consisted of layers of different colours with a small round seed at the centre. It was an amusing pastime to keep half a dozen on the go at once, suck each to a different layer and then place them along the groove of the desk in a range of size and hue. They had a special appeal for two very good reasons. They were the best buy, both in quantity and in sucking time, for my 3d. a week pocket money; and they were conveniently small for escaping detection. Thus, 'Are you eating, boy?' was answered with a quick swallow and a more or less honest 'No, sir!' Discovery, of course, meant confiscation and usually total loss.

For an especially daring piece of mischief we chose our mathematics master as the most suitable victim. It involved boring a hole down the centre of a stick of chalk, inserting a live match, and leaving it ready for use on the board. As we had no drill, the hole was made with the point of a compass; this required hours of patient probing, mostly during lessons, and resulted in many failures and much broken chalk before the device was complete. A hush of expectation enveloped the class when the master entered; he must surely have wondered at the unprecedented quiet! As he launched into geometrical theorem and reached for the chalk, the hush became almost solid. Thirty pairs of eyes were focused tensely on the point of contact between chalk and board, eager for success yet nervous of its consequences. When the chalk refused to write, he pressed harder and then – a burst of flame and smoke, a flash of astonishment across his face, and suppressed giggles from the class as the tension broke. We were too startled ourselves to laugh openly, and too doubtful about consequences yet to come. But there were none. After surveying us with his customary air of incredulity, he took another stick of chalk from the box and continued his explanation. This, I now recognise, was a masterly piece of self-control and wise pedagogy.

Our pranks and misdemeanours did not go unpunished. Detention came not infrequently; this we could evade on occasion by feigning sickness and spending the day at home. Lines were a regular penalty, imposed by both staff and prefects. Their phrasing was sufficiently constant to enable the more prudent of us to anticipate demand by writing up a store of them from which to draw as needed. It was even possible to write lines for other boys if their handwriting was unknown (as it might be to a prefect) or similar to one's own and sell them at so much per 50. An alternative to lines, and even more mindless, was copying out chapters from the Old Testament – a practice which no doubt contributed to my strong boyhood aversion to the Hebrew scriptures.

Apart from the very occasional evening lecture and the annual Mayor's Ball (of which more later) the only out-of-class activities were the games and sports considered appropriate for a boys' grammar school. These were rugger once a week during the two winter terms, cricket in the summer, an annual sports day and a cross-country. The first two of these were taken very seriously by the school, but at that time I had little interest and scant proficiency in any of them; I accepted them as part of the required routine. It was at Kingswood some years later that I discovered I had the stamina for long-distance running and came to enjoy it.

Skirts were a rarity at Magnus. Apart from the secretary, the headmaster's wife, the one female teacher and the cleaners, the last of whom were necessarily timed to follow our departure, they appeared only on Sports Day and similar occasions. This almost total absence of females we accepted insensibly as part of the established order: girls belonged to a different world; they went to the high school; and they played hockey. Moreover the years eleven to thirteen are a time of minimal mutual attraction between the sexes (or *were* – it may be different in these days of advanced precocity). Hence our segregation was not noticed as such, nor did we feel deprived.

But we were not without interest, though it was spasmodic, ignorant and often blatantly vulgar. For me in particular, having no sister, the nature and outward appearance of the female anatomy was still a mystery posing something of an intellectual problem. I was aware by now that it was connected with babies and reproduction, but the mechanism of procreation and the function of the male and female genitals remained totally obscure. Neither the school nor my parents took any steps to inform me; nude photography and sexy magazines were not the commonplace they are today. The mystery was deepened when I burst into the bathroom one day and was confronted with my mother standing facing me in the bath. Of course, I retreated hastily and shut the door firmly behind me, but the dark patch above her groin left me for days in a state of profound puzzlement. For I was ignorant still of pubic hair and had visualised the adult body as bald as mine – how could it be otherwise?

And so for three years at Magnus I had virtually no association with girls of my own age. For me they remained denizens of another world, skirted instead of trousered, long-haired and fuller in the chest, different, remote, unknowable. This was emphasised by the one occasion when, in my first year at the school, I attended the Mayor's Ball. Such was the inflated title of an annual party given by the Mayor of Newark to the boys of Magnus and the High School girls (there was no similar provision for the rest of the school population). It was held in the Town Hall. I remember it with a sense of utter, helpless futility. I arrived, presented my ticket and was ushered into a vast room. Sitting along one side of it were about 100 boys; opposite them along the other was a rather larger number of girls; in the intervening space were a few couples, mostly pairs of girls, dancing to music which for the rest of us was without meaning or motive. We sat there – it must have been for an hour or more – immobile, uneasy, pathetically unaware of our social illiteracy, just waiting for something to happen. Came the food – something we could at least understand and respond to with enthusiasm. After that I went home.

There were girls at the Wesleyan chapel we attended down the street from the manse, but no words passed between us – only the occasional glance and giggle from pew to pew. Some of them lived nearby, and as they skipped and played their ball games in the street, I would sometimes race through on my bicycle, swerving crazily around them in mock bravado and laughing gaily as they scattered to the pavement. Some older girls met weekly at the manse under my mother's leadership as members of a Methodist organisation called the Girls' League. Its purpose, as I remember it, was to promote friendship, discussion and good works. The meetings occupied the sitting-room for an hour or two on winter evenings, thus depriving me of the only fire we could afford to keep burning after tea. Whether to vent my annoyance or (more likely) to attract attention, I would crouch outside the door holding our cat firmly between my knees and squeezing the end of his tail until his complaints brought out a girl to let him in. If he were absent on one of his copulatory missions, my simulated howls could produce the same result. By such devious means did my incipient adolescence contrive to satisfy a need, unrecognised as such, to know and meet the other sex.

Throughout these years at Newark home and family provided a secure base for my later childhood. For a time there were four of us, for my brother had left Kingswood and was now working in a bank at Retford (just up the line from Newark) before entering the Wesleyan ministry. Not that I saw a great deal of the others except at meal times and on Sundays (when we kept to our traditional lunch of Yorkshire pudding – always eaten first with gravy as an appetiser – roast joint and two veg.). My father was out most evenings, my mother often, and my brother had his own friends and interests. In any case, I led a fairly self-contained life – homework every evening for an hour or so, followed in the winter by play with Hornby trains or Meccano or a book by the fire, in summer by games outside with friends or cycle rides in the nearer countryside. We had no radio; television was not invented. Just once a year we had the excitement of listening in: my father took me to a neighbour's to hear the broadcast of the FA Cup Final; it was a crystal set, which required a delicate probing with the 'whisker' before the sound came through.

Occasionally there were shopping expeditions by train (the old LMS) to Nottingham or Lincoln; at one or the other there was a Foster Brothers where, as I have already explained, my clothes were charged to Uncle Jack's account. Among the delights of shopping in those pre-electronic days were the systems of cash and change which operated in some of the larger stores. The cashier sat at a desk which was sited at the back or centre of the shop and raised well above floor level. This was connected to the service counters by stout wires, up and down which ran little metal containers; these took the customer's payment to the cashier and brought back his receipt and change. The assistant despatched them from the counter by pulling a handle as if he were flushing a lavatory; he thus released a spring which zipped them up the wire until they clicked to a stop at the cash desk; thence they returned more sedately by gravity. At a busy time dozens of these containers were sizzing to and fro along the wires like miniature cable-cars or bustling spiders on a mesh of metal threads. Such antiquated mechanisms have long since disappeared – before the war, I think; but to the boys of the 1920s they were a source of endless fascination from which we dragged ourselves reluctantly when purchases were complete. Antiquated they certainly were by modern standards and clumsily inefficient in their demands on time and space. Yet they possessed a certain lively humanity; more accurately than their 1980 counterparts they mirrored openly and visibly the reality of the situation – transactions overtly in progress, people actively involved in buying and selling; so different from the green impersonality of the figures that flicker momentarily on the microchip cash-computers!

Twice a year Uncle Jack and Auntie Kate came over from West Bromwich in their Daimler; for the period of their stay the standard of our eating was noticeably improved; and there were luxurious trips to more distant places of interest – the Peak, the coast, and south to Belvoir and into Rutland. (For me their visits brought the further bonus of the half-crown which they always gave me when they left.) In summer too there were family picnics by the Trent; these were infrequent but enjoyable, for there was a variety of river traffic – tugs and barges punctuated by the occasional yacht or launch. But how different was the deep, masterful, polluted flow of the industrialised Trent from the peat-dark Tees whose tree-lined banks had delighted our picnics at Barny!

Our style of life was plain despite subsidy from our relations, but not by the standards of the time impoverished. The weekly joint lasted through till Wednesday and ended in the inevitable shepherd's pie. Too late on one occasion; for despite its protective cage of metal gauze the flies won through and I found the resultant maggots emerging on to my plate. After the initial shock of disbelief my mother swept out of the room with the remains of the joint and returned to serve us with bread and cheese. (Why is this incident so vividly imprinted on my memory? – I can see us at the table, maggots and all, as if it were yesterday!) A goose at Christmas was the Wesleyan circuit's gift to its ministers; the puddings, of course, were my mother's, always ceremoniously stirred in the making, and always concealing a threepenny piece for each of us. A special treat, perpetuated through these years of childhood and beyond, was the strawberries and cream provided for my birthday tea and eaten, if the weather allowed, in the shade of the garden sycamore tree.

Milk also fell victim sometimes to the forces of nature. There were no pinta bottles then. The milkman clattered up the street with his horse and cart and a great jangling of cans. Arrived at the door, he ladled our request (unpasteurised) from a large, oval, flat-bottomed pail into a waiting basin and left it on the doorstep. Thence it was taken to the larder and covered with a gauze cloth edged with beads to weigh it down. In midsummer's heat it was not infrequently 'off' or even solid by next morning.

Week by week, after lunch on Saturdays, I received what was known within the family as my 'Saturday penny'; in fact it was 3d. and remained so throughout those non-inflationary years at Newark. Armed with this I raced to the corner shop and peered through its misted, fly-blown window at the great glass jars of assorted confection displayed within. Aniseed balls I must have, for they were cheap at 20 a 1d., but tasty too and long-lasting. But what else? Choice was difficult, requiring discrimination and a careful balancing of pro and con; often it took me to the next shop and the next again in my effort to find the most economical compromise between resources and desire.

I was not entirely free from illness, still less from the fear of it. Scarlet fever was more virulent then than now; it was sometimes fatal and was as much dreaded as polio in the 1950s when the annual epidemic approached. Morning and evening I inspected my chest and was horrified one day to find (as I thought) my worst fears realised in the tell-tale rash. It was like a death knell, the end of the world; but it was not scarlet fever!

The subsequent brief period which I spent in bed was memorable for two things. I was reading a book about the Spanish conquest of South America, when I came to a passage on human sacrifice which described how the hearts of living persons were torn from their breasts as they screamed and struggled and died in the welter of their own blood. I was numbed into immobility, frozen open-mouthed by the chill penetrating dread of it which somehow made me the very victim of the sacrifice. Needless to say, I turned to other reading.

My other memory is very different. Our house was only a few hundred yards from the LNER railway station. In those days delivery of freight and parcels was by horse and dray – huge shaggy-maned horses which clopped their ponderous way along the streets and left their piles of rich dark dung steaming in the roadway (of which more anon). Some time previously I had found in the fields an unexploded shot-gun cartridge from which I had extracted the powder and pellets; the former I had made into a squib and let off in the garden, but the pellets still awaited the inspiration which would put them to use.

My normal dress at the time was short trousers and knee-length stockings; the latter were supported by garters of three-quarter-inch black elastic. In a flash horse, garter and pellets clicked together in unexpected convergence of focus, and I rushed to the window to await the next delivery dray. The trees in the front garden gave me cover and at the same time provided a convenient gap for sighting my target; the horse appeared in full view while I was still hidden from the driver. And so, until my ammunition was exhausted, I amused myself by shooting at the horses and delighting in their antics as they reacted to the sting of the pellets on their flanks and buttocks. No less entertaining was the vocabulary of the drivers as they flung curses at their frisky beasts which reared and tossed inexplicably between the shafts.

As in Redruth and Barny family life was permeated and structured by the Wesleyan Church and its demands on time and commitment. Morning prayers remained an essential part of the daily routine. I almost wrote 'ritual', but that would be unfair; for my parents it was far more than that: the life of a Christian minister would be incomplete without it. Table talk was of the circuit and its various chapels, of Synod and Conference and, increasingly towards the end of our stay in Newark, of Methodist Union. (This proposal to unite the separate Wesleyan, Primitive and United Methodist Churches into one Methodist Church with a single organisation and one hymn-book seemed to me, even at that tender age, to be an eminently sensible arrangement; but my father was opposed to it. The union was consummated in 1932.) The study was an integral part of this as of all our other manses, though its influence was intangible and hardly recognised as such; an aura of prayer, theology, books and sermon preparation overflowed its door and subtly flavoured the rest of the house. I have written above of the bias which I believe this gave me towards books and learning. I am deeply grateful for it, and I hope that the study will remain an indispensable item in Methodism's provision for its ministers and so continue to influence younger generations of children of the manse as it has influenced me.

Chapel activities determined the pattern of daily life; inevitably the weight of the working day was shifted to the evening; morning was for reading and for sermons, the afternoon for visiting; after an early tea came services, prayer meetings, committees, concerts in one or another of the chapels in and around Newark. Sunday was a full working day, often a 'three-decker' of morning, afternoon and evening worship conducted in different chapels. For my father leisure, if any, came on Saturdays and Monday afternoons – though weddings frequently interrupted the former, and the incidence of funerals was unpredictable. A consequence of this was that I saw less of my father than do most boys; he seemed always to be out when I was in and *vice versa*, and there was little opportunity for shared leisure activity; an exception was our occasional visit to the local football match.

Our chapel was North End, an undistinguished redbrick building at the bottom of the street; nearer the centre of the town was Barnby Gate, the principal chapel of the circuit, and in the surrounding countryside were a number of village Zions – Winthorpe, Collingham, Beckingham, Balderton, Claypole and others – to which my father cycled for the weekly meetings and Sunday services. Inside, North End conformed to the normal Methodist furnishing of varnished pine, gallery and elevated pulpit; behind the preacher was the choir and below him, within the communion rail, a table bright with flowers. (Communion, or the Sacrament of the Lord's Supper, was reserved to full members of the church; I had, therefore, to wait fidgeting in the pew while my mother went to the rail and received the bread and wine – the latter non-alcoholic and distributed in tiny individual glasses.) Here we attended worship morning and evening, Sunday by Sunday, receiving the customary Methodist sandwich fare of prayers, lessons and sermon between five hymns, and following the recurrent annual cycle of Christmas, Easter and the various anniversaries for Chapel, Overseas Missions, Home Missions, Sunday School and Harvest. In all this I occupied a curiously anomalous position, being both within the church and yet, because of my family connection, in a strange sense outside it. I could never feel entirely at home; always I was 'the minister's son'.

Our first appearance at North End was notable for an incident of light relief as unexpected as it was untoward. There was at that time a widely used soap or scouring powder known as 'Monkey Brand'. It carried on its packet the picture of a squat little man with grey pointed beard, moustache to match, and a slightly startled, droll appearance which gave him a fair resemblance to the name of the product. When the stewards rose to receive our offerings and one of them approached us with his plate, my brother nudged me and whispered, 'Monkey Brand'. Whereupon I collapsed into uncontrollable giggles. For there he was, the very image of the man on the packet, as if he had walked straight out of it! The earnestness of his bearing and the incongruity of the resemblance combined to give an overwhelming sense of comedy to the situation. It took some minutes to stifle my laughter, and not before it had attracted the disapproving attention of neighbouring worshippers.

Barnby Gate we attended only on special occasions. One such was the visit of 'Gypsy Smith', a popular exponent of emotive evangelism whose services were much sought after at that time. Certainly he was a master of his trade: by skilful use of voice, gesture and a primitive but effective psychology he could rouse his packed congregations to a compulsive fervour of devotion and induce in the uncommitted a profound experience of 'conversion'. He had a valuable ally in the Wesleyan hymn-book which, as I mentioned earlier, contained hymns of superb rhythmic and melodic quality. The impact of these hymns, a great surging volume of song issuing from a massed congregation of several hundred already lifted by dynamic oratory to a high crest of emotion, is almost irresistible. Such, of course, was the intention. Before the last hymn was sung the Gypsy appealed to the unconverted to give themselves to Jesus and to make public their confession by coming forward to the communion rail. And many were those who did.

I was a boy as well as a minister's son, as must be obvious from the preceding pages; and I had the normal interests of boyhood, some more or less permanent, others transient, spasmodic or briefly recurrent. Among the last were fireworks, then readily available on open counters in the weeks before the Fifth and a source of eagerly anticipated pleasure. My limited funds could afford but few and these were chosen from the assortment on the counter with the same calculating discrimination as the product of my 'Saturday penny'. From time to time I would array them lovingly on my bed or dressing-table – Little Demons, Cannons, Volcanoes, Golden Fountains, rockets, sparklers and the rest – ranking them together by price, colour or size as the whim took me and visualising with mounting excitement the moment when their promise would be discharged by the delicate touch of match on twisted blue fuse. On the night itself the treasured package was taken to the garden and its contents there deployed in an exhilarating medley of explosions and vibrant scintillation. Delicious was the drifting smell of burning powder, the sweet scent of wood smoke, the ghoulish flicker of half-lit faces, the vicarious release of imprisoned energy – delights perpetuated undiminished when shared in later years with children and grandchildren.

A similar pleasure, but not confined to date or darkness, was afforded by toy bombs. These were inch-long metal eggs divided horizontally into two halves which were held together by an elastic band. A length of string passing through a central hole and knotted at both ends served both as a means of propulsion and as a fin to guide the missile in its descent. The bombs were armed by small percussion caps, pink with a black explosive dot, which were sold in round green penny boxes. Since a hard surface was needed for detonation, our battlegrounds were the local streets, then blessedly unencumbered by press of traffic. We hurled our bombs at imaginary German lines, recovered and re-armed them, and advanced again until victory was assured. Alternatively we could simulate aerial attack by dropping our bombs from bicycles on targets marked in the roadway. Police intervention (the bobby on his beat) occasionally forced a tactical withdrawal; but our skirmishes, unlike the brutal vandalism of today, were devoid of any malice or destructive intent.

The cinema provided occasional diversion. Films of World War One were common and I delighted in them; but I can remember only one, about the German cruiser *Emden* which wrought havoc on British shipping until it was sunk off the coast of Ceylon. In the 1920s and 1930s there was still an Empire and a Royal Navy to protect it. Those great coal-fired battleships, steaming in line across the screen and releasing their devastating salvoes, had a magnificence of aesthetic grandeur and destructive power which awed, uplifted, and filled one with a sense of pride; the harsher realities of war were carefully obscured. These were silent films. 'Talkies' arrived during the latter part of our stay in Newark. The first I saw (if I remember rightly) was 'The Desert Song'; I went incredulously and was thrilled by the novel conjunction of sight and sound which gave substance to the empty mouthings of silent dialogue.

These various pleasures were shared with friends. As most of them lived nearby, I was rarely at a loss for companionship; and although I could be content with my own company, I was as gregarious as most boys of that age. One of my friends was blessed with a large untidy garden in which we could do as we liked, including shooting at empty bottles with an air rifle. Another lived across the road in Appletongate; behind his house was a malting factory against whose great brick walls we played endless games of cricket on summer evenings. There were many others whose names I have now forgotten; but remembered or forgotten, dead or alive, may God bless them all for the many hours of boyhood happiness which we shared together.

A transient interest, not shared with other boys, arose from my father's enthusiasm for manuring the garden. To buy manure was beyond his means; but another source was available, provided free by the huge railway horses. For several autumn weeks of 1929 I rode back and forth through the streets of Newark, bucket and spade in one hand, the other on my handlebars, shovelling up the piles of dung and carrying it back to the garden. Since the horses were large, their droppings were correspondingly generous – two lots could fill a bucket; and, conveniently for me, they usually paused to defecate instead of scattering their gifts along yards of roadway. No doubt our cabbages and potatoes grew bigger and better because of it, but at that period of my life I had little interest in gardening.

The railway provided a constant source of pleasure in the trains that roared and rattled up and down the main LNER line. A few hundred yards north of the station the track is crossed by the main road to Lincoln; at that time there was a level-crossing with a pedestrian footbridge, but the line has long since been fully bridged. Northwards still it runs straight for three miles, crossing the LMS line to Lincoln and then a couple of bridges over the Trent; to the south, beyond the station and Ransom and Marles, it curves eastwards and disappears behind the slopes of Beacon Hill. Hours, indeed days, we spent on the footbridge, a group of local boys competitively collecting the names of engines. From here we could keep a train in sight for four miles or more – and what anticipation, what excitement as it came! At first a soundless black dot capped with steam, the engine grew to an identifiable Pacific, Atlantic or Mogul shrieking its approach in the swelling clamour of separable items of sound – the smooth repetitive flow of pistons, the hiss of steam, the plangent din of wheels vibrating perceptibly ahead through the metal of the rails. There followed the clackety-clack of bogeys as the carriages sped past beneath us, the swish of wind, the swoop of paper swirled in the blast, the opening of the crossing-gate, the fading roar until sight and sound merged again into the contours of the countryside.

There was no British Rail, of course; the companies had their different styles and liveries for engines and rolling-stock. The Pacifics which dominated the LNER main lines were majestic instruments; their huge driving wheels, exposed machinery and rapid susurrous puffing all combined in a manifest impression of power. They had beauty too, of line and colour, of solid, compact strength and disciplined purpose, an aesthetic appeal far greater than the massively ponderous diesels of today whose driving force is concealed from view. A streamlined version of them was introduced during our last year at Newark; it became a point of honour to see the first of them pass through, and I spent the lunch hour at the bottom of Beacon Hill waiting for the thrill of its emergence from the cutting – but I have forgotten its name! The carriages behind them displayed their destination on long boards above the windows – Hull, Grimsby, Newcastle, Edinburgh, Perth, Aberdeen, all of them as remote to me as the moon, but familiar enough in later years.

Cycling was another pleasure, sometimes solitary, sometimes shared. For this the countryside round Newark is ideal; there is an abundance of country roads, and even on main roads the traffic then was negligible compared with today's oppressive and perilous burden of metal; motorways and long vehicles did not exist. Apart from the abrupt descent of Beacon Hill and the more distant escarpment of the Lincoln Ridge the contours are gently undulating. There were shorter rides on summer evenings, to Winthorpe and Langford, Stapleford, Coddington, Beckingham and Barmby in the Willows. Delicious it was to float along free-wheeling in the scented twilight, the moon above the hedgerows and the moths flitting one's face, enfolded into the deep peace of a world seeking rest! Longer excursions took us occasionally to the Vale of Belvoir, more often eastwards to Cranwell where we enjoyed the aerobatics of the little trainer biplanes looping, banking, spiralling and spinning at speeds which now seem impossibly slow. From Cranwell we returned to race top speed down Beacon Hill, both arms widespread into the wind in emulation of the aerial antics we had rejoiced to observe.

It is difficult for the car-borne adult to appreciate the heady delight a youngster gets from his bicycle – more so in those easy traffic-free days when safety-training was nonexistent and scarcely necessary. The mastery of skill, the novel freedom of movement, the expansion of horizons, the acceptance into a peer-fraternity of riders – it was like an escape from confinement (which indeed it was), the discovery of a new dimension. Care of the cycle was also part of the joy; for here too were new skills, new mastery, pride of possession, pride in an instrument shining clean and smooth-oiled to function at the acme of performance. Lamps were not then the simple plastic battery-containers they have since become; they were a (comparatively) complex system of carbide and water, requiring careful cleaning, adjustment and assessment of quantities to secure satisfactory illumination. And then it was a thrill as intense as it was rare to ride forth beyond the streets, preceded by the pale oval of acetylene and cocooned in a microcosm of velvet darkness containing only oneself, the cycle, the soft brush of its tyres on the road surface, and the wind's whispering tug at one's ears.

Other open-air diversions included walking, fishing and boating. The immediate environs of Newark do not offer the pleasant variety of walks that we enjoyed round Barny (and the valley of the Trent is hardly comparable with the woods and waters of Teesdale); but there was countryside accessible by foot along the river north to Winthorpe and eastwards towards Stapleford woods. It was the former direction I took most often, usually alone but sometimes with my father, for whom walking was still a major recreation and means of relaxation. Fishing, with a length of cane, string and a bent pin, offered some variation from the normal routine. Poised on the bank with a penn'orth of maggots, I would hook the occasional minnow and transfer it triumphantly to the large jam-jar beside me. At home they gaped out their remaining days in a tin bath under the sycamore tree; here, their white bellies uppermost, they were overtaken by premature mortality and interred with due ceremony beneath the turf. It amazes me, looking back, that I was allowed such freedom to wander alone along the banks of the deep and swift-flowing Trent; for I could not swim, and my own death would have been certain had I fallen in. Whether or not there were public baths in Newark at the time I do not know; if there were, neither Magnus nor my parents encouraged me to visit them.

Boating I was not allowed to indulge in unaccompanied. My brother was an enthusiast for rowing (and also a strong swimmer), and on half days and summer evenings he would take me with him as steersman. The boathouse was at a junction of the Trent with a tributary, the Devon (pronounced Deevon), just south of Newark. Sometimes we rowed south along the Trent on a stretch of water unobstructed for several miles by locks and weirs. More often we chose the Devon which, unlike the Trent, is slow-moving, clear and overhung with willows. Here we could drift smoothly, hands trailing in the water, watching for the silver flash of fishes or the mallards, bill beneath wing, asleep on the bank. Occasionally a kingfisher flashed its blue-green brilliance in front of us or a heron beat its ponderous ascent from the adjacent water-meadows. It was not unlike the Granta above Cambridge, as I later came to know it (indeed my memory may have confused the two) –

> . . . the thrilling-sweet and rotten
> Unforgettable, unforgotten
> River-smell.

But there was no Grantchester to reward one's toil; upstream the Devon narrowed between banks of reed and willowherb and soon became impassable to oars.

One windy evening, while waiting for our boat, we watched two lads attempting to sail their yacht in the Trent just off the boathouse. Their spaniel was with them, paws on gunwale, balancing delicately as the boat careened this way and that, sail almost touching the water in the stiff gusts. Suddenly there was contact; the cloth clung sodden and the boat filled; in a flash its frolicking partnership with the breeze was frozen into numb surrender to an element which clawed, absorbed and sucked it down. A line was thrown from the bank, the yacht pulled in and the lads rescued, wet, cold, frightened, but unharmed; the dog was dead. From behind us, as we stared at the brown and white waterlogged body motionless on the landing-stage, came reproachfully their father's voice: 'You've lost your dog, then.' There was a finality in the words which emphasised the fact of death, darkened the summer sky, and diminished our anticipation of enjoyment. Again I felt the oppression of mystery, an incompleteness, evil and impenetrable. We rowed away in silence and spoke little for the rest of the evening.

For the male sex the years from ten to thirteen are perhaps the least romantic of any – if by that is meant insensitivity to tender emotion and to mystery of the numinous kind. Emotion there certainly is in these years, expressed in loyalty to gang, team, school or family, in the spirit of adventure and daredevilry, in the ebullient *joie de vivre* of overflowing physical vitality; nor are they without mystery of the more practical variety – the explorer, the detective, the enemy agent, the curiosities of wild-life and astronomy. This is a plateau-period of comparative stability, a prepubertal poise *pour mieux sauter*; the numinous does not intrude overmuch. Yet there were times even in these years when I felt the presence that disturbs.

A favourite cycle ride was out along the Lincoln road, then right towards Stapleford, through the woods to Coddington, and back down Beacon Hill. It was seven or eight miles in all – enough to fill pleasantly a summer evening between homework and bedtime. For a mile there was deep wood on both sides, into whose darkness the columns of imprisoned pines receded inscrutably. The wide grass verges were gay with foxgloves, ragwort, harebells, dog-daisies and clover; in the ditches, promising an autumn richness of berry, were honeysuckle and bramble. The soft cooing of wood-pigeons came like answering echoes from the trees on either side; on to its soothing ebb and flow a late warbler imposed a lively pattern of cadence, and a pheasant the contrast of its jarring honk. In the warm, moist air of evening the scents of summer were enriched and amplified; they flowed past, successively and intermingled, a rich, enfolding flux of hay, honeysuckle, clover, meadowsweet and the balmy fragrance of resin. And all this medley of sight, sound and scent was held and concentrated within the enclosing walls of pinewood which, as they tapered to the point where the road emerged, seemed to channel it upon me, compel me to absorb it, identify with it. (Looking back I would liken it to a multisensory symphony; but I was ignorant of music at that time and the imagery would have been meaningless.) I felt then the presence of a reality both disturbing by its mystery, its urgent vitality, its transcendence of the here and now, and at the same time refreshing, comforting, invigorating, a source of power. As I rode from the woods into the open countryside, I knew that I was not alone.

It came to me again along still stretches of the Devon as I sat steering the boat over its clear, placid waters, bordered by lush water-meadows and overhanging willows. There was not here the rich medley of the road through Stapleford woods, but something quieter, more of a kind (a dominance of green and aquatic growth), the tranquillity of deep water, slow-moving, caressing one's hand as it trailed alongside. But the presence and the message were the same.

Shortly before leaving Newark we spent a fortnight as paying guests at a farm a few miles to the east. This holiday was memorable for the deep satisfaction that came to me, during those two weeks, from total immersion in the activities and experience of farm life. I was given the daily round of egg-collecting (no battery hens – they laid anywhere, in hedgebottoms, under haystacks, in any hole or corner where they could scrape together enough straw and feathers for a nest); I shared in the feeding, the watering, the milking; I watched the grooming of the horses (no tractors) and the repair of machinery; but most of all I involved myself in the harvesting which was then in full swing. Here my chief task was to help build the stooks in which the sheaves were left standing in the fields to dry before stacking. The different patterns and perspectives of adjacent fields thus laid out in rows of stooks provided a scene of great visual attraction; but it has virtually disappeared from the English landscape.

It was brilliant August weather and the work went on all day till after sunset, interrupted only to feed and water the horses. The machinery was primitive by modern standards; the day of the combine-harvester had not yet come. A revolving cylinder of horizontal wooden arms thrust down into the standing corn and held it firm; as the teeth of the cutter scissored into it, the stalks fell on to a moving belt, piled themselves into a sheaf's weight, and were then bound and dropped to the ground; and it was all open to the eye. For hours on end when I was not required for stooking, I followed the binder round and round the diminishing acres of corn, fascinated by the endless repetitive precision of the machinery, by the flowers exposed by the cutting – pimpernel, speedwell and dwarf convolvulus – by the fieldmice scampering to cover and the occasional partridge decapitated as it crouched protectively on its nest. There came a point where the rabbits, which had been retreating to the centre of the field, were forced to take their chance and race for the hedgerows. Then the guns were ready, tumbling them one after another in ungainly somersaults of useless limbs and scattered fur.

When the day's work was done, the clatter of the binder ceased and the horses led away, I would sometimes stay behind in the half-reaped field and wait, just wait – why, I could not have explained either to myself or anyone else. It felt good to be there; I wanted to be there. It was warm, beautiful, and a little eerie; for the farm was out of sight and I was alone, the wide, darkening countryside around me and the vast sky above. But not wholly dark or silent; for the orange disk of the rising moon was etching sharply black the twigs and runners of the hedgerow; and the owls were hastening nightfall with their wavering calls. I was part of it all and it of me – the quietness, the beauty, the forces of growth, harvest and husbandry; it held me, and I was reluctant to go.

The end of our holiday came too soon. We returned to a manse stripped of all but the furniture officially provided by the circuit; our own possessions, previously packed, were already en route for their next destination. This was Ilkeston, a mining town in the Derbyshire coalfield, which I remember chiefly for its spoil heaps and winding-gear. It was not to be my home as Newark had been; for there began for me now a wholly new stage in my education, five years at Kingswood, a Methodist boarding school on the slopes of Lansdown, overlooking the city of Bath.

CHAPTER V

Kingswood (i)

I LEFT FOR KINGSWOOD IN SEPTEMBER 1930 at the age of thirteen. On this first departure I was accompanied by my father; thenceforth I travelled alone or in the company of boys who lived along the route. I remember little of it beyond the uneasy sense of foreboding which oppressed those last few days at home and grew, as we neared our destination, into a sickening apprehension which tugged at my stomach and kept me close to tears. One recollection, however, remains with clarity undiminished as if of yesterday – the sight of my mother standing alone on the platform at Ilkeston Town station, smiling and waving with a show of cheerfulness as the train chuffed out towards the junction with the main line. Waving back I leaned to the last out of the carriage window until her figure dwindled to a blur of colour and was finally absorbed into the steam from the engine. Unrecognised then by either of us, our parting had an ultimacy inevitable as the passage of time or the severing of the umbilical cord (which in a sense it was), and frustrating as the vain yearning of Virgil's ghosts for that unattainable further shore.

In contrast, my goodbye to my father was brief and perfunctory; once delivered to the school I was too preoccupied with novelty and with finding my way around to spare thought for other matters. New boys arrived at the school a day earlier than the rest to enable them to settle in and learn the geography of the buildings. We were introduced to the headmaster, the matron and our various Housemasters, fed and taken on a conducted tour. Then, after a forlorn night in (to us) vast dormitories which echoed emptiness, we awaited with trepidation the arrival of the older boys. However, they were less concerned with us than with one another, with the renewal of friendships and the exchange of their experiences during the seven weeks of the summer holiday. Suddenly the dormant buildings sprang into bustle and stir – boys excitedly chattering in the corridors, dashing up and down stairs, shouting across the playground, a surge of recharged energy not yet canalised into the formal daily routine. All of which, since as yet we knew no names, served only to accentuate the isolation, the confusion, the lack of status of us new boys caught up in this bewildering pressure of anonymity.

I was extremely homesick that first term. Many a time after lights-out I pulled the bedclothes over my head, imagined myself at home, and wept myself to sleep. When I was not preoccupied with the exigencies of the moment, there would well up from deep inside me a gnawing, helpless wretchedness which saw no end to my imprisonment. The 91 days of term (each thankfully deleted from the calendar as it ended) stretched interminably towards a Christmas that seemed impossibly remote; the weekly letter from home did little to diminish the sense of isolation. Again and again the paradigms of Greek verbs (which I was learning for the first time) were dimmed by tears; and while my teachers laboured to expound their lessons, my mind, rejecting the unreality of the alien world about me, was focused far beyond them on familiar scenes and friends of a Magnus now irretrievably lost.

I must not exaggerate. Boyhood is irrepressible; merriment and laughter there certainly were in those thirteen weeks; but the adjustment from one form of life to another was difficult and unhappy. Yet the adjustment once made, the balance was reversed: before the year was out I had begun to prefer school to home (except for food); I had no friends in Ilkeston; we had no radio; there was nothing to do but read or walk the dog along the cinder towpaths of overgrown canals or cycle out alone into an unattractive countryside. At school there was companionship, activity, interest; life was organised, decisions made for one; carried comfortably along on the smooth flow of bell-governed routine, one rarely had to think what to do next.

The journeyings six times a year between home and school became part of an established pattern of life which was prolonged, with a change of destination, by four years at Cambridge. In 1933 we moved to Horncastle, in Lincolnshire, but a major part of the journey, between Bath and Birmingham, remained the same. By constant repetition (thirty times in the five years) the route acquired the familiarity of a well-known film, unreeling its episodes – towns, stations, farms, factories and tunnels – in predictable succession. There was a junction then at Mangotsfield, northeast of Bristol, and a spur running from the main LMS line round the foot of Kelston Round Hill to its own station in Bath. These have now disappeared. At Mangotsfield, coming and going, we changed trains; it was a dismal, nondescript little station whose name resounds for me with a strangely blending reminiscence of doom and release. For either way, to or from school, it was both a beginning and an end, the point of transition from one settled way of life, one kind of intimacy, one kind of enclosure, to another; and the meeting of the little branch line with the main route to the north was itself somehow symbolic of the contrast.

The original Kingswood School was opened by John Wesley on midsummer day, 1748, with a sermon on the text: 'Train up a child in the way he should go; and when he is old he will not depart from it' (Proverbs 22, 6).[1] Dissatisfied with existing boarding schools, in particular their lack of supervision and consequent indiscipline, he decided to establish a school of his own based firmly on Christian principles and practice. A suitable site was found at Kingswood, then in open country east of Bristol but long since submerged by urban sprawl. In addition to its Christian purpose the school was intended 'with God's assistance, to train up children in every branch of useful learning'. It was built to house fifty boarders, and its pupils (including some girls who were boarded separately) were mainly children of Wesley's friends and others associated with his religious movement.

If we in the 1930s thought our life was hard (as inevitably we did during those bitter windswept winter runs when severe frost had made rugger impossible), it was luxury compared with the regime of those early years: up at 4 am for private prayers, then public devotions in the adjacent chapel at five, breakfast at six, manual work for an hour, and lessons for the rest of the day with breaks only for meals and further religious exercises – no play, no holidays! A century later changes in educational thought and practice had greatly reduced these initial rigours; they also brought an increasing realisation that the site and buildings of the school were inadequate to its purpose. In 1845 a specially appointed committee resolved in principle to transfer it to a new site; land was bought on the slopes of Lansdown overlooking Bath and the new buildings were formally opened in October 1852. The entire cost, including furnishings, was £16,000![2]

This, with many later additions, is the Kingswood that I knew. Set a few hundred yards below the crest of Lansdown, its imposing stone frontage overlooks the spires and crescents of the city, the wooded combes immediately south, and beyond these the green uplands of Wiltshire. A central tower with a huge oriel window at its base contributes notably to the aesthetic impact of the building. (Originally it

---

[1] Wesley's views on education and his intentions for the school can be found in his tract, *Instructions for Children* (1745), which expounds 'the true principles of the Christian education of children'; in *A Short Account of the School in Kingswood*, which contains the rules approved at the Wesleyan Conference of 1748; and in his later pamphlet, *A Plain Account of Kingswood School*.

[2] For historical details here and elsewhere in this chapter I am indebted to Ives, A. G., *Kingswood School in Wesley's Day and Since* (Epworth Press, 1970).

Kingswood in the 1930s: top left, *the Ferens Building;*
bottom right, *the school chapel*

had also a utilitarian function, incorporating a heating and ventilation system which failed to work.) Below were extensive gardens in which sixth formers were allowed to wander on summer Sunday afternoons; for reasons of economy these have been converted into a vast sward of lawn. Behind the school a private road leads to open fields (where I sampled my first cigarette) and to wide views over countryside south and west; and behind this is an acre or two of woodland which we could explore at will on free afternoons. Kingswood, it has been rightly said, is a place of wide horizons. Even at night the eye is drawn to the long chains of lights, dipping and curving and intersecting, which are the streets of Bath.

Lansdown is a small plateau about 750 feet high. Across it runs the main road which comes up the long hill from Bath, past the school and on northwards to the M4. Here are the playing-fields (and also those of the Girls' Royal School which is lower down the hill); here too is the racecourse, forbidden to us when in use, but forming part of the school's cross-country course and at other times an easy route to Prospect Stile and Kelston Round Hill. The plateau itself is exposed and almost bare of trees; grey walls of limestone line the roads and divide the fields. In the winter term it could be bleak and bitter – a hostile place it seemed to us as

Kingswood in the 1980s

we forced our way through driving snow or rain. In summer it was a different world; its broad spaciousness gave a sense of freedom, of expansion, which prompted vigorous expression in physical exertion; and then one could lie in lazy ease on the warm turf, caressed by the flower-laden breeze that flowed up from the valley-pastures below. Enfolded in its steep escarpments are sheltered combes and copses where primrose and anemone make an early showing and blackberries abound in September. These it was a delight to explore, one in particular, conveniently near, which drops down sharply into the village of Charlcombe; but there are others, round Upper Weston on the Swainswick side, all of them accessible on our free half days.

Wesley's intention for the original school was that it should be 'not too far from a great town . . . nor yet too near, and much less in it'. The new Kingswood satisfied his educational caution, and still does more than a century later. For us much of the time the city was 'out of bounds'; for there was always the risk of infection, and epidemics can play havoc with a boarding school. When it was not, the freedom of Bath was ours in exchange for the little pink permits obtained from our Housemaster. It was not, I must add, the city's architectural beauties that attracted us, though I would like to think that we were not wholly oblivious to them –

the Abbey, the Pulteney Bridge, the magnificent Georgian crescents. Rather it was the bustle of shops and streets, trams and buses, and the temporary release from constriction.

The headmaster throughout my time at Kingswood was A. B. Sackett, the son of a Methodist chaplain and himself a former captain of rugby at the school. After service and severe wounding in the 1914-18 war he had returned to his studies at Merton College, Oxford. He then taught at Christ's Hospital until his appointment to Kingswood in 1928. The previous head was H. A. Wootton, appointed in 1919. Both men were reformers.

Wootton found major deficiencies in discipline, classroom provision and even such basic items as drainage and sick-room accommodation. To put things right required a regime which now seems rigorous, restrictive and even harsh. 'I do not believe in sparing the rod,' he wrote to the secretary of the governors.[1] Yet he was a man of warm humanity and educational vision; it was his prompting that secured the addition of the Ferens Building (see on, p. 92); this in turn enabled the older classrooms to be converted into dayrooms, and the huge old single schoolroom into the splendid Moulton Hall to be used for lectures and musical and dramatic performances. To such an extent did Wootton transform the school that in 1922 he was elected to the Headmasters' Conference and Kingswood became a 'public school'. It already had many of the accoutrements of the public school and of its traditions. There were, of course, a school tie, blazer and cap. There was also a coat of arms and a Latin motto reflecting the purposes of the founder: *in gloriam Dei optimi maximi; in usum ecclesiae et reipublicae* (usually abbreviated to the second phrase).

Sackett came to a situation on which he could build a more humane regime. Restrictions were relaxed, the cane all but disappeared, and an altogether more friendly atmosphere was established. Better provision was made for resident Housemasters; in the boys' dayrooms there appeared leather chairs, pictures and curtains; school societies proliferated; discussion was encouraged on all manner of subjects – an unaccustomed educational *glasnost*. 'Life at the school became more civilised,' writes A. G. Ives in his history of Kingswood. More of Sackett's refining influence will become apparent in the pages that follow.

As a pupil at the school I was quite unaware of Sackett's reforms or of any contrast between his regime and Wootton's. Perhaps it would be more accurate to say that I did not recognise his reforms as such, but simply enjoyed the benefits of them. As a child and adolescent one

[1] Ives, A. G., *op. cit.*, p. 198.

assumes that what is has always been. It would not, I think, be unfair to Sackett to say that his successors, building on his achievement, have brought Kingswood still further towards the goal of a humane and civilised society, not least by introducing coeducation.

From the 1780s the school had been increasingly, and was eventually exclusively, filled with the sons of Wesleyan preachers, who paid nothing for the privilege. But from 1922 it was opened to the sons of laymen, and ministers' sons were charged £15 a year; in 1930 my father's account book shows that this had risen to £25 plus small additional items like pocket-money – well below the actual cost.

For thirty years the original building of 1852 was sufficient for the needs of the school; it contained dormitories, schoolrooms and accommodation for the Governor but not for the headmaster, whose position at that time was distinct and subordinate. Advances in educational thinking and an increase in the number of pupils demanded additional buildings; these were sited at the rear and in my time included a swimming bath, gymnasium, sanatorium and (mundane but necessary) a laundry and bakery. Alongside the latter ran the back way into the school, which was the normal route for non-prefects; here the smell of soapy steam and hot yeasty bread mingled incongruously and unforgettably as we passed to and from the games field. Most prominent of the later buildings was the huge gaunt dormitory block whose stone is now weathered to a dull uniform grey; four storeys high, it was built in 1883 at right angles to the main building.

By this time the house system was well established in many public schools, but not yet at Kingswood, where it was introduced in the 1890s. Initially boys were assigned to the dormitories according to their position in the school. Later the structure of the buildings suggested an obvious division into three Houses, Upper, Middle and Lower, with a fourth, School House, occupying the main building. Mine was Upper.

Those who have not known dormitory life can never fully capture the feel of it. Sixty of us slept in two cavernous compartments, seniors in one, juniors in the other; each had fifteen beds to a side. Between the two were baths and toilets; at the northern end was the Housemaster's sitting-room and bedroom. Every boy had his own small wooden cubicle with its wash-basin (cold water only), mirror, and a locker for odds and ends of possessions. This gave some privacy to those who wanted it; otherwise we were exposed to the chatter, pranks, snores, nightmares and other idiosyncrasies of our twenty-nine co-sleepers. Occasionally, in the hottest of summer weather, there emerged from our cubicle plugholes, like visitants from a subterrestrial underworld, a repulsive, red, coagulated mass of what were presumably worms – the product, no doubt, of the complex biochemistry of unsterilised waste. After the first impulse of nausea we rushed to queue for the water-can and swilled away the invaders with a gallon or two of hot water from the bathrooms. This was usually enough to dispel them until the following year.

The day began with the strident clamour of a handbell. Distant at first, it grew in volume as Bob, our caller, climbed the stairs, and ended with a shattering blast as he opened the door into our dormitories. Then came the prefect's shout, 'All up now!', a scurried chase into our clothes and a final frantic stampede, four steps at a time, down the spiral stairs at the far end. After breakfast we returned to make our beds (prefects were relieved of this by 'dumbs' – our word for maids since there was a rule of silence between us); these inspected, we descended once more to chapel and the daily routine. At the other end of the day we toiled up the central zigzag staircase, undressed, and chatted or read until the prefect's 'Silence!' and lights-out cut us short. After that there was no leaving our beds unless the duty-prefect granted a plea of 'bed please' or 'lavatory please'. (I am not clear what the former signified – perhaps to get a handkerchief or a drink; we could not, surely, have had chamber-pots, for they would have been dropped from the windows or used as missiles, and I have no recollection of this.)[1]

We had a weekly bath by rota in addition to our thrice-weekly shower after games. Cleanliness we certainly did not lack; even during a period of severe drought and water restriction we continued our baths, carefully eyeing the black line painted below the taps to indicate the permitted level. At appropriate intervals there appeared on the end of our beds little bundles of clean clothes, deposited there by the unseen hands of 'dumbs'; those we shed we tossed into huge wicker baskets as we raced to breakfast next morning.

It was a simple, austere, communal, regimented existence in our dormitories. At first, straight from the privacy of home, one felt acutely the pressure of numbers, the exposure to public scrutiny, the lack of simple amenities like curtains and carpets. It was cold, too, in winter; only very rarely, in the severest of weather, was the heating turned on – and this, I suspect, was more to protect the pipes than us against the frost. But there was some concession to comfort: on my first arrival the long passage between the beds was bare, splintery wood; we returned one September to find it neatly covered with brown linoleum which slid

[1] In fact we did have them, so I have been told; they were taken with the school when it was evacuated to Uppingham at the start of the war and there 'disposed of'. They would surely have been worth a fortune now!

smoothly beneath our stockinged feet. Once inured to the life, however, one accepted it as of the nature of things, and there were no complaints. Looking back from a different climate of adolescence I am surprised at our docility.

Yet there were compensations. Up there at the top of the building we could look far, east and west, over the surrounding countryside. Sunrise and sunset were at our pleasure, and many a time in later years I watched the sun drop down into the Avon valley and waited while rural Somerset darkened into velvet night. Nor did sunrise escape me when, as a prefect, I was up early swotting for exams. The air was good too; it drifted in refreshingly on sultry days when down below was heavy with the threat of thunder. And of the storms when they came we had a grandstand view. There was one magnificent occasion when almost the whole thirty of us crept from our beds to watch the lightning scour the slopes around us with blaze after blaze of brilliant effulgence while the building beneath us shook with reverberant blasts.

At a less exalted level there were a number of stunts and escapades which provided amusement and relief. The structure of Upper dormitory (but not of those below) offered a trial of strength which was undertaken from time to time by older boys in response to challenge or to satisfy their own self-esteem. The ceiling was supported at intervals by a pair of thick iron rods, each about twelve feet long, which sloped down to the walls on either side at an angle of about 30° to the horizontal. The test was to work one's way up one bar from wall to ceiling and down the other, hanging on by hands alone. Coming down from the centre was easy, but the upward passage I found surprisingly difficult; it required the use not only of hands and arms but of the whole body to provide the necessary momentum.

'Spotting the red' was a pastime reserved for prefects; its nature restricted it to times after lights-out when all others were in bed. The main zigzag staircase had a central well from top to bottom; the floor below was paved with red and black tiles about nine inches square. The game was played by leaning over the banisters and trying by judicious expectoration to hit one of the red tiles some fifty feet below. It was a matter of luck as much as skill; for however accurate one's initial aim, the spittle was easily deflected by gusts of air from the intervening dormitories or from the doors at the base of the well. There was some risk involved too; masters were still about, and the echo of footsteps approaching down the ground floor corridor would enforce a rapid retreat and pretended innocence.

Dormitories are only a small (but not unimportant) part of life in boarding-schools. For leisure time and the many shorter intervals between various activities we had our House day-rooms, senior and junior. Here we could read, play games or simply mooch around waiting for the next bell. Our senior room had lino and curtains, but the junior room as I remember it was stark, cheerless and dominantly wooden – oiled wooden floor and wooden forms, chairs, tables, lockers and reading-desk (for newspapers); it was not exactly a home from home.

The day-rooms were also used for the evening preparation periods, one hour for juniors, two for seniors. These were supervised by prefects who sat at separate tables and combined their own studies with a watchful eye on the rest. Three minutes before the end of the first hour a junior boy left to collect a basket of buns from the dining hall; this he brought back and held at the door while we all filed past and took a bun or not as we chose. They were a kind of rock-bun with currants and not infrequently stale; on one's first introduction to them they had a certain deceptive appeal; later the sight of the bun-boy at the door induced a temporary anorexia which shrugged the basket aside. Exceptionally there would appear the odd piece of cake, doughnut or sandwich left over from a House party or a team tea. Then there was a scramble through the contents of the basket to unearth whatever other delicacies might be concealed.

For games we had table-tennis, chess, dominoes, l'Attaque and the like; in the senior day-room we somehow acquired a small billiard-table whose popularity soon wore it threadbare. And, of course, we invented our own amusements. Obstacle races, for instance: we arranged the tables, forms and chairs in a course around the room and timed each other's frantic efforts, through, under and over the various items of furniture, to beat the clock. One Sunday in the interval between chapel and lunch we devised a more sophisticated ploy. We attached a piece of wire to each of the terminals of a light switch; a dozen of us joined hands, leaving a boy at either end to complete the circuit by grasping a wire with his free hand; the light was then switched on. The bulb glowed faintly and we felt a pleasant tingle as the current passed through us. One by one boys dropped out of the circuit; the bulb glowed more brightly, the tingle grew to a vibrant throb, and eventually, as the number reduced to three and two, it became a painful shudder which we could sustain for only a few seconds. (Since the current was passing through the bulb, and the floor provided reasonable insulation, there was no great risk. Nevertheless, it was a foolish prank which it would be unwise to imitate.)

Another important focus of life in any boarding-school is the dining-hall. During my time at Kingswood it could accommodate the whole school at one sitting; the tables, each for about a dozen boys and a prefect, were arranged in parallel rows at right angles to the walls with a central aisle between. The walls themselves were lined with huge Honours Boards on which were inscribed the names, whether for veneration or emulation, of senior prefects, captains of rugger and cricket, and winners of university scholarships, major school prizes and similar distinctions.

We were served by 'dumbs', who stood against the walls between the tables and spoke only when speech was unavoidable. They had skirts, and their hair, however coiffured, was obviously longer than ours; but we scarcely thought of them as female. They were black and white automata to whom we held out an empty dish or water jug with a brief request for more; and when the meal was over, they removed our pile of dirty plates. They appeared thus partly because they *were* 'dumbs', partly because few had any pretence to beauty (a lack which may, perhaps, have been a criterion for their appointment), and partly because the most conspicuous features of normal femininity were disguised by dresses with shapeless, blousy tops. There was one exception, who either rebelled against the rule or had breasts too large to be thus concealed. 'Flossy', as we knew her, was noticeably good-looking and there was some competition to secure her services (at table); but our attempts to attract her attention she treated with haughty disdain.

About our food it is perhaps better not to particularise in too great a detail; my memory may be at fault and is certainly prejudiced, for our diet is the aspect of boarding life on which I look back with most distaste. It was simple, tedious, repetitive and unimaginative, though not, save in one or two respects, seriously deficient.

There was not then the miscellany of packet cereals that line the grocers' shelves today. Breakfast began invariably with porridge, usually of a medium consistency but sometimes a thin gruel interspersed with undigested lumps of oatmeal. On one occasion a lump had a tail attached which, on closer inspection, was seen to belong to a mouse; the discovery prompted shouts of incredulous laughter and was a principal theme of the day's gossip. Was there a second course? I can vaguely picture bowls of cracked eggs oozing out their hard-boiled contents and kippers, complete with heads and tails, staring vacantly at us with flat, fishy eyes; but I cannot remember whether this was a regular feature of breakfast; bacon we never had.

There was bread, of course, and a round of butter which the prefect carefully marked into the dozen or so required portions and then passed round for each to take his share. We could have as much bread as we liked, but no more butter; marmalade appeared only on Sundays. This and other spreadables we could bring from home or have them sent; they were passed to friends at the same table or, if the owner were in a generous mood, to every boy – and even to the prefect unless he were grievously disliked. Among these spreadables Marmite was a special favourite, for a little went a long way and provided savour for as many slices as our butter would spread.

The two-course lunch menu followed a regular rota; we knew what to expect each day and this alone was enough to dampen our appetites. The food itself was unattractive and we were offered no choice; we ate it because we had to – or go without. For tea there was a meat or egg dish of some sort and bread and butter, but no jam or cake except on Sundays. The bread, for breakfast and tea, was always white – or almost always, for very occasionally a brown loaf appeared and was devoured with appreciative gusto. The cake was invariably the same oblong, tin-baked, sultana-loaf variety, undeviating in colour and texture. Tea boys, who ate later, served our cups from enormous brown enamel pots.

Any variant from the normal menu was welcomed with acclaim, until it too became part of the routine and was eaten only in preference to hunger. For one novelty, however, we found an alternative use. This was a small red-skinned polony about three inches long; appetising at first, it soon lost its appeal and the number left on the dish increased week by week. But its size and weight made it an ideal missile: it fitted neatly between thumb and forefinger, was not too heavy, and was unlikely to cause injury. We began surreptitiously to pocket the remnants and secrete them in day-room and dormitory; here they delighted our idle moments as we threw, dodged and returned fire until inevitably the skins ruptured under the strain and spattered their contents on walls and tables. The culmination of this affair was a pitched battle in the playground, during which the air was filled with flying polonies and the ground littered with their limp, eviscerated corpses. Eventually authority intervened; the battle was stopped and the casualties swept up. We saw no more polonies.

Relief from the repetitive monotony of our diet was, of course, received with delight. One's heart leapt at the unexpected summons to collect a parcel – who was it from? and (more important) what could be in it? Like hungry dogs a group of onlookers gathered round and scrutinised the contents as they were laid on the day-room table. If they were lucky there might be an immediate distribution of some portion before the rest was put away to be eked out privately or shared with a few close friends. The rarity of the event precluded a more open-handed generosity. Relief came also from the tuckshop, but here it had to be purchased. Money could be brought from home, deposited in the 'bank' and withdrawn at intervals; and we had a weekly allowance of pocket-money. My own funds were scant and my visits to the tuckshop infrequent; but the occasional bar of chocolate sucked with deliberate unhaste or the tub of ice-cream scraped clean of its last extractable fragment were like ambrosia to a palate unaccustomed to delicacy. Prefecthood brought further relief as one of its privileges. There was a prefects' 'supper' in the interval between preparation periods; it was no more than a snack – biscuits, little cubes of hard cheese, a bun and synthetic lemonade; but it was different. And there was evidently butter to spare; using our knife blades we vied with each other in trying to flick small chunks of it on to the lofty ceiling beams – a difficult task and a matter for congratulation if accomplished. Here it stuck for months, even years, and was pointed out with pride by Old Boys returning to the school.

All this was fifty years ago and Kingswood fare has vastly improved since then, as I know from recent visits to the school. There have been great advances too in culinary and nutritional science; dinners in state and independent schools are appetising, well cooked and dietetically balanced; and there is choice of menus. By modern standards our diet was unsatisfactory; nevertheless, we kept remarkably healthy, hardened perhaps by regular exercise and the rigours of Lansdown. Inevitably, in our close community, epidemics took their toll, and the sanatorium occasionally overflowed; but there was little serious illness. One must acknowledge too (and gratefully) the problems of feeding 300 boys, many of them paying less than cost, on a limited budget. Kingswood, I am sure, was no worse than other schools in the 1930s.

Games were part of our life at Kingswood, recurring on Mondays, Wednesdays and Fridays as part of a routine which no one questioned. On these three days, our stomachs stodged with various forms of carbohydrate, we trudged up the hill to the 'Upper' (our playing-fields), where we spent the afternoon loping to and fro across the turf in pursuit of one or the other kind of leather ball according to season. After which we ambled back again, varying our route sometimes by a path which took us through open fields along the south-west corner of Lansdown.

For rugger it was 'colours' against 'blacks' (nothing racialist, only a convenient nomenclature for the teams and their jerseys – broad red and black stripes for the former, black (or more often a faded blue-grey) for the latter; jerseys with narrower, wasp-like hoops were reserved for the School XVs). If we were unfit for games but not sick enough for the sanatorium, we were made to walk, under prefectorial supervision, to a point about half a mile beyond the village of Charlcombe. If the ground was unfit, we were sent on a run. In the summer term there was the same straggle to and from the 'Upper', save that now it was a uniform white. And there was warmth and sunshine; the comings and goings of successive batsmen provided intervals of idleness for lazing on the turf and sucking nonchalantly on a stem of grass; or, if luckily placed, one could day-dream upright on the boundary, while the game assumed an unreality of which one was a distant and impartial spectator.

Games were not an obsession at Kingswood, as they are said to have been at other public schools; but they were a major focus of interest for those who played, or had some hope of playing, in House or School teams; and even the rest were enthusiastic enough to watch and cheer their teams against a rival or to clap success when it was announced in the dining-hall. Games were also a criterion of one's standing in the school; to be no good at games was to be a 'wet' and regarded with disdain; to excel was to command admiration, respect and early elevation to prefecthood. Especially were the members of the First XV, its captain above all, the objects of veneration and hero-worship to younger boys. Victory in one of the 'big' matches against Taunton School or Wycliffe enlarged their stature still further; clad in an aura of semi-divinity they dwelt in a world apart.

In my early days at Kingswood I found as little joy in rugby football as I had at Magnus. The sweating, panting line-outs, the heaving scrums which bruised one's ears between bony bottoms and confined one's vision to grass, mud and a score of disembodied boots – it gave me a kind of claustrophobic nausea coupled with a keen sense of futility. What *was* the point of it? To give another boy the pleasure of scoring? That was a distant altruism of which I was as yet incapable. Team spirit? But the lists differed from week to week; we were not *teams* and could feel no loyalty towards a rotation of strangers. And the balls we played with were not the taut, light-tan ovoids of the School XVs, which responded crisply to hand and foot. Ours were soft, care-worn, blown-out specimens possessed, so it seemed to us, of more than their due share of gravity.

Eventually, however, I managed to establish myself as a full-back. I had neither the weight nor the strength for scrummages; nor was I fast or nimble enough for half-back or three-quarter play. But I could catch and kick, and though I lacked the spontaneous courage of the good player, I could bring myself to make a tackle when I saw the need for it and was forced into a calculated decision. Thus I found my way into School and House teams, and in my last year was playing regularly for the School Second XV and the House First XV. Then, of course, my attitude changed. It was not so much that I came to enjoy rugger for itself – though pleasure I did find in the physical activity, the sense of release, the spectator-like view of the game that I enjoyed as full-back, the occasional brisk tackle that stopped a certain try. Rather it was the concomitant delights of away matches, extra teas, and the prestige attached to membership of a team; I felt that I had 'made it'.

The team teas that followed a match were indeed a prize worth having. They were far from banquets; but they were different, and they included savoury items which were absent from our daily diet. Best of all were the special teas ('progs' as we knew them) which were given to the whole House as a reward for winning any of the inter-House championships. In these the catering staff excelled themselves with trifles, jellies and other delicacies; and our Housemaster rounded them off, amid boisterous cheers, with romantic stories about mythical heroes of Upper House.

Away matches – perhaps no more than half a dozen for the Second XV during the two winter terms – were, like the teas, an enjoyable departure from normality. There was a curious thrill of pleasure in that sense of exposure, blending unease with the will to win, as we lined up on an alien pitch surrounded by strangers all shouting for the opposing team. Moreover, they introduced us briefly to worlds contrasting with our own – in geography, architecture, food, dress, routine and human components. There was educational advantage in this as well as pleasure for boys who for most of the year were confined to a single close community with its own peculiarities of tradition and conformity; it was a pity that the benefit was limited to the few of us who played for School teams. At Prior Park, a Catholic school on the other side of Bath, we reacted with boyish mirth to the sight of the fathers stamping along the touch-line in full clerical habit. Sidcot, a coeducational school near Winscombe, aroused surprise and curiosity by the unwonted presence of girls in corridors, dining hall and playing fields. It was foreign to our conception of life that boys and girls could live and work together thus *and* regard it as nothing extraordinary; and we thought it 'sissy' to be so closely associated with the female sex.

The return journey, especially after a victory, was an event in itself. Bruised, tired and sleepy, but cheered by success and a change of fare, we sang our well-worn songs, exchanged ribaldries, chattered excitedly about incidents in the match or simply dozed in a corner seat until the proud moment of arrival and the announcement of success. Defeat was less exhilarating, but it had its compensations; and after all it was the game that mattered – so we were persuaded – and the manner of our losing it.

Cricket, for me, was disastrous. I was never taught to bat or bowl; a good eye, which I had by nature, was no substitute for practised skill; hence my performance at the crease was usually brief and ignominious.

Moreover, the slow pace of the game and the tedium of protracted inactivity left me bored and irritated; my concentration was so erratic that I could not be trusted even as a scorer. Until one reached the sixth form there was no alternative; then one was allowed to switch to tennis, and this with immense relief I did, shrugging off the stigma of what, in the popular view, was a second-class game. But it was one for which I was temperamentally suited and could thoroughly enjoy; moreover, the courts were in the main school grounds; there was no tedious trek to and from the Upper.

Swimming too one could enjoy within the precincts of the school. The baths, built in 1908, were antiquated and somewhat cramped; they were a boon none the less. From that time on few boys, if any, left Kingswood unable to swim; I was certainly not among them, for once I had learnt the rudiments I found enormous pleasure in this activity. Not that I excelled in it, or wished to do so; I was content simply to enjoy the mastery and concomitant freedom of a new element, the increasing strength which culminated, for me, in the coveted completion of 22 lengths (440 yards) and the receipt, if I remember rightly, of a medal for so doing. There was also the sheer sensuous pleasure of yielding oneself wholly to the water's embrace, floating easily on its surface or gliding smoothly through its enfolding caress. These are sexual images, the product of hindsight from adult years; at the time we were unaware of any such implications, but they may yet have been present. For it was here, with my contemporaries, that I discovered the delights of swimming in the nude. At first for bravado (because it was forbidden), later we shed our costumes to indulge in that distinctive quality of pleasure that naked swimming gives – perhaps from the total yielding of oneself with total lack of restraint, or possibly there lingers still in the subconscious, recalling us to primeval simplicity, some echo of that aqueous womb in which life began.

Long-distance running was the one physical activity I found I could excel in. The discovery came by accident and was as much of a surprise to me as to anyone else. The cross-country was an inter-House event and took place in the middle term when rugger was often impossible because of frost or snow. Preparation started about a month before; a group of about a dozen from each House were put through a rigorous programme of training which culminated in runs of up to five or six miles and finally the race itself (which was nearer four). From these dozen a team of eight was finally selected.

For the first few days, until lungs and wind were adjusted, it was agonising; trots of a quarter of a mile or so were interspersed with sharp sprints of 100 yards which left us gasping, racked with stitch and wishing the world would end. When the afternoon's drill was finished, our legs stiffened until we walked with difficulty and climbed stairs like rheumatic octogenarians. Once this stage was passed, I began to enjoy it; there was a sense of release as the whole body responded to increasing demands, of freedom as we cantered mile after mile over the openness of Lansdown. In the steady rhythm of legs and lungs – breathe in four strides, breathe out four strides – the mind too found escape, drifting along easily and comfortably on a random flow of thoughts and images. Then, back at school, came the hot shower, the clean, warm afterglow, the mug of sweet re-energising tea. Yes, this was good! For the first time I had found genuine delight in the efficient, top-level functioning of a healthy body; it was among the best things that Kingswood gave me.

My first race found me bunched outside the games pavilion with thirty-one other competitors all waiting nervously for the starting signal; I had been chosen, so I supposed, simply to make up the eight, and the sooner it was over the better. Amid the cheers of supporters we set off on the first stage to the Blathwayt Arms. By the time we reached the pub the initial bunch had trailed out to a long line with a few stragglers toiling in the rear. Thence we turned into the racecourse and for the next mile followed its white guard-rails. It was here that, incredulously, I found myself catching up and passing other boys; one after the other I left them behind, moving from about 25th to somewhere in the first half. Came the road to Weston; over the stiles, across the three fields, up a last dragging slope, and there was the finishing funnel and a mass of cheering boys through whom I strained those last painful steps before flopping thankfully on the grass. I was 13th.

Next year I did better, and in my third year was expected to win. A week before the race I was attending one of our weekly sixth form science lectures when I suddenly noticed a large red spot on the inside of my left wrist, then another, and another. There was german measles in the school at the time, but surely, I thought, my extra fitness would see me clear. However, when I looked at my chest there could be no doubt. Here indeed was a dilemma: if I told no one, I might be fit to run, for the infection was trifling in itself and scarcely raised either temperature or pulse-rate; but could I conceal the spots? There was a training run that afternoon; in the changing rooms and the showers one was open to public scrutiny and my condition would be obvious. In the end I gave myself up and spent the next week, including the day of the race, in the sanatorium.

This was not the end of my running. Already in the previous year I had found sufficient pleasure in it to set off alone or with one or two companions on long, easy runs over Lansdown, stopping when we chose, to get our breath or just to look around. This was during the summer when we were training for athletics; but we had no thought of competition. So now, in my last term at Kingswood, many times we ran the level miles along road and racecourse to Prospect Stile and on to Kelston Round Hill. Here we lay for a while contentedly in the long grass, relaxed, carefree, delighting in the cool touch of the breeze on sweating limbs and faces. Like gods we gazed out over Bath and the Avon valley and beyond these to the Wiltshire Downs and the White Horse of Westbury which we could dimly see through the summer haze. Refreshed, we trotted back below the wooded edge of the escarpment, through combes and fields decked out in their full array of summer flowers – clovers white and red, dog-daisies, knapweed, buttercups and bedstraws, whose pollen stained our running-shoes as they brushed through them. Then came the cold shower, a mug of tea, and a leisurely book to fill the hour until our evening meal. It was delectable – the freedom, the wide horizons, summer's plenitude, and the blood pulsing vigorously through healthy bodies. Like the poet, but for a different reason, we knew that to be young was very heaven!

Closely associated with games was an event in my last year at Kingswood which was unusual in providing opportunity for the practical application of my classical education. The school is built on sloping ground which has been levelled to meet the needs of each phase of construction. Beyond and below the main teaching block, the Ferens Building, was an area of grass rather smaller than a full-size rugger pitch but large enough, had it been level, for useful practice. It was used for pasturing the horses which pulled the mowers on the Upper and was known as the 'moke field' because 'moke', for reasons unknown, was our word for horse (and donkey). The captain of the First XV at the time was J. L. Halstead, a fearless player, a good classical scholar and in my eyes a paragon of combined physical and intellectual excellence. It was his idea to level the field.

It would be an ambitious undertaking, for there was no money to hire labour and no machines of the kind which would now complete the work in weeks or even days. The only means available were boy-power, spades and a few wheelbarrows. But the decision was made and planning began. The first stage was to remove the turf and pile it at the top of the slope; gangs of boys were organised to dig, others to wheel and stack. When work began, it soon became obvious that the uphill push with the loaded barrows was beyond their strength; the only alternative was to carry the turf by hand. Our problem was to devise a method combining the maximum load with the minimum effort.

It so happened that Jimmy Halstead and I, as members of the same year of the classical sixth, had recently been reading Book IV of Thucydides' *History of the Peloponnesian War*, in which he describes how

Athenian soldiers fortified the promontory of Pylos on the west coast of the Peloponnese. Having no hods or buckets the soldiers carried the mortar on their backs, 'stooping down to make it stay on, and clasping their hands [behind them] to prevent it falling off.' Could not we, I suggested to Jimmy, adopt the same technique? We did, and it worked well. The next afternoon of operations saw lines of crouching boys plod slowly up the slope with their back-fulls of turf, release their burden, and then race gaily downhill to collect another from the diggers. It had been explained to them that they were playing the part of Athenian soldiers; they responded with alacrity and the work lost much of its chore. This was in 1935. When I left at the end of the summer term, we had barely scratched the surface of the task; it was completed mechanically and the field was opened for use in 1952.

A boarding school, where several hundred pupils spend the whole of their daily life on or near the premises, requires delegation of authority from masters to boys. This remains true even where the school is divided, as Kingswood was not (but is now), into physically separate Houses; and it is no doubt equally true of girls' schools. Otherwise there must be either a larger staff or greater demands on existing staff (including many trifling duties which can as well be performed by boys) or risk of serious misdemeanour, as was common in the 18th and 19th centuries. Heads like Thomas Arnold (though he was not the first) recognised the need for such delegation and institutionalised it in the prefect system which thenceforth became an integral part of the public school tradition. It was given a somewhat dubious educational justification by arguing that valuable lessons (for instance, in responsibility, judgement, attention to duty) were learnt from the exercise of authority, and that in any case it is bad for youngsters to be constantly supervised by adults.

Popularly associated with the prefect system – a product of generations of schoolboy fiction – are images of small boys rushing down corridors to answer an imperious call of 'fa-a-ag', or lighting fires and making toast for their seniors (who lounge meanwhile in easy chairs), cleaning their shoes, making their beds, and receiving a thrashing for failure in these and other servilities. There was no fagging at Kingswood, though boys could be required, as a punishment, to clean a prefect's shoes or perform similar menial tasks; there were no separate studies, no fires, and no beatings. There were School Prefects and House Prefects. The former, a select few of about eight, had authority throughout the school and a room of their own. House Prefects were more numerous, about half a dozen to each House, and their authority was confined almost exclusively to their own House.

I was a House Prefect throughout my last year at Kingswood, possibly for a term or two earlier than that. I was late in reaching this elevation partly because I was young for my age and correspondingly immature, partly because I commanded little respect from other boys in the physical prowess which our ethos expected. A prefect must not only have authority but be able to enforce it; otherwise he would be 'fooled'; he would be the target of snide sarcasms and open disobedience; his rule, particularly in the dormitories where he might be outnumbered by thirty to one, would degenerate into chaos. He would then be a liability to himself, his colleagues (who rescued him from his own ineffectiveness) and his Housemaster. Obviously it was important that this should not happen. Fortunately (or by the wise judgement of my superiors) I escaped such indignity; although my authority was often tested and sometimes tenuously maintained, it held and I survived.

Our duties were not arduous; they centred on dining-hall, day-rooms and dormitories. We sat at the head of tables and portioned out food; we supervised the evening preparation periods; we saw juniors and seniors to bed, called 'lights-out' and imposed silence thereafter. In addition there was a general responsibility to see that school rules were obeyed, at least by members of our own House. Nor were our privileges impressive; we had status; we were not subject to 'lights-out'; we had a prefects' 'supper' in the prep interval; we could use the side entrance to and from chapel; we had our separate prefects' room; and we enjoyed a certain camaraderie arising from community of interest, responsibility and enlarged freedom. To these must be added the weekly meetings with our Housemaster which took place in his room after senior 'lights-out'. At these 'ups', as we called them, we discussed House matters and other topics over tea and biscuits. The latter, a variety called Wantage Cakes, were offered to us in full-size double tins. Regrettably, we took advantage of this generosity by consuming them in excessive quantity; a few we even pocketed surreptitiously for future consumption in our cubicles.

The sanctions available to us against disobedience, defiance or breaking the rules were limited; shoe cleaning I have already mentioned. This particular penalty could redound on the punisher: I was once ordered by a prefect whom I specially disliked to clean his shoes for a week; on the first day I not only cleaned the outside but also put dollops of blacking inside, well up the toe where they would not be seen until too late. Strangely, he either did not notice – a sad reflection, perhaps, on his personal cleanliness – or was too baffled by this audacity to devise suitable retaliation. We could also impose detention; this took place on half holidays under staff supervision. Our response to common misdemeanours like talking after 'lights-out', eating during prep or fighting in the corridors was normally one 'mark' (30 minutes detention) or two 'marks' (45) for repetition of an offence or for answering back. 'Marks' were recorded and totted up; too great an accumulation might bring further punitive measures and comment on the end-of-term report.

Does prefectship, as an institution, still serve any useful function (assuming that it ever did) or is it, where it survives, a mere relic of antique furniture? I find it difficult to make judgement on the traditional arguments to support it ('training for leadership', etc.) and on the benefits I received from my own brief spell as a prefect. It boosted my self-confidence and gave me a sense of obligation, of duties to be punctually and responsibly performed; but I suspect little else. Of day schools some retain it, others have abolished it either on egalitarian principles or because, in the present climate of thuggery, it exposes prefects to the risk of personal assault. In many boarding schools it survives for the practical reasons mentioned above; but even here there is a shift away from the exercise of authority and the enforcement of rules to a broader role of pastoral supervision.

CHAPTER VI

Kingswood (ii)

MUCH OF OUR LIFE AT KINGSWOOD was centred on the classroom; we were expected to work, and academic success was highly regarded. Well before the end of the 19th century Kingswood boys had achieved a reputation for the school by winning an impressive number of scholarships at Oxford and Cambridge and by distinguished careers thereafter. When I arrived in 1930 the Oxbridge tradition was well established; an open award was held up before us as the supreme goal of the academically able and, for impoverished ministers' sons, virtually the only route to university.

The importance attached to academic work was reflected in the new teaching block which had been opened by the Prince of Wales in 1926. It was named the Ferens Building after its donor, T. R. Ferens, a prominent Methodist and chairman of Reckitts, the Hull pharmaceutical firm. Magnificently sited on open ground to the west of the main school, it commands broad views over Bath and the Avon Valley. It is also a beautiful building in itself, made of local stone and underlining by its simple dignity the directness of scholarly purpose for which it was intended. Yet purpose-built though it was to the highest standards of its time, it would not satisfy today's pedagogy. It was designed, like the classrooms at Magnus but more elegantly, for a teacher-centred concept of instruction based on talk, chalk and pupils sitting at desks. This was not, of course, the fault of the architect, who could not forsee the changes in educational practice and the advances in technology which the next fifty years would bring.

Our curriculum too, judged by modern standards, would be thought unduly restricted, at least on the classical side. My School Certificate (handwritten in a script whose graceful loops and flourishes have an old-fashioned beauty of their own) records passes in English, History, Latin, Greek, French and Elementary Mathematics; this was the whole extent of my examination studies. In addition we had weekly sessions in the

92

gymnasium and a period of Scripture, but no art or music, and no craft of any kind. At Magnus I had been learning physics and chemistry as well as Latin, French and the normal core of general subjects. When I transferred to Kingswood, I was assigned to the classical fifth, began learning Greek and for the next two years lost all contact with the sciences. I did not question this curricular limitation – how could I? I had a goal – 'School Cert.', with the five credits we were told were a necessary passport to the sixth form, 'Higher Cert.' and university. I was content with this distant, but increasingly urgent objective and preoccupied more immediately with the routine of learning and the tussle of marks and termly orders.

I can remember little of the detail of this run-up to School Certificate. On the classical side our main concentration was on Latin and Greek; the latter, despite the greater complexity of its grammar, I found no more difficult than Latin; memorisation was no problem – the parts of Greek verbs have a rhythmic and melodic quality which swings trippingly and unforgettably off the tongue. They still bring me a strange comfort – an illusion of security perhaps – when I recite them to myself to relieve the tedium of motorway driving.

As at Magnus the classical teaching was based on grammar and syntax and imposed on us a succession of mechanical exercises in translation to and from Latin and Greek. Later we were introduced to passages from original texts, but we read them in such snail-pace driblets that their content was lost amid the labour of deciphering. Our groans were audible, though good-humoured, when we were asked to 'take out your Petries'. This was an unattractive grey-bound book of Latin extracts edited by a scholar of that name; publishers have since learnt the skilful use of colour and design to enliven the external appearance of even the dreariest textbook. We read only a few pages in the course of a year, mainly from Cornelius Nepos's biographies of famous generals. The laborious, dragging hours which we spent disentangling the exploits of Themistocles and Miltiades from their bewildering web of vocabulary and inflexion brought us little nearer to the men themselves and their doughty deeds. These remained for the most part shadowy unrealities. Of Greek and Roman culture and the greatness of the classical past we had only the rarest glimpses. It was not revealed to us how these people lived, loved and fought; how, without trains, cars, electricity, radio, cinema, flush toilets and Heinz 57 varieties, they satisfied and rose triumphantly beyond the needs of everyday life. Even Roman bathing habits remained a mystery to us, despite the proximity of the baths of Aquae Sulis in the valley below. As for Greek sculpture and vase-painting (what little we saw of them in illustration), these were a source of prurient rather than aesthetic interest. Our teachers were not to blame; they were conforming to the conception of classics teaching prevalent in the 1930s. The fault lay partly in the examination syllabus, which required only linguistic competence, partly in a long tradition which for centuries had exalted means above end, grammatical minutiae above cultural appreciation and the enjoyment of literature.

French I never enjoyed – though I am grateful for such competence in the language as I still retain. In mathematics I found geometry intriguing and arithmetic at least tolerable; algebra both mystified and repelled me – what *was* the sense, I asked myself, of this alphabetical jugglery? Calculus baffled me, I despaired and gave up trying.

English I remember chiefly for the tedious practice in précis required by the Certificate syllabus. Tedious indeed it was at the time, and exasperating too, for I could never be sure that I had got to the heart of the matter (and when I thought I had, as often as not my teacher deemed otherwise). But I have since learnt its worth: to extract the core of argument or exposition and express it in one's own words with clarity and concision is an invaluable, and much underrated, exercise in understanding and in logical and verbal skills. Essays were also required of us. These too I found tiresome, for I had no natural fluency in writing, no easy flow of ideas or inventive imagination. When I tried to express myself, my mind became all thumbs; it was seized by vacuity, a fumbling aphasia and verbal penury from which eventually it tortured out a series of banalities rigged up in desiccated verbiage. Delight in wrestling with words, in chiselling away at language until it fits exactly the shape of thought and feeling – this was remote from my boyhood experience, a joy for the distant future.

Of the literature that we read in our English lessons I can recall only *Julius Caesar* and Palgrave's *Golden Treasury*. Familiarity with the former, which we had read at Magnus, made this second reading both easy and pleasurable; I even bought my own second-hand copy, carried it round with me and, of my own volition, committed to memory a further store of notable passages. Alone in the fields and out of earshot I declaimed them to myself, savouring the rhythms and cadences of the majestic verse and perceiving in it something of that universal truth which makes Shakespeare a poet for every time and place.

> There is a tide in the affairs of men
> Which taken at the flood leads on to fortune,
> Omitted, all the voyage of their life
> Is bound in shallows and in miseries.

The words spoke, so it seemed, even to my condition as I moved towards the critical juncture of School Certificate – and I worked the harder because of it. Palgrave had no such attraction for me ; it struck no chord within the stirring of my adolescent emotions.

I have no recollection of our Scripture lessons during those two years ; yet lessons there must have been, for we had half an hour's Scripture prep on Sunday afternoons and the one would have been pointless without the other. Later, in the classical sixth, we were introduced to the Greek text of St Paul's letters ; this was a welcome variation from Thucydides and Plato, but the convolutions of the apostle's style made this more of a linguistic than a theological exercise. It was John Wesley's intention in founding the original Kingswood to train up 'rational, scriptural Christians'. Rational some of us may have been, but scriptural we were not ; Wesley would have been surprised and disappointed at our ignorance of vast areas of Holy Scripture and even of the New Testament. (I am not suggesting that he was right – I fancy he knew more about the Bible than about children.)

Our history syllabus for the School Certificate was in two parts, English 19th century and classical. I failed in the former but passed sufficiently well in the latter to secure a credit with the combined marks. For me, English history was a wasteland of names, facts and dates. Corn Laws, Factory Acts and Reform Bills, Wilberforce and Gladstone, Waterloo and the Crimea, all of them slotted, date-tagged and mortified between the red covers of the dreariest of textbooks – my immaturity could see no sense in them, no illuminating purpose, no thread of coherence. Memory rebelled against them, rejected them like incompatible transplants.

In contrast, the past of Greece and Rome had a quality which made it acceptable. Distance gave it not only enchantment but perspective, a simplicity of outline which made it intelligible ; motives were transparent, events stood out in bold relationship ; it was as if time had somehow sifted out the real stuff of history from a cloudy murk of impurity. Marathon, Thermopylae, Salamis, Plataea, and the frustration of Persian imperialism ; the rise and fall of Athens, tyranny to democracy, Peisistratus to Pericles, Nicias and the debacle of Syracuse ; the legendary kings of the Seven Hills, the emergence of the Roman republic and the battles that conquered Italy – here, in the clash of purpose and personality, the adventure, the intrigue, the valorous last stand, here indeed was meaning, drama, romance, all of it pulsating with an exuberance which matched that of my own boyhood. And, of course, it provided context and relevance for our linguistic studies.

Our history master for the Certificate year was a dear, gentle, scholarly soul, a real Christian gentleman ; but unfortunately he was unable to control our class (which was, I believe, an especially difficult one). So we did what we liked, and for most of us this was anything but history (until the summer term and the imminence of examinations). The few who wished to learn grouped themselves earnestly round the dais, an oasis of attention amid the prevailing hubbub; the rest of us read, chatted, played cards and indulged in various other forms of amusement. My own contribution to the fun included the manufacture of fireworks and the organising of beetle races.

The ingredients for the former were supplied by friends on the science side; powdered magnesium was among them; the rest, for obvious reasons, I must refrain from mentioning. These were packed into tightly rolled tubes of graph paper and ignited later in surreptitious corners of the school grounds and the surrounding fields. Beetle races were dependent on a supply of suitable competitors; these could usually be found in sufficient quantity – half a dozen at a time, black and about an inch long – in the woods above the school. We raced them along the aisle between two rows of desks whose metal bases formed a confining barrier to keep the runners on course. But first we stuck to each of them a tiny paper disc marked with its number (easier said than done – patience and gentle fingers were needed to restrain their vigour); then we lined them up and let them go.

Beetles are not accustomed to moving in straight lines; Euclid's 'shortest distance between two points' is not part of their mental equipment; consequently, though they leapt energetically from the starting-line, thenceforth the race became a tangle of wild meanderings. They darted criss-cross this way and that, collided, paused to feeler each other, and moved off again in a variety of curves, u-turns and gyrations which delighted the spectators. Some escaped through gaps in the barriers; these we pursued across the classroom, weaving and heaving our way through the huddle of legs and desks in our frantic efforts at recapture. Finishers were few, and this rare achievement was greeted with a burst of uninhibited cheering; the studious few looked up from their notes; the master interrupted his discourse to deliver a mild rebuke. The beetles, their brief days doubly numbered, scurried away into nooks and crevices of the classroom and were quickly forgotten. Regretfully, we had no concern for these elegant and charming creatures whose innocence we so wantonly abused.

There was no malice in this, just a huge sigh of escape from the tram-lines of normal class routine; we held our teacher in grateful affection for permitting this relief. And his lessons, though most of us learnt little history in them, were not without ultimate educational value. In the summer term we became aware of the approach of examinations and of our own ignorance. We set to work, those of us who had our sights set on university, and began to teach ourselves. For myself I plodded drearily through the arid boredom of English history and found unexpected pleasure in Greece and Rome. In the process I learnt to make notes, to sift, abbreviate and rearrange the content of textbooks into meaningful and memorisable patterns of information. This was a lesson in self-instruction which proved invaluable in later years.

This was not typical of our teaching, most of which was good, much of it excellent. As at Magnus the teaching was instruction-based – formal exposition reinforced by practice, competitive form orders, the deterrent of failure and the prestige of success. Such was the prevailing pedagogical ethos. Discovery methods, projects, information packs, work sheets, group activity and team-teaching were not widely known or practised in secondary schools. But we learnt none the less; passively perhaps and uncritically, but we learnt, we passed our examinations and some of us won our way to university. That we did so reflects the conscientiousness, efficiency and patience, as well as the scholarship, of those who taught us.

Five credits in School Certificate (history gave me one to spare) assured my elevation to the classical sixth; here my objectives were Higher Certificate and a university scholarship. Promotion brought some sense of status but little in the way of privilege – a move up the dormitory nearer to the Housemaster's quarters and the use of the sixth form walk, a pleasant shrub-lined path behind the Ferens Building. In the classroom effort was inevitably concentrated on Latin and Greek, the languages and the literature. A minimum of French was added, since a third language was a likely requirement of our scholarship examination, and English essays for the same reason; religious education came through the medium of Greek. In my second and third years in the sixth form we attended lectures in general science; this was a wise and welcome addition to our studies, of which more later.

There were four or five of us in that first year of the classical sixth. At once the contrast was obvious, not only between our own small group and the full class of the previous year, but even more between the fully timetabled routine of the latter and the large quota of 'spare' periods which we now found at our disposal. Supposedly these were for private study and preparation, but we had no guidance in their use. Consequently, since human nature inclines to do no more than is asked of it, we wasted much of our time in idle chatter, playing cards or chess, reading light novels or simply looking out of the window. The transition from

W. I. Tidswell: 'qui doctus indoctos docebas'

heteronomy in learning to autonomy is necessary, but it is difficult and needs to be gradual; it is best begun in the primary school.

Our principal teacher in that year was a genial, paternal, pipe-smoking gentleman who could be relied on to arrive a few minutes late for a proportion of his lessons. This gave us extra time for whatever amusement occupied us; it also reduced the number of lines of Sophocles or Virgil that our calculations deemed it needful to prepare. His scholarly touch and gentle correction eased us through the formidable labour of learning to render passages of English into a semblance of idiomatic Latin and Greek. One by one we took our versions to his desk and there, inhaling the reek of his last pipe, we watched his kindly pencil transform our stumbling solecisms into a rhythmic flow of grammatically correct prose. I have a photograph of him, taken in the act and without his knowledge, through a hole in the back of a file; with it is a Horatian ode composed by a younger colleague to mark his retirement:

O tu per annos vix numerabiles
antiquitatis cultor et artium,
qui doctus indoctos docebas. . . .
Num quid senescis?[1]

'Surely you don't grow older?' The answer is yes and no. Old he seemed to us at the time, and he is dead now together with most of the others who taught us. Yet he retains a certain immortality, a composite flavour of scholarship, classical antiquity and paternal concern which is preserved in the photograph and in the nostalgic memories of those of us who survive.

In this first and subsequent years we read, either in class or on our own, the obvious Greek and Roman authors – dramatists and historians, epic and lyric poetry. We marched with Hannibal through the Alps and with Agricola in Britain, fought with the Spartans at Thermopylae and the Athenians in Sicily, accompanied Odysseus and Aeneas in their wanderings, rejoiced and grieved with Horace and Catullus, and shared Socratic subtleties in Plato's *Apology* and the minor dialogues. In addition we wrote a weekly prose and unseen in each language. It was hard, slow work, but interesting, sometimes exciting – especially prose composition, in which I developed some facility; I enjoyed manipulating words and phrases to fit the exact tone of meaning and at the same time to make them attractive in rhythm and cadence. My regret is that we had little or no instruction in Greek and Roman antiquities: coins, architecture, sculpture, Roman roads and aqueducts, mosaics and hypocausts, Greek science and mathematics – the fascination of these and the concept of language as part of a culture we were left to discover for ourselves.

For our second and third years we had a change of staff and of venue. The former was a firm, efficient, kindly teacher with a number of mannerisms which we delighted to mimic; he was almost completely bald and was nicknamed 'Eggum'. Instead of a classroom in the Ferens Building we met in the reference library, which was then housed in the main school block. It was a stimulating move, for we worked now for most of the day in a pervading atmosphere of books, and for the first time we had at our finger-tips the literary resources to support and extend our learning. From the windows we looked out over the headmaster's garden – trees, flowers and velvet lawns – and the city of Bath. Summer and winter alike it was warm, comfortable, secure; we belonged to a world of our own, whose distance in time and difference of language made it an exclusive possession.

---

[1] Learned patron of antiquity and the arts, who for years almost beyond reckoning taught the unlearned. . . . Surely you don't grow older?

An important feature of my last two years in the sixth was the general science course newly introduced for the arts side. I had lacked all contact with the sciences during the run-up to School Certificate; likewise my fellow pupils. The headmaster was a historian with strong aesthetic interests, and no doubt this innovation was a response to his own need as well as ours (he did in fact attend some of the lectures). They were carefully organised, briskly delivered and well supported by experiments on the bench in front of us; I found them fascinating. We were invited to present our own questions, and regular answer-sessions were set aside for this. The course as a whole, and the answer-sessions in particular, brought science home to me, made it a reality, in a manner that had been lost to me since leaving Magnus.

The twin targets of my sixth form classics were Higher Certificate and a university scholarship. I was scheduled for the former in the summer term of 1935, then in my fourth year of the sixth I would sit for Oxbridge scholarships. However, we were encouraged to practise for the latter by taking the examinations in the third year; we would thus gain useful experience in examination techniques, interviews and the 'feel' of the two universities (which to most of us were unknown territories harbouring strange conventions and were only remotely attainable). Hence in the winter term of 1935 I found myself at Queens' College, Cambridge, competing for an open scholarship. I remember almost nothing of the occasion or of the journey to and from Cambridge. We wrote the examination in the college dining-hall, which was odorous with stale roasts and puddings; later we had tea, a small group of us, with one of the tutors. The rest is forgotten; but never to be forgotten is the sense of utter, mocking incredulity which possessed me when, walking up from chapel a few days later, I was met by Eggum and told that an award to me was announced in the day's *Times*. It was a mistake, surely, or a sour joke; impossible to be true!

But true it was, a scholarship of £100, which meant that, with further help from the County of Lindsey where my parents were now living, I would go to Cambridge the following autumn. The school's reaction was amused surprise, combined with a measure of self-congratulation both for its teaching and for the headmaster's recommendation (which, however good my prose composition, must surely have tipped the balance!). My parents, of course, were delighted; it had long been their ambition that I should go to university, but without scholarships it was impossible. For me an immediate result was that I need not sit the Higher Certificate; I had in front of me, therefore, the agreeable prospect of a summer term devoid of onerous academic commitments. I returned for that last term determined to enjoy it – and succeeded. Much of the routine of work and play went on as before – composition, unseens, translation, tennis, prefect duties in dormitory and dining-hall. Most of this was unavoidable, but all was vested in a new atmosphere; the ties were loosening, I would not be here next term. Academic work no longer claimed me for the sake of further goals but for its own enjoyment, to savour the taste of words, the feel of poetry, the thrust of argument; it was a new experience. So rewarding was it that I resolved to read the *Aeneid* right through.

It was hard work and slow at first; today I can read it fluently, then only two or three lines without pause for notes or dictionary. Living with Virgil for a period of weeks is an education into subtleties of inflexion, cadence, rhythm, characterisation, structure which one misses when reading only single books. The impression grows of a cultured epic, a piece of imperial propaganda, contrasting with the rude, first-hand vigour of Homer, yet an epic as much in contact with human reality (of a different kind) – *sunt lacrimae rerum et mentem mortalia tangunt.*[1]

I have read it through at least twice more, each time more enjoyably. The last occasion was a mountain-walking holiday in Scotland when I needed protracted reading to occupy the rainy days. By chance I came to Book VI, Aeneas' journey to the underworld, on a wet, misty day at the head of Glencoe; the hills were wreathed in turbulent cloud which opened and closed on dark vistas of glen and crag. It was a scene of desolation whose visual impact and historical associations entirely matched the reading. This was an experience well worth the labour of learning classics! But the *Aeneid* was not the only book I read that term; I discovered English literature. I read the novels of Thomas Hardy, whose sad sentimentality suited my mood in that last term at school. I also enjoyed *Moby Dick.* On sunny afternoons I retired with this beneath a philadelphus bush below the sixth form walk; the scent of its honey-sweet blossom languoured delectably around me as I read, full of 'the murmur of innumerable bees'. The scene was of summer tranquillity and delicious ease, which gave a fictional air of unreality to the bitter salt-sea struggles of the whalers.

The curriculum to which I was exposed at Kingswood had many virtues and some obvious deficiencies; of the latter, science (below the sixth form) was one, sex was another. During my five years at the school nothing was done to advance our knowledge of biological reproduction, human or animal; we received no explicit sex instruction, no moral

---

[1] Like all great poetry, the words are untranslatable! The sense they convey is something like this: 'A sadness pervades the world and our experience of it; human affairs touch the heart with pity'.

guidance. Yet Kingswood was not a hotbed of homosexuality, as some books suggest of public schools. Male nudity was commonplace and unremarkable in changing-rooms, showers and baths; there was no display nor any shyness save in those who lacked pubic hair. Perhaps it was indeed our strenuous physical activity that kept our instincts at bay!

Skirts were less of a rarity than at Magnus. The headmaster's wife was seen occasionally, his secretary more often, and the two matrons (one for clothing, one for catering) more often still; these last were delightful middle-aged ladies whom we greatly admired, but not sexually. There were also the 'dumbs' who served our tables and made our beds; few of these had any charm, and full blouses obscured their breasts; Flossy, above mentioned, was an exception. In the sanatorium many of the nurses were charming, and their charm was more than that of mother to boy; we recognised their femininity and they responded, especially a dark-haired Irish girl whose eyes and voice were softly winsome.

Another source of femininity was the Royal School whose playing fields were adjacent to ours; we passed the girls on our way to and from the Upper; conversation with them was forbidden. Apart from their skirts, long hair and hockey sticks we scarcely recognised them as different from ourselves; their larger hips and bottoms were hardly noticeable, their breasts were obscured; their goalkeepers wore chest-shields, but we asked not nor wondered why. This isolation from the other sex must surely have delayed our social development (mine, at least, who had no sisters) by some years. I left the school in a pathetic state of social immaturity and almost total sexual ignorance; fortunately instinct and curiosity eventually made good what schooling failed to provide. Kingswood is now coeducational.

Some small relief to my ignorance came from a booklet which my father gave me to read. More practical enlightenment came quite unexpectedly during a holiday we spent with farmer friends at Beckingham, near Newark; during this I assisted in delivering a calf and castrating some pigs. For the former we set off from the farm one evening, the farmer with a rope over his shoulder and I wondering why on earth it was needed. For although he had told me briefly what he was going to do, I had not the slightest idea how it was to be accomplished. The cow was in the middle of a large and otherwise empty field, mooing and heaving in the throes of birth. When we reached it, the back legs of the calf were already protruding; the farmer tied the rope to them and bade me join him in pulling. After two or three minutes of steady tugging, accompanied by agonised complaints from the cow, the calf burst out with a gush of bloody fluid and flopped soggily on to the grass, a shapeless mass of sodden skin scarcely recognisable as bovine. For a few seconds it lay there motionless, until, miraculously, as the cow began to lick it, its sides expanded with its first breath and gradually it struggled to its feet.

So that was the mystery of birth – a sodden bundle dragged bloodily and painfully out of a cow's backside! Was human birth like this? Did one use a rope for it? And did it hurt my mother so when I was born? These and other unanswerable questions swirled through my mind as we walked back to the farm. I was too shy to ask the farmer; my parents I dare not ask, for they would have been shocked even to have known what I had taken part in. I myself was shocked by the experience, though I was unaware of it at the time; perhaps this is why I could never bring myself to witness the birth of my own children.

By contrast, the castration was far less traumatic, even lighthearted. The farmer entered the sty, seized and straddled a resisting, squealing pig and sat on it with his face to its rear. From his pocket he took a penknife, previously sharpened to a razor's edge on the farm grindstone; then, grabbing the animal's tail, he made a neat vertical slit, and extracted the testicles, flicking them neatly through the open upper half of the door. The surgery was repeated on the remaining pigs and we left them loudly lamenting their lost boarhood.

I have already quoted John Wesley's intention of training up 'rational, scriptural Christians'; his means to this end was 'by instilling the principles of true religion, speculative and practical'. Adjacent to the original Kingswood was the school chapel, which until 1844 also served the local Wesleyan Society. Here the pupils attended worship every weekday at 5 am and 7 pm and on Sundays at 8 am; later on Sunday mornings they made their way (presumably on foot and not without risk of molestation by the riotous Kingswood miners) to a parish church. The chapel planned in 1851 for the new Kingswood School was postponed for lack of funds; it was built at last as a memorial for World War One and opened in 1922. Previous to this there was no Wesleyan chapel nearer than King Street and Walcot in Bath, and for generations, in all but the most inclement weather, the boys had walked the mile and a half down the hill for Sunday morning service and back to lunch. The religious observances imposed on my generation were far less onerous than those of Wesley's time – morning prayers in chapel on weekdays *after* breakfast and worship twice on Sundays; evening prayers were taken by Housemaster or prefect in the dormitories. Occasionally, if one had homework to complete or an absorbing book, one could escape from morning prayers by hiding in the 'pets' (toilets); but generally attendance at chapel was accepted without question or resistance as part of life's established pattern.

The school chapel

How little of it remains in memory! I spent five years at Kingswood; during that time I was present at (I cannot honestly say 'listened to') some 370 sermons, many of them delivered by the most eminent preachers within the Methodist Church. Of all those sermons I cannot remember the text or theme of a single one. Six words alone stand out from oblivion, spoken by the headmaster one Sunday evening during my final year. I can see him now, a regal figure in his Oxford robes, uttering them with solemn passion: 'the cotton wool of intellectual hypocrisy'. But what he was attacking, and why these words, out of so many scores of thousands should be retained, I have not the slightest notion – unless it was the fascination of their imagery that caught my mental eye. Most of the sermons were beyond my comprehension, for there was little allowance for our wide differences in age and understanding nor any attempt, so far as I was aware, to plan the Sunday services according to our interest or request.[1]

---

[1] I could well be wrong! R. E. Davies writes in *Methodism* (Penguin 1963) that the headmaster (A. B. Sackett) 'took immense pains' over 'the carefully-ordered services of the School Chapel' (p. 179). Indeed I suspect that he was increasingly aware that the chapel services were not having the impact he had hoped for, and because of this persuaded the governors to appoint a chaplain to the school. This first chaplain, appointed shortly after I had left, was the Rev. R. E. Davies, author of *Methodism* and later to become Principal of Wesley College, Bristol, and President of the Methodist Conference.

During these same five years I sang or suffered nearly 3000 hymns. Many of them were favourites, repeated again and again; these we sang with gusto, even with genuine feeling which went beyond the tune to embrace the sentiments of the writer. It was an experience not soon forgotten to join with 350 others, men and boys, in the singing of Charles Wesley's 'Love Divine' to either of the Welsh tunes Hyfrydol or Blaernwern. The great, pulsing volume of harmony stormed into every cranny of the chapel, binding it and us together in irresistible emotional bonds. Addison's 'The spacious firmament on high', sung to Walford Davies' tune, was another which gripped and moved us, myself especially in whose love of nature it found immediate response. And there was Blake's 'Jerusalem'. Oh how we sang it, with ardour of passionately felt commitment to its pledge of unremitting mental fight! (These last two were not in the Wesleyan hymn-book but were distributed to us on duplicated sheets; that they were included in the 1933 Methodist hymn-book is an indication of the spiritual and musical wisdom of those who arranged our worship. Regrettably, 'Jerusalem' has not been given a place in the 1983 *Hymns and Psalms*.)

There were others, however, whose language, imagery and theology were so much of the 18th century as to baffle and repel us and even arouse our ridicule. 'Come, Thou Fount of every blessing', a great hymn and unexceptionable in its first and last verses, begins its second with the line, 'Here I raise my Ebenezer'; to us, not having been trained to Wesley's 'scriptural Christianity', this was meaningless and was regularly parodied to 'Here I raise my lemon-squeezer'.

For most of us the direct religious impact of chapel services was, I believe, minimal; either they washed over our heads incomprehensibly or else, after uplifting us temporarily on a comforting swell of emotion, they abandoned us breathless on the even strand of daily commonplace – there was no obvious continuity from the one level to the other. What influence they had was aesthetic and habitual.

The chapel is a beautiful building in a beautiful setting. Built of the same Bath stone as the rest of the school, its exterior is simple, chaste and unassuming. It stands at the end of a sloping line of chestnuts which shed at our feet their richness of summer petal and autumn gold; westwards it faced in my time through pillars of rambling rose into the headmaster's garden, itself a model of ordered loveliness. Within is a contrasting world of stained glass, dark oak, reverberating organ music and choral euphony. This, repeated week by week and year by year throughout the impressionable years of adolescence, habituated us to an expectancy of order and beauty as a normal part of the human environment. And if order and beauty are among the attributes of divinity, then to that extent the impact of chapel was indeed religious. But I suspect there was more to it than that; for the daily routine of attendance at chapel, however overtly inscrutable at the time, penetrated by constant repetition to levels of mentality beneath consciousness and emerged later, for many of us, in profound religious and moral commitment.

There are other and more effective ways of educating children into religion than by direct inculcation of scripture or theological dogma. Undoubtedly the routine of chapel made us aware of a religious dimension to our lives and, as we grew older, stimulated intellectual questioning which might not otherwise have arisen; its subconscious influence may, as I have suggested, have been far more powerful.

Perhaps the most potent of all educational instruments, whether for religious, moral, or any other purpose, is the permeation into daily life of constant environmental influences, of values, attitudes and modes of behaviour incorporated into the structure of communal living. Implicit in the Kingswood regime were standards of conduct which reflected its religious foundation: courtesy, loyalty, kindliness, tolerance, honesty and, at the root of these and other virtues, a personal concern for the individual, of which we ourselves were not fully aware. But it was brought home to me, both at the time, and even more in retrospect, by an episode in my final year.

It was the headmaster's custom to interview every boy individually at the end of each term, for five or fifty minutes as the occasion required. This, surely, was an expression of religious purpose: if God cares for individuals, so too must any school which claims a Christian motivation; and here was one way of doing it.[1] At the end of one of the terms in that last year I came to the head in his private study late in the evening after the concluding school concert. On his desk were two things that took my notice: a carving of a tree, beautiful in its detail of foliage, which he himself, he told me, had cut from its block of wood; and a red-bound edition of St Mark's Gospel, finely printed and illustrated with woodcuts. At the time I was beset with sceptical doubts which questioned every aspect of the Christian faith, from God's existence to the possibility of life after death. It was these doubts we discussed.

Eventually, when it was clear that argument would not resolve my scepticism, he pointed to the gospel lying open on his desk and said, 'But

[1] F. C. Pritchard writes thus in ch. 8 of *A History of the Methodist Church* vol. 3 (Epworth 1983), p. 306: 'Sackett and his colleagues imparted to the school a distinctive flavour by their patient and determined attempt to bring the best out of every boy individually, whether his bent lay in academic pursuits, artistic expression, or making things with his hands. . . .'

surely *there* is something you can believe!' I looked and I read: 'The beginning of the gospel of Jesus Christ, the son of God'. That was the end of the interview but not of my doubts; yet the words were not forgotten, neither his words nor the evangelist's. And I suspect that it was that brief incident, unpremeditated and seemingly inconclusive, which, more than all the hundreds of chapel hymns and sermons, brought me ultimately into membership of the Methodist Church.

The tree which I saw on the headmaster's desk that evening was an indication, as well as a product, of his interest and performance in the visual arts. It was in middle life, I believe, that he came to carving and also to painting; he was secretive about his work and preferred not to publicise it; few of us therefore knew him as a creative artist. For music he had a deep love but no practical skill. To us these aesthetic interests were manifest mainly in the various concerts arranged throughout the year in the school assembly hall. By these he attempted both to share his own interests and to extend our educational experience beyond the classroom and games field into regions of imagination, emotion and professional skills of which most of us (coming from the impoverishment of the manse) were pathetically ignorant. Especially welcomed was the annual visit of the Wookey Hole Male Voice Choir, whose buoyant singing and rustic mien we cheered to the echo of enthusiasm. No less popular were the Oxford Balliol Players; they delighted us with Aristophanes (outside if weather permitted, in a natural amphitheatre below the playground), performed with a boisterous gaiety which brought us close to the spirit of the original. At a different level of sophistication was the visit of the great pianist Myra Hess, whose professional excellence, manifest even to our musical illiteracy, held us utterly enthralled.

A further extension of educative experience came from the 'occupations' or leisure activities which were made available to us on three evenings a week. Among these were the Junior and Senior Literary Associations which met to read plays, listen to papers by boys, masters and visiting speakers, and once a year to perform plays before the rest of the school. The Senior Association also published a magazine of poems and essays obscurely titled *Piazza*. There was a Scientific Society which organised lectures, many of them illustrated by bench demonstrations, on topics of current interest. Art, craft and music rooms might 'occupy' those who were financed for them; library and reading-room were open to all; there were clubs for games and other activities, whose number and variety were greatly increased in later years. The chess club attracted me; I was a regular attender and eventually became captain of the School team – for reasons of seniority rather than skill, for I rarely won.

In addition to official 'occupations' there were others illicitly pursued. A particular friend of mine was in charge of a games store in the school basement; here for many months we brewed a home-made beer. The recipe was simple, our methods rudimentary. Yeast was cajoled from the genial school baker, sugar 'borrowed' from the dining-hall; these, with water, were the sole ingredients. We had no notion of quantities but guessed them into bottles, filled up with water, tied on the corks and awaited eagerly the resultant 'fizz'. Not without anxiety, however; for bottles are not designed to resist the pressures of brewing; bursts were frequent, spilling the sticky concoction over shelves and floor, and stuffing the windowless room with a rancid, clinging effluvium.

Though most of our days followed an organised pattern of routine – chapel, meals, lessons, games and the rest – we were left with many vacant hours to fill as we chose. Much of this unoccupied time was of brief duration, gaps of up to an hour between one timetabled activity and the next, during which we were confined to the school and its precincts. Here we played our various indoor and outdoor games, read, chatted or slouched against the radiators until the next bell; there was no radio or TV to provide instant diversion. But on the three weekday afternoons when we were not required for games we could do and go as we pleased – and as far as we pleased within the limits of available time. Indeed our freedom was remarkable; apart from Bath itself, which might be temporarily out of bounds and for which a permit was always necessary, we could wander at will over the countryside; no one questioned our comings and goings.

Many were the rambles I enjoyed with my friends in the surrounding lanes and fields. On a long Thursday or Saturday afternoon there was time enough to explore the eastern scarps and combes of Lansdown as far as Woolley and Langridge, or on the Weston side to Prospect Stile and Kelston Round Hill. We would set off after lunch in a happy state of indecision about direction and destination; we had no care, no sense of urgency, of *having* to go anywhere; tea was at 5.30, distant enough to forget meanwhile, and hunger was sure to bring us back for that!

We soon became familiar with the ins and outs and ups and downs of Lansdown (an accurate description this, for although the plateau itself is flat, the escarpment is broken by grassy bluffs and coves, copses and gullies which add variety to the landscape – and distance to the feet). But familiarity did not diminish our pleasure; always there was fresh interest in the changing aspects of the countryside, its flowers and wild life and seasonal growth; in summer our shoes tugged through the rough grasp of long grass; in autumn we lunged merrily through deep drifts of crisp new-fallen leaves; there were blackberries in September for us to pick and share out later at tea; and in the woods were 'ground-nuts' to reward our

Kelston Round Hill and Prospect Stile

patient grubbing with sticks and fingers.[1] Nor were our routes ever twice the same, for we had no map but made our way by eye and instinct, over walls and through hedges, regardless of public footpaths.

If asked, we could not readily have formulated our pleasure in these walks. Apart from the obvious attraction of the countryside, it derived in part from temporary escape from the close regulation of our bell-dominated communal life into a more relaxed rhythm of existence; in part from the release of energy in physical activity, from companionship, from delight in exploration. And during the darker months there was a special pleasure in emerging from the chill damp of dusk to rejoin the bright warmth and bustle of the school and our evening meal. For me the walks reinforced and extended that felt affinity with nature already deeply rooted in me by the moors and Barny and Newark. In later years I ventured out on my own and came to love the tranquillity, the remoteness, the open horizons.

Kelston Round Hill became a place of special pilgrimage which I revisited time and again. It stands out, island-like and tree-crowned, a

[1] Our 'ground-nuts' were the tubers of *conopodium majus*, also known as earth-nut or pig-nut; the tubers are blackish and resemble a chestnut; they can be eaten raw (as we did) or boiled or roasted.

few hundred yards from the south-western edge of Lansdown. On its summit there came to me an agreeable sense of isolation, of possession – this for a few brief minutes was my world, the whole of it, and my *own* world, inviolable. The school amid the distant trees, the streets and buildings of Bath, these I could survey with detached equanimity, a kind of Epicurean *ataraxia*,[1] which lifted me temporarily above their trivialities. But it was not only the sense of detachment that attracted me; I experienced there moments of profound intimacy with the natural world. In the dormancy of winter when the wind was a whispered sifting through bare branches, in the fullness of July's profusion of growth and insect hum, on gusty October days which blasted the yellowing leaves headlong down the hillside – the voice was always there, speaking with powerful insistence of a reality, mysterious yet reassuring, of which I was a part and it of me, and whose being and beauty I was invited to share.

Adolescent fantasy the sceptical reader may again object, or the upsurge of nascent sexual impulse. Be that as it may, to me at the time the experiences were vivid and compelling; they repeated and confirmed the message that had come to me in the woods at Barny and in the lanes and harvest fields of Newark. But they puzzled me too; I could not explain them nor share them; nor, so far as I knew, had they come to others – until by chance I picked up second-hand a copy of Richard Jefferies' *The Story of My Heart*. Here in the first chapter he writes of a hill that he frequented and of the spiritual exaltation that he experienced there as he yielded to 'the embrace of the earth' and was 'absorbed into the being . . . . of the universe'. Here at least was something kindred, told in words I could not find for myself. Later, of course, I discovered it in Wordsworth.

Walks and runs about Lansdown were not the only means of enjoying the freedom of our half holidays. Half way up the bank at one end of the sixth form walk was the philadelphus under which I read *Moby Dick*. In July it was a mass of bloom; within its shade I lay for whole afternoons cocooned in a private world of drowsy warmth, the sun a flicker of light through the leaves, the air honey-sweet with the scent of its blossom. Sprawled in lazy content I drifted through time, overhearing with distant unconcern brief snatches of conversation from the path above and all the manifold sounds of summer activity around me. Or else I read, finding delight not only in *Moby Dick*, but also in Hardy's novels. The latter's descriptions of the countryside and of rural life, as well as his pervasive air of regretful resignation, found in me a sympathetic response.

[1] Undisturbedness

'Whole holidays' gave us even greater freedom to explore the countryside. These were granted two or (in summer) three times a term and allowed us a full day's absence, from after morning chapel until six or seven in the evening. Their incidence was unpredictable, for it depended partly on the weather. However, although the precise day was not known in advance, it was a fair guess when one would come. If three or four weeks had passed without a 'whole hol', and if the weather looked set for fine, our expectations would build up to a sustained simmer of anticipation which could be felt throughout the school. Conclusive evidence came when we peered through the kitchen windows and saw the 'dumbs' preparing sandwiches for our lunch bags. Excitement became irrepressible; as we dawdled across to the Ferens Building supposedly for our first lesson, our ears were cocked for the announcing bell, and when it came, there were great cheers, a scramble back to the day-rooms to deposit our books, and a rush to the assembly hall for the headmaster's final confirmation (usually disguised by some preliminary bantering which deceived no one and was greeted with roars of applause). Marvellous was the sense of liberation! For a whole blessed day we could cast off the trammels of classroom, games and all other obligations and venture out, under a blue heaven bright with sunshine, to go and do as we pleased.

Most of us had our plans already made. It remained only to collect lunch-bags and pocket-money, declare our intended destination, and then away! Again it must be said that our freedom was remarkable. It was an obvious precaution to require some statement of intention, though it was often tentative and even on occasion fictitious; but there was no forbidden territory (except the cinemas); time and distance were the only restraints. And finance of course, which restricted most of us to our feet; but train, tram, bus, and even taxi were permitted for those who had the money; cycles could be hired cheaply in Bath, and for many this was a favoured means of extending the range of their wanderings. I cannot remember any specific exhortation aimed at our behaviour or safety; nor can I recall any incident involving injury or serious misdemeanour. We had to take, if not to wear, our school caps; these both identified us as Kingswood boys and perhaps served as a restraint on our more adventurous propensities.

Sometimes there was a problem of finding companions. I took advantage of this one glorious June day, hired a bicycle for half-a-crown, and set off on my own for Wells and Wookey Hole. I knew of their fame – cathedral and caves – and they offered a reasonable round trip of about fifty miles. I wish I could do justice to the splendour of that ride. It was cloudless and very warm – the fecund, somnolent warmth of rural

Somerset. Summer was approaching its peak of burgeoning growth; the roads were lined with hawthorn in full blossom, and the air was heady with its scent and the fragrance of fresh-cut hay. Fields and trees were luxuriant with verdure newly rain-washed and as yet undimmed by heat or dust. From the hedges came the lilting cadence of willow warblers and the cheerful outburst of the chaffinch's ripple of song (among the few I could then identify). Everything – sight, sound, scent and the exhilaration of release – combined into the perfection of a summer's day.

Usually we went out in twos and threes and visited well known places of local interest – Solsbury Hill (an ancient camp just north of Bath), Sham Castle, Hampton Rocks, St Catherine's Valley, Bath itself and the villages near by. A favourite walk was along the towpath of the Kennet-Avon canal to Bathampton. This was pleasant enough in itself, but a further attraction was Harbutt's Plasticine factory, a mile or two from Bath. The plasticine, we were told, was made entirely from vegetable components and the process was secret; but we were welcome to visit the showroom, and here we were fascinated by the beauty and artistry of what could be made from such seemingly unpromising material. Another popular outing was by tram to Batheaston. These trams were ancient vehicles whose top deck was open to the sky. Since on these occasions the sky was always blue, we rejoiced in the openness, the breeze on our faces, the clatter and clang of rails and bell, the privileged views across the countryside. From Batheaston it was a short walk to Bathford and the wooded hills above.

A more ambitious holiday venture for summer days was to hire a boat and row it up the Avon to 'third weir' at Limpley Stoke. This required a party of four or more to share the expense (and the labour); and it was an option available only to those who had reached a certain seniority in the school and of attainment in the swimming bath. 'First weir', so called only as our point of departure, was at Batheaston where the road from Bathford crosses the Avon. Here we hired a boat from an attendant whose air of tardy reluctance impressed on us (intentionally no doubt) his concern for our safety. Thence we rowed over the deep, still water above the weir, through the echoing arch of the bridge and away upstream.

At first, edged with willows and alders, the river winds through level pastures which in July were profuse with flowers; later it swings due south under the main GWR line (as it then was) and into the steepening wooded valley that leads to Bradford. 'Second weir' is at Warleigh, where at one time there was a ford and a ferry across to Claverton. These have long since disappeared, but the river is broad and open here, the trees taller and more graceful. At one side of the weir was a shallow, graded slipway up which we lugged the boat to the next stretch of level water; for this we stripped to our pants and heaved and hauled at our reluctant craft which seemed transformed at once into a monster of dead wood shrugging off our efforts to shift it. But success at last, another transformation, and with the boat restored to life we glided smoothly on towards Limpley Stoke. After a mile or two we passed under the aqueduct which carries the canal; another mile and we were at 'third weir' and the end of our journey. Whether it was possible to take the boat further we did not know; in any case time would not allow, so we turned and began the easy passage downstream.

Those were delightful days that the river gave us. There was the novelty of a different element demanding unwonted skills; there was the merriment of exuberant youth rejoicing in its freedom; there were the larks and skirmishes with other boats, the cheerful blasphemies as boys were pushed, fell or dived clothed and unclothed into the water; above us was the blue, sun-drenched sky, around us the warm, lush river-smell of the gently drifting Avon. When we were not rowing, we could lie back at ease, luxuriously trailing our hands in the water and surveying with contented indolence the gliding banks and trees. And if there was time, we could enjoy the final delight of swimming at 'first weir', our toes tingling deliciously with the consciousness of unknown depths of water beneath us. On the bank above I can picture the ghost of Wesley with his long white hair and black preacher's gown. Brooding over the scene with sombre disapproval he intones his warning: 'He that plays when he is a child will play when he is a man'. Dear John! He who does *not* play when he is a child will never *be* a man!

The final days of my last summer term at Kingswood were a time of high sentiment, a strangely uneasy mixture of cheerful expectancy at the prospect of a new life at Cambridge and of fatalistic regret. I said goodbye to the familiar scenes where for five years I had found enjoyment and security; they were still part of me, yet between us there was now interposed a widening, Styx-like gulf which was tearing them irrevocably away. Once again, as at that parting from my mother on the station platform at Ilkeston, it was like a severing of the umbilical cord, but now it was separation from a surrogate womb which had nurtured my adolescence. My unease was further complicated by the ominous rumbling of world events which came from beyond our secluded horizon. For by now Mussolini was dropping bombs on Abyssinia and Hitler's storm-troopers were goose-stepping defiantly down the Unter den Linden. Dismiss them as we might, our adolescent insouciance could not wholly shrug off the chill of gathering war-clouds.

Temporarily, however, they were forgotten in the surge of emotion which crested to its climax at the leavers' service in the school chapel and that last triumphant singing of 'Jerusalem' which uplifted the hearts and moistened the eyes even of the most brazen. In that moment of exaltation we indeed meant what we sang – a total commitment, in mental and physical strife, to the service of England's green and pleasant land; but the sword we pledged ourselves to wield on her behalf was to become for many of my friends the instrument of their own extinction.

Of home life during those five years there is not much to say; there was not much of it. After the initial shock of separation Kingswood became my home, the focus of my interest and activity; relationships with masters and boys gradually encroached on and largely superseded those of family. From my parents, despite the weekly exchange of letters, I was increasingly estranged, partly (and inevitably) by adolescence, but more by absence and diversity of experience: my world of boarding school was totally foreign to them, and their weekly routine of house and chapel I no longer shared, or only spasmodically and with growing reluctance. Home life had become a breach of normality, though I was unaware of it at the time (at least in such words); looking back I see this now as a sad consequence of my boarding education.

Ilkeston is a drab little town half way between Nottingham and Derby and sandwiched grittily between their two coalfields. There was nothing to do there during the holidays apart from solitary walks and cycle rides in a countryside as uninspiring as the town itself. (I once got as far as Derby, where I bought a secondhand copy of Aeschylus.) My memory is chiefly of slag-heaps and winding-gear, of black cinder towpaths by the side of derelict canals overgrown with wild iris and willowherb, which lent a fleeting beauty to this scene of squalor; a few miles to the south was the vast devastation of the Stanton ironworks. This last, incidentally, was the source of some relief. One of the managerial staff was a staunch Wesleyan whose home, though near the works, was well shielded by trees and extensive gardens. My parents and I were sometimes invited to have tea there; with his two boys, of about my age and likewise at boarding school, I formed a somewhat intermittent friendship. Here was a serene, elegant beauty contrasting with the industrial spoliation outside, and a style of life (and food) into which I thankfully escaped. A further attraction to adolescent curiosity was their buxom maid who would obligingly stand at her bedroom window and bare her breasts to our gaze. (Ilkeston had a coeducational grammar school, and I have often wondered how different my life might have been if I had been sent there.)

In 1933 my father was posted to Horncastle, in the heart of rural Lincolnshire. This is a small, unremarkable town which serves, as it did in Roman times, as a centre for the surrounding villages and farms. It would be unkind to call it drab, and it was untouched then by industrial pollution (save for the summer traffic roaring through to Skegness); but it lacks distinction. Yet I found a certain attraction in its old, red-brick, terraced streets, its parish church of contrasting stone, its tall trees, and its somnolent air of contented detachment from the larger world. Moreover, it seemed an integral part of the countryside it served, and this not only as a market and a hub of roads, but by the almost indistinguishable merging of its streets and houses with the lanes and pastures that fringed it.

For my father the move to Horncastle meant the superintendence, with one colleague, of an extensive circuit of some thirty chapels. Methodist union had been ratified the previous year, but in many of the villages there were still two chapels within a few hundred yards, each insisting on its independence and requiring separate services for worship with their different Wesleyan and Primitive hymn-books. So much for the spirit of Christian unity – but perhaps it was early days for a united Methodism! Many of the villages were served by public transport (now virtually extinct); to most it was either walk or cycle, as far as eight miles to Scamblesby on the edge of the wolds or Hagworthingham towards the coast. It was hard work but healthy, and my father enjoyed it despite the frictions which sometimes arose from Wesleyans and Primitives not yet firmly bonded together in Christ. Neither here nor in any other circuit except possibly his last one, Padiham in Lancashire, did he have a telephone.

With the Methodist chapels in Horncastle I had no contact save the twice-a-Sunday worship which I was expected to attend. I had no friends at all; and although we now had a wireless, the gift of Uncle Jack, it worked off an accumulator which required frequent recharging, and my father was reluctant to use it for anything but the evening news, the Boat Race and the Cup Final. (Electricity was a fairly recent comer to Horncastle; the manse was converted to it in 1935; gramophones were powered by a spring which had to be rewound for each playing; the local dentist used a pedal drill, chugging away like a one-legged cyclist as he ground out one's molars.) There was not, so far as I remember, a cinema in the town; if there was, I never visited it. Recreation was first-hand; it did not flow to the turn of a knob, but had to be actively sought, contrived. For me, apart from reading in the winter evenings, it consisted almost entirely, as at Ilkeston, of solitary walks and cycle rides. There were footpaths in plenty, the natural village-to-village cross-country links, relics of a passing age but not yet obliterated by disuse and aggressive ploughing. And there was a network of country lanes which provided almost endless alternatives for cycling.

Although I had ventured into Lincolnshire from Newark, this area was new to me and I revelled in exploring it. And what a beautiful countryside it was! – and is, for the mechanisation of farming has left it largely unspoilt. It offers nothing spectacular; but in its broad expanse of varied husbandry one finds still the tranquil ebb and flow of the perennial rhythm of growth harnessed productively to human need. To the south and west are the flatlands bordering on the fens; here are great open skies, dikes, dark soil and, in my time there, toiling windmills (I counted a dozen one day from a vantage-point near Hameringham). North and east are the wolds and, cupped within them, Tennyson's country of 'coot and hern' and a straggle of hamlets whose names seem all to end in -by: Hemingby, Fulletby, Salmonby, Somersby, Aswardby, Raithby and Mavis Enderby. I came to know it all by heart; I loved it, and it spoke to me with the same quiet insistence I had known so often before. During the weeks of the holidays my bicycle (a new one now, and three-speed) became my best friend and shared it with me. There was one discordant note, however, which jarred even on my meagre conscience; this was the flow of tramps, ragged and unshaven, who trudged in abject beggary along the verges of the main roads from one workhouse to the next. From time to time they came knocking at our door, knowing they would not be refused the bread and cheese they begged.

In August and September there was harvesting (unpaid) on local farms. This was real harvesting, the kind I had enjoyed during our Newark holidays, in which human labour played a decisive role and horses were the motive power. The sheaves were gathered and stooked (or starked) by hand; days later, when they had dried out, they were pitchforked on to wagons to be taken to the stackyard. This latter was an agreeable task, day-long but not too demanding of teenage strength. The two curving prongs must be correctly placed in the sheaf to balance its weight (often bottom-heavy with the compacted growth of weeds); then comes the easy, two-armed upward swing, a quick turn of the wrist to release the sheaf, and back to the stook for the next. It became an almost tireless rhythm of the whole body, with every limb and muscle working in close, satisfying harmony. Above on the wagon one's partner received the sheaves, turned them ears-inward, and built up gradually round himself a golden turret which swayed precariously as the wagon tipped and tilted in the corrugations of the field.

At the farm meanwhile the sheaves were transferred from wagon to stack; at first they were tossed easily down to ground level, where two stack-men disposed them round a base of straw and dried branches; later, as the stack grew, they were thrust up and further up with increasing arms-length effort until they topped the culminating ridge. There was art as well as skill in the building of the stack, an element of beauty which gave grace to the work and lifted it above mere economics. For protection against rain and gale the stack was shaped with rounded corners like a crusty loaf and thatched with straw held down with wooden pegs and twine. I took part in all these operations except the last – stooking, carting and stacking; and when I was not required for these it was my job to 'lead', that is, conduct the massive horses in their jingling harness back and forth between field and farm. This too was a delight; the horses became friends and partners in a common task, and the visit to the trough to slake our thirst was a shared pleasure which they seemed to recognise as such. Farming was mechanised then but not motorised; horses were universal, the tractor scarcely known. But for threshing, the final stage of the long process of harvesting, there were steam traction engines which moved from farm to farm. These were magnificent instruments with their gleaming brass, whirring fly-wheels and tall chimneys – but dangerous if the sparks flew too readily. (They were sometimes used for ploughing, two at a time dragging the plough from side to side across the field on a steel rope.)

Such was harvesting as I knew it: long hours of physical activity in sun and open air; sweat blinked from the eyes and sucked salty from the lips; men and animals joined in community of purpose; chat, laughter, tea-breaks, and a shy piss in the hedge; and pervading all was the rich, subtle smell of ripe corn successfully garnered. Motorisation and the combine reaper have made harvesting quicker, less dependent on the weather and no doubt more profitable; but they have also impoverished it, reduced it to an inferior level of human experience.

It was during the years at Ilkeston and Horncastle that I was introduced to mountain-walking. My brother and I went on two week-long Youth Hostelling holidays in the Lake District and Snowdonia. The details I have forgotten, nor can I remember which came first. We climbed the Langdale Pikes, Great Gable, Helvellyn by Striding Edge and Snowdon by the Pig Track. During one or other of the two weeks it rained constantly. There were no light-weight anoraks and trousers then, no waterproof rucksacks; zip-fasteners were not in common use and nylon was not invented; our clumsy oilskins were no barrier to persistent wind and rain. We arrived at each hostel soaked to the skin and left next day with wet clothes clinging uncomfortably. For me the result was acute inflammation of the knees which kept me in bed for a week and gave me a somewhat tarnished image of the hills – but not enough to keep me from them.

The summer holidays of 1935 were more protracted than usual, for the Cambridge term did not begin until the second week of October. I had little idea what the Classical Tripos would require of me and made no attempt to prepare for it. When harvesting was over, I walked and cycled through miles of mellow countryside which was resting, so it seemed, from the labours of fruition and gathering strength for a final orgasmic burst of autumn beauty before sinking peacefully to sleep. It was a kind of no-man's-time, both for me and for the rural scene around me. Gone was the luxuriance of high summer; the bold colours of July had faded to tired greens and pallid stubble. One season was passing, another arriving; there was a temporary loss of impetus, an indeterminacy combined with a strong underflow of anticipation. I too was caught between two worlds; Janus-like I looked back to Kingswood, Kelston Round Hill, and the receding world of boyhood, while in front of me and eagerly awaited were Cambridge, Queens' and a novel, semi-adult world of college conventions and classical scholarship in which I must work my own way to success ('You'll get nowhere without a First,' I was told). The day came, goodbyes were said, and I was chugged away uneasily along the little branch line, through embankments draped with scarlet hips and hawthorn berries, towards the placid, academic Cam and the last stage of my formal education.

CHAPTER VII

Cambridge

IN THE TRANSITION FROM BOARDING SCHOOL TO COLLEGE there was both similarity and contrast. It was a change from one form of institutionalised life to another – to greater freedom and greater responsibility for one's own affairs, but to a life still governed by rules and bells (less frequent) and in which we were still officially *in statu pupillari*. One similarity to public school life was especially obvious: it was a dominantly male environment; women were limited to a total of 500 in the two women's colleges and were not admitted to degrees (until 1948); they were allowed into men's rooms only up to 11 pm.

It was a strangely equivocal world. The age of majority was twenty-one; neither adult nor adolescent, we played the part of both. In college we were 'gentlemen', each with our suite of two rooms and a 'bedder', who was shared through the staircase; in hall we were served by waiters in evening dress; we shopped for our own clothes and food, save for the daily 'commons' supplied by the college to protect us from undernourishment; time was abundant, and within the limits of academic and college rules we came and went as we pleased. Yet we must pay 'caution money' to cover prospective damage and debts, 'keep' fifty-nine nights during 'term' three times a year for three years (otherwise no BA), and obtain a tutor's exeat to be absent for a night. College gates were shut at 10 pm; after 11 pm we were signed in, fined and, if it occurred too often, reported to our tutor. Gowns were worn for all official purposes – lectures, supervisions, tutorial visits; after dusk beyond the college bounds we wore both gown and 'square' (mortar-board in common parlance); the last was enforced by proctors and human 'bull-dogs'. How much of this still persists I do not know.

There was also a prevailing air of mediaevalism, which was enhanced by the grievous spikes placed strategically to deter illicit nocturnal entry. Perhaps if I had attended a more traditional public school, the differences

119

would have been less noticeable; and maybe the kindliness of time has since diminished their number. As it was, I found them unsettling; but like my fellow 'freshers' I accepted the conventions and was quickly acclimatised to them. Vocabulary too we quickly assimilated; in addition to 'commons' and 'bedders' and the rest already mentioned we learnt to speak of 'going up' and 'going down', of 'sporting one's oak' (closing the heavy black outer door to one's room), to refer to the University Library as 'the cocoa factory' (which it resembles), and to Oxford as 'the other place'. Colleges quickly became Cats, Emmer and Pemmer; we began to speak unselfconsciously of Jesus and Christ's Pieces.

Queens' is one of the smaller and certainly among the most beautiful of the Cambridge colleges. From Queens' Lane one enters through a huge battlemented gatehouse with massive doors (of which only a small segment opened to us after 10 pm). The first court remains more or less as it was when the builders removed their scaffolding over half a millennium ago, in the form of a mediaeval half-fortified manor-house; its red brick, set off by cobbles and velvet lawn, has darkened to a rich loveliness. (The elaborate sundial over the library passage is two centuries later.) Erasmus lodged in one of its turrets during his stay in Cambridge; in the 20th century I saw the Lion of Judah, Haile Selassie of Abyssinia, stepping in exile down its central paving – black and very regal but unexpectedly small! Beyond the buttery and hall is Cloister Court, again uniquely beautiful; on one side is the timbered President's Gallery, beyond it the 'mathematical' bridge anachronistically attributed to Newton.

As an impoverished scholar I was assigned an inexpensive suite in the fourth floor of Friar's Building. Its aspect was delightful: Walnut Tree Court, the President's Lodge and Fellows' Garden, and the tall trees of the Backs across the river. In early Spring the foot of the walnut tree was a mass of crocuses. From my bedroom the pinnacles of King's Chapel pierced the roof-tops. Yet there were disadvantages: if I remember rightly, there was no running water in the bedroom, no hot water in the building; the nearest lavatories were across the court and these were sometimes, as a wit put it, 'out of ordure'. We were supplied with chamber-pots which the 'bedders' emptied down the sink in each storey. I believe there are women students in this building now; if so, they no doubt demand to be more civilised than we were. (Not that we complained; these conditions differed little from those in the public schools which most of us came from.)

Each morning my 'bedder' toiled up the stairs, set out my simple 'commons' (bread, butter and milk), cleaned and laid the fire, and called 'Sir!' at eight o'clock. 'Laid' the fire because our source of heat was coal, and the external pollution was appalling. Firelighters were sticks wired

Queens' College: the 'Mathematical Bridge'

Queens' College: the President's Lodging

over a wad of chips and naphtha; the stench of tar and naphtha in King's Lane at 9 am was sometimes unbearable. Central Cambridge has since gone smokeless, no doubt with much benefit to health. There was a gas-ring for simple cooking – a necessity for avoiding the expensive meals served from the buttery; dinner in hall was paid for anyway, and it was a good meal.

To see one's name displayed on the wall at the bottom of the staircase, to 'sport one's oak' and settle down before one's personal fireside with books, papers and privacy, to admit and exclude whom one wished, come and go as one pleased within the very liberal limits of lectures and tutorials – this was indeed an agreeable contrast with the communal life of school in day-room and dormitory. Time was a problem at first – what to do with it? Half a dozen lectures a week and a couple of tutorials were the total of my timetable; there were weekly proses and unseens and an abundance of classical reading; but these were the occupation of evenings and weekends. The afternoons were vacant.

For a time I sampled cross-country running, but the pace and distance of the leaders were too much for me, and I soon turned elsewhere for recreation and exercise. There was squash and tennis and, in summer, an occasional swim at the university bathing pool (men only) half a mile up the Granta – but the cold, turgid green of the water specked with gobbets of scum was unenticing. More attractive was to skim the surface in a hired canoe, gliding deliciously between the willows as far as the open pastures and there to recline at ease in the sweet, sun-warmed grass.

Mostly I relied on walking and cycling. The Backs were a ready source for short breathers before evening hall or after toiling through essay or prose; and further afield to east and south are gentle slopes and undulations which pass for hills and offer some relief from the flat monotony of fenland. It was pleasant of an afternoon to stroll out to Grantchester, mentally rehearsing Brooke's nostalgic lines, and on to the weir and Byron's Pool; or to Coton and Madingley where there were trees in abundance and a sense of rural seclusion. But it was my bicycle which gave me the greatest pleasure. With it I explored the villages south and west – Hardwick and Highfields, Camberton, Kingston and Caldecote, and back along the St Neots road or, more dangerously, on the long, straight stretch from Huntingdon where moneyed under-graduates raced their MGs. Even in the fens there was beauty – in the restful somnolence of autumn, in the luxuriant growth of early summer, in the great dome of the open sky (Bridges' 'unresting cloudland'), and in the wide horizons broken only by copse and farm and the distant towers of Ely.

Walks and cycle rides combined conveniently with another interest which burgeoned in my Cambridge years, the identification of bird songs. Precisely how and when it started I cannot remember, but it became an engrossing hobby which gave me long hours of enjoyment. With the help of two gramophone records of bird songs, a pair of cheap binoculars and endless patience I was soon able to distinguish the song-patterns of most of the common birds, resident and migrant, including some of the more elusive warblers. I joined an ornithological society and through this had access to a small reserve, an acre or two of overgrown shrubs and trees and a small patch of water, where I could wait, watch and listen for the birds to reveal themselves. Though not far from the centre of Cambridge, it was quiet and secluded – I saw no one else in all my visits – a place of restful intimacy with nature's growth and activity.

Once in early May I dragged myself from bed long before sunrise to listen to the dawn chorus – not in the reserve but on a bridge nearby in a suburban road. It was an unforgettable experience, waiting there as darkness paled and warmed into Homer's 'rosy-fingered dawn', listening with intense anticipation for the first chirp of song (a robin I think it was) and then a rapid crescendo to the full volume of intricately interweaving patterns as thrush and blackbird, chaffinch, willow-warbler, white-throat, blackcap and many another all woke to make their orchestral contribution.

Memorable too was my introduction to the nightingale. This was in Madingley woods in the spring of 1939. For the past year I had been collecting passages describing the nightingale and its song from a variety of poets from Homer to the present day; this, together with my ornithological interests, had kindled in me an urgent desire to hear one for myself – partly for the sheer delight of it (for delightful it must surely be if so many had found inspiration in it), partly for its literary and romantic associations, and partly for the novelty of hearing a bird in full song at midnight. I was not disappointed. I listened enthralled to bursts of song which it is impossible to describe even in poetry, but whose power, quality and phrasing, once heard, are immediately distinguishable from all others. Here it was at last, the same song which had echoed down the centuries from the simplicity of Homeric simile, through the sentimental classicism of Keats and Arnold, to the plain matter-of-factness of Harold Monro, whose 'Nightingale near the House' comes nearer than any other to capturing the reality.

I have listened to it many times since, most memorably one night in 1941. I was sitting in a wood in Hertfordshire enveloped in the sweet fragrance of bluebells while overhead the German bombers throbbed their way to unseen targets. Rapt in my shadowy microcosm of sound and scent I felt intensely the contrast of its beauty with the sufferings of the crucified world outside. But as for the nightingale, here was no song of despair, no *miserabile carmen* that Virgil wrote of nor Arnold's 'wild, unquenched . . . old-world pain', but rather a brilliant, triumphant, defiant protest, issuing from the very heart of things, against the brutal insanity of human purposes.

Walking, cycling and bird-watching were solitary activities, but there was social life as well. I arranged lunch parties in my room at Queens', shopped at Fitzbilly's for scotch eggs and cakes, and learnt to make a respectable cup of coffee. I was invited back in turn and thus found my way into most of the colleges. There was also the Methodist Church and its associated fellowship groups, of which I shall have more to say in chapter 9. But money was always short, and I missed much of normal Cambridge life through lack of it. Not for me were the May Balls nor the term-time concerts and entertainments; even the cinema was a rare event. But I bought a gramophone (spring-wind) and a few records and with these began my musical self-education.

Money apart, I was not at ease during my first terms at the university; I was younger than most, poorer than most, socially and athletically ill-equipped, and alien to the central core of ancient public school tradition – Kingswood was not like the rest. Or perhaps it was myself! One incident in particular stands out in memory to emphasise my social inadequacy. After one of our lectures at St John's a dark-haired girl in a green skirt and jumper (one of a small minority of women) approached me shyly and asked me to lunch. I was taken completely by surprise and so startled and embarrassed that I could only mumble a refusal and turn away in haste. The invitation was not repeated. Sadly, my education had left me totally unprepared for contact, metaphorical or otherwise, with the other sex. It was not until my fourth year that I made friends with a girl, a nurse at Addenbrooke's Hospital whom I met at a church fellowship group, and established something like a normal relationship.

In my third year I moved to lodgings on the eastern side of Cambridge; they were quiet and comfortable, and I retained them for the rest of my four years at the university. The change made little difference to my manner of life: I was subject to the same hours of lock-up, received the same 'commons' and ate dinner in hall as before; instead of coal I had a gas fire and meter. At first the squat, terraced, yellow-brick houses of suburban Cambridge contrasted sadly with the green courts and antique charm of Queens'. I missed the ready access to the small stretch of Backs behind the college where, on warm spring and autumn afternoons and after hall in summer, I had strolled up and down reading poetry or delighting in the flowers, the birds and the peace of the riverside scene.

But the eastern side of Cambridge has its beauty – Midsummer Common and the river towpath; and I was able to explore further towards Swaffham Prior and Wicken Fen.

The Backs were still a constant source of pleasure to me at all times of the year – and they are of course one of the chief glories of Cambridge. (Richard Bentley, the notorious Master of Trinity, was mainly responsible for their creation; 'he found a fen,' it has been written of him, 'and he left a garden'.) Queens' owns only a small area, wholly surrounded by water and bounded on the south by buildings of differing age and style; hence the Backs stretch northwards along the Cam past King's, Clare and Trinity to the New Court of St John's. Here were enormous elms flanking the main road, graceful avenues of lime brilliant in spring with massed crocuses. Here in January the drooping branches are silver-etched with frost; in April they are jewelled with the green, rust and umber of swelling buds which burgeon later to full summer luxuriance; October brings a manifold richness of crisp reds and golds; and in November the trees play ghostly hide-and-seek amid the wreathing mist. Within enclosing waters are smooth lawns immaculately kept, groves and glades where one can stroll inviolate from traffic; willows drift their branches in the placid Cam; mallards trail scrabbling youngsters or wander gormless on the banks or cleave the air in swift, efficient take-off. The grey stone of the college buildings, the various bridges (not least the 'Bridge of Sighs' that links the old and new of St John's), the ubiquity of water and of civilised elegance – in these the Backs are like an excerpt from Venice with the addition of arboreal splendour (and without the pollution). Inevitably they were a favourite area for revision; in May and June recumbent bodies, sprawled on the grass or more expensively in punts, grasped books and papers and, in various states of discreet undress, sought to combine the absorption of information with leisurely exposure to sun and beauty.

It was while I was loitering in Queens' Backs one evening after dinner in hall that there occurred the bizarre incident of the chamber-pots. A gravel path runs from the 'mathematical' bridge alongside the river towards King's, where it ends in a stone bridge across the river. Here the BBC had arranged to broadcast live a programme of madrigals sung by a university choir. It was a perfect setting: the clear light of early summer was mellowing to dusk as the last rays of the sun filtered over Laundress Green; around were the manifold fresh greens of trees and shrubs, and across the water the flowers of the Fellows' Garden – all of them doubling their beauty by reflection in the still water; in the background the pinnacles of King's Chapel were catching the last glow of sunset. The programme was half way through when we glimpsed upstream a dozen small circles of light carried slowly towards us on the tardy flow of the current. Enthralled by the singing we took little notice; but as the circles approached and we saw them for what they were – chamber-pots with lighted night-lights within – an initial ripple of surprised amusement grew to a billowing roar of approving laughter which engulfed the madrigals and forced the BBC to fade them out. There followed a jubilant contest to sink the pots with paddles and punt poles. The scene remains indelibly in memory as vivid as at the time of its occurrence – the grotesque contrast of elegant beauty with droll vulgarity, the sudden eruption of coarse laughter, the abrupt termination of the programme. It was worthy of Aristophanes!

Of course, there was work to be done, a great deal of it. It was hard work that had got me to Cambridge; the same must justify my being there and win for me, as I hoped, the First that would ensure my employment. I wanted to teach; this was my 'call' and I had nothing else in mind; but the 1930s were a low ebb for the teaching profession and without sporting prowess, of which I had none, academic distinction was a vital qualification.

I was fortunate in my supervisor. This was A. B. Cook, Emeritus Professor of Classical Archaeology and currently Vice-President of Queens'. He was in his 60s then, a small, grey-haired, stoutish man, whose welcoming friendliness (the outflow, as I learnt later, of a deep Christian piety) invariably made one at home in his presence. With other students of the college I was invited to take Sunday tea at his home two or three times in the year. He was a scholar of enormous erudition; his life's work was a huge three-volume publication, *Zeus: a Study in Ancient Religion*, prompted partly by personal interest, partly by his friendship with Sir James Frazer, the social anthropologist and author of *The Golden Bough*. His room in college housed a collection of Greek pottery, coins, gems and other archaeological specimens which would have done justice to the British Museum (where perhaps they now are); all of them, I was told at the time of his death in 1952, were uninsured. One item in his collection I remember especially vividly. It was not an original; it was a replica of a Mycenaean bronze dagger whose blade was inlaid with a lion hunt in silver and gold (after the style of Achilles' shield in the *Iliad*). To hold it was a thrill of joy; even as a replica its art was superb and its value unimaginable. At the end of my second year he presented me with a piece of pottery, the base of a *krater* or wine-mixing bowl, Sicilian-made in the 4th century BC.

Yet his immense learning was never felt oppressive by his students. He lectured to his small Queens' company of classicists with easy informality, great clarity and abundant visual illustration, enlivening his exposition meanwhile with pleasant touches of wit. When I looked him up recently in the Dictionary of National Biography, I found him described as possessed of 'a puckish humour which went with the twinkle of his keen eyes' – a precise portrayal. It adds that he was 'supremely helpful to younger men'; this too was true of ABC as I knew him. When we met him weekly as individuals for correction of unseens and proses, he invariably combined correction, even of blatant howlers, with courteous consideration for difference of view.

Another lecturer remembered with affection was T. R. Glover who taught us ancient history at St John's. At the time I found him tedious and perplexing; his discourse lacked the clarity and cohesion of A. B. Cook's; it was rambling, digressive, directionless (so it seemed); to take notes was impossible. Because I respected him for his religious writings, notably *The Jesus of History*, I persevered and in the end learnt to respect his historical scholarship. I also learnt that there are two kinds of historian. Some, like Thucydides, present facts critically and economically in a swift-moving, structured narrative which compels attention by its style and dramatic force. Others, like Herodotus, wander amiably through the vagaries of events, alert always for the good story, the eccentric character, offering history as a pageant of human activity in which no episode is too small to have possible significance, and leaving the diligent reader to search out his own interpretation. The latter, to whom Glover belonged, are in the long run probably more educative; but to appreciate them requires a greater maturity of mind than I possessed in my first undergraduate year.

A lecturer whom I enjoyed from the start was Charles Seltman, a Fellow of Queens', who gave a course on certain aspects of Greek archaeology. His lectures were well illustrated by slides, and an important lesson I learnt from them (reinforced by A. B. Cook) was the necessity of visual aids for successful teaching. He was the author of a delightful book, *Women in Antiquity*. Also remembered with affectionate gratitude is C. F. Angus, peering through his thick spectacles like a wise old Socratic owl as he lectured to us on the early Greek philosophers. His manner was gentle, tentative, almost laboured, as if he were himself oppressed by the mysteries which intrigued those philosophical pioneers and which they explored with such brilliant shafts of imagination. His lectures reinforced and gave direction to my own amateurish probing of these mysteries and laid the foundations of a lifelong fascination with philosophical problems.

Most of my work, of course, was private study; this, apart from the regular proses and unseens, consisted mainly in extensive reading of classical authors. There were no set books for Part One of the Tripos; our syllabus was Greek and Roman literature, and we could be required to translate from any of the principal authors. Much of the reading I greatly enjoyed. Now, instead of stumbling through a few paragraphs at a time, I read straight through the *Peloponnesian War* of Thucydides and Caesar's *Gallic War*. Thus I came to see them for what they are – masterpieces, respectively, of historical and military exposition (and the latter of political propaganda). Livy too, read at the same pace, I found enthralling, especially Rome's war with Hannibal, which reveals him as a descriptive writer equal to any. Euripides, Catullus, Homer (of whom we read little at Kingswood), Herodotus, Virgil of course, and many another I read with great pleasure and personal enrichment. Others I found distasteful: the urbane elegance of Horace, the snide cynicism of Juvenal had no appeal for me; nor had Pindar's abstruse and tortuous lyrics nor the comedies of Plautus (which ill compared, I thought, with the subtleties of Aristophanes).

Plato's *Apology* and *Phaedo* I had read at school; now for the first time I read the *Republic*. It was at home at Horncastle that I started reading it one summer vacation. 'Yesterday,' it begins, 'I went down to the Peiraeus with Glaucon, Ariston's son, to make my prayers to the goddess and to see how they organised the festival' – a sentence which Plato is reputed to have written and rewritten time and again until he thought it perfect in rhythm and cadence. Such is the unpretentious start to a literary and philosophical masterpiece which it was a privilege to read. Not that its logic is flawless or its politics wholly laudable; but it has an overriding greatness of metaphysical vision and educative purpose which atones for its defects. Another book, also great of its kind, that I read through with profit (but less immediate enjoyment) was Aristotle's *Ethics*. Packed and ponderous in style, it is nevertheless the best of all introductions to ethical philosophy; and though it lacks the *Republic's* aesthetic appeal, it rivals it in educative power.

I learnt during these years the value of memorisation. The memory is a faculty nowadays much neglected; but for fluency in reading a foreign language it is essential to command a wide vocabulary and to distinguish immediately between words which look the same but differ in meaning. From my reading I composed in each language a list of about 3000 words in addition to those I felt I safely knew, and set to work systematically to learn and revise them, to and from their English equivalent, until their meaning was automatic. This was a task to which I devoted half an hour daily before breakfast. Much else I also learnt by heart: Pericles' funeral speech, delivered over the Athenian dead of 431 BC, I could recite from beginning to end, and I came thus, in the only possible way, to appreciate fully its magnificence of rhetorical style; passages from Euripides, Virgil, Catullus, Lucretius, Homer further enriched my memory and gave me pleasure as I recalled them in leisure moments. Of them all I remember now only Callimachus' lament for Heraclitus: 'They told me, Heraclitus, they told me you were dead', and especially that last brilliant, poignant image, 'your nightingales live on'.

In all this, a shadow at my shoulder, were the impending examinations and the pressure to excel; a utilitarian purpose invaded my studies and infected their pleasure. In the last two or three weeks before Part One of the Tripos examination I never slept beyond 5 am, suffered perpetual flatulence, and spent much of the day wandering through the Backs in a state of restless anxiety. Clearly the examinations were to be a test of mental and physical stamina as well as of academic performance. When they were over, my eyes were so sore as to be virtually unusable; they remained so for nearly a month. However, the toil and tribulation were amply compensated by the telegram which brought the result to Horncastle.

In the following year the shadow was less oppressive; what I had done once I could do again; and with language study reduced to a minimum I was able to concentrate on my option of Greek philosophy. This was where my interest lay, but I was not mature enough to benefit fully from it; and Plato's *Theaetetus*, the text required for detailed study, is a difficult dialogue whose epistemological issues I found unattractive. Yet my interest in philosophy remained and deepened into permanence. Reduction of pressure left me time at last for reading outside classics, mainly in English literature, science and religion. This reading made an important contribution to my intellectual growth which had been restricted in the two previous years by intense concentration on a limited, though immensely valuable, area of knowledge.

The result of Part Two of the Tripos was the same; I had achieved my goal. In fact I had unexpectedly achieved rather more, for students with a First and limited means were able to apply for a grant to travel in Italy or Greece. I was awarded £50 for the summer of 1938 and chose to visit Greece.

There were no package tours in those days, no regular air services to Athens (and few anywhere); I went alone and made my own arrangements. It was a six day journey by rail across France and sea from Marseilles; but this is surely the best way to make one's first visit. For the Greeks were a seafaring people and their country is a land of capes and gulfs and islands deeply interwoven by the sea, as is their history. The voyage itself was a delight. For four days under cloudless skies the ship cut through the sparkling waves of Homer's wine-bright sea. I wondered at the porpoises, the flying-fish, the incredible silken blue of the water; and then, late one afternon, came that first thrilling, unforgettable glimpse, emerging from the violet mist of the horizon, of the Hellas of my dreams.

There is no need to recount all the details of my journeyings. By bus and train I visited the major sites in Athens and mainland Greece; a brief sea trip took me to Mykonos and Delos in the Aegean. It is impossible to describe the surging excitement of anticipation as I approached each site for the first time and as the meagre mental image which perforce had satisfied me for years was now transformed into glorious actuality. The marvel of it! – to stand on the Acropolis where centuries before had walked the feet of Socrates and Plato, Euripides, Pericles and all those other giants of the ancient world; to feast one's eyes, as they had done, on the splendour of the Parthenon and lift them further to the honey-sweet slopes of Hymettus and the blue waters encircling Salamis. It was the same at Delphi amid its awesome cliffs, at Corinth, Mycenae, Olympia, Sounion, Delos. (At the last I was startled by my first sight of a phallic symbol, massively erect in glistening marble at the side of the sacred way.) I learnt in these encounters what had never before been impressed upon me, the contextuality of human beings and the impossibility of understanding their history and their experience without visiting the environment which had cradled them.

Memorable too, but for different reasons, was the journey by mule from Sparta, in the central Peloponnese, to Kalamata on the coast. (The motor road which now links the two was then just snaking its first coils through the foot of the pass.) From five in the morning until sunset I clung to the wooden saddle, lightly covered with sheepskin, as the guide walked the full twenty miles at my side. Exhilarating it was to rise from the verdant heat of the Eurotas valley into the cool, pine-scented mountain air of Taygetus, zigzagging precariously above the tree-tops on the slow, slip-proof animal, until at last, cupped in a cleft, came the first cheering glimpse of the sea. I thought of Xenophon's 10,000 and their cry of *'thalassa, thalassa!'* as they emerged foot-weary on the shores of the Euxine after their long, long march from Cunaxa.

August is not the time to visit Greece; the countryside is parched and brown save for the grey of olives and the few watered valleys; the roads are dusty and the heat oppressive. Forty years later I went again, in April, and I found a land green and aglow with flowers; and at Olympia the nightingales were vying in bursts of vibrant song. But at least in the 1930s there were few tourists; I could stand alone on the Acropolis in quiet contemplation of history, alone too at Sounion and watch the sunset glow on Poseidon's temple. The hotels, though few, were clean and comfortable and the people welcoming and friendly (as they still are). 'Travelling in the younger sort,' wrote Francis Bacon, 'is a part of education.' How right he was!

I returned from Greece to two events of great importance: one was my parents' move from Horncastle to Portessie on the coast of the Moray Firth; the other was the Munich crisis, the aftermath of which overshadowed my fourth year at university and proved, as we know, the prelude to global tragedy. Although it was my intention to teach after leaving Cambridge, I did not register for a Postgraduate Certificate course (which was not then a necessary professional qualification). Instead I chose to read for Part Two of the English Tripos. There was now no pressure to obtain a First; I had time to read, ruminate and digest the authors set for study who included the whole of Chaucer (thoroughly delightful) and most of the English metaphysical poets (an austere coterie). I also read widely in English literature – Wordsworth, Tennyson, Malory's *Morte D'Arthur*, much of Dickens, most of Shakespeare, a great deal of contemporary English poetry and much else besides. Lectures were few – I remember only F. R. Leavis – and I attended or not at will. It was a pleasant, relaxed year which enabled me to catch up with my intellectual growth, retarded by the pressures of the previous three years, and greatly to extend its range.

In August 1938 my parents moved to Portessie, a village in Banffshire on the southern shore of the Moray Firth. My father's period of service at Horncastle had come to an end; he had received no invitations from other circuits (or none that he felt able to accept), and was directed to this distant outpost of British Methodism which comprised a number of small congregations scattered along the coast and a 'central' church in Aberdeen some seventy miles away. None of us had ever previously heard of Portessie or even crossed the border into Scotland; Aberdeen was no more than a name vaguely associated with grey granite and the destination boards of express trains ('The Granite City' was among them). The move was therefore accompanied by much foreboding and much peering at the map; it was like departure for a foreign land (which in some respects it was – and still is). But we were comforted to find that Portessie had a station on the coastal line to Elgin (now axed); and the manse, we were told, was well equipped and overlooked the sea.

In fact, for my parents the move was a disguised blessing. Portessie proved a blissful haven for them during the years of war; the sirens rarely sounded; and rationing meant little, for the fishermen were well supplied with food and generous in disposing of their surplus and of their fish. The inconveniences were minor – black-out and ration books, the general shortage of almost everything, and the special passes required for holidays in the restricted area north of Inverness. Occasionally the reality of war came near, as for instance in the early days when a trainload of bewildered children arrived from Aberdeen and we helped to settle them for the night in the local school. Or again when German spies were landed from a submarine and went to buy their tickets at Portgordon station a few miles to the west; here, through some error of language or currency, they were spotted by the booking-clerk and quickly arrested. (My father was also picked up and questioned about this, for he had a habit, suspicious in wartime, of taking a stroll along the cliffs.) And inevitably there were deaths and loss among our little congregation at Portessie. But all this was still in the future.

The journey north was an adventure in itself. Our misgivings temporarily laid aside, we settled down to enjoy this penetration into the unknown. A night's stop at Edinburgh gave us no time to explore the city; but next day we gazed fascinated as we crossed the Forth Bridge and saw for the first time how marvellously its poised webs of interlocking steel combine engineering skill and aesthetic appeal in a single superb act of artistry (there was, of course, no road bridge then to rival it). Then came the long stretch across the Tay, a bridge whose prosaic structure nevertheless impresses by its sheer length and bold defiance of earlier tragedy. From Aberdeen onwards the countryside was strange and novel – mile upon mile of unharvested oats, and in amongst it sweeps of heather richly purple still and clumps of pine. At last came the sea, peeping blue over the yellow fields, then Cullen viaduct, and finally we stopped at the little wind-swept platform at Portessie and were welcomed by the local Methodists.

Many a time in the following years I stepped down on to that platform and always with the same unutterable sense of blessed relief. After the oppression of dark, war-blasted London, the scream of sirens, the ugly rumble of guns and bombs; after the tedious discomfort of those seemingly interminable night journeys in crowded, semi-lit trains which crawled through blacked-out towns and waited endlessly at signals until the raids were over; after all this, to emerge into the sunset colours of a quiet summer evening or, as once I did on Christmas Eve, into the crisp grip of frosted snow which sparkled in brilliant starlight, to breathe the silence and the fresh tang of the sea – this was a healing and a balm beyond all telling.

Portessie and its environs are reminiscent of Cornwall – sea and moors, stone-built houses, drifters in the harbours, fish on the quays and the ever-present clamour of gulls. But there is also contrast. Here there is no drowsy *douceur* of the south-west that gives us daffodils in January and our earliest potatoes. Spring comes tardily and it can be early June before the trees and hedges are fully reclothed. The light is different too ; here it has a halcyon quality characteristic of the north, a calm lucidity which distributes more evenly the colours of the landscape – except at sunset, which flames out in the richest of reds, golds and purples beyond the Sutherland hills and the waters of Moray. In midsummer the days are long ; there is almost no darkness. In winter they are short and bleak and the wind blows bitter from the north – not all the time, of course, for there were nights of calm starlight when, leaning over the garden wall, I watched the streamers of the aurora like searchlights over the sea.

The people were mostly fishermen and farmers, warm-hearted, generous and welcoming to us 'foreigners'. Oddly, the prevalent name was Smith, so many indeed that they had to be distinguished by forenames and street numbers and sometimes by occupation too. Of the rest many were Flett. They were not Gaelic speaking, but when they spoke between themselves, pronunciation and regional dialect made them unintelligible to us ('squeal' for school, and 'quines' and 'loons' for girls and boys). Virtually they had two languages, and for our benefit they would speak in 'normal' Scots. There were oddities too in their Methodism ; they had no chapel service on Christmas Day, which went unmarked by any act of worship until my father persuaded them otherwise. For us, comers from the distant south, it was a strangely fascinating world, simpler, closer to the roots of life and, above all, hospitable and beautiful.

Looking back I am surprised that my father adapted so easily to the change. Here was a new life, a new culture, of which he had no previous experience save possibly in the fisher villages of Cornwall – but that was many years ago. Yet his own origins were humble ; and though he loved reading and intellectual study, this was never a barrier between himself and the people he served. His was a simple Gospel which could be preached in simple terms to men and women of all kinds and classes ; and not only preached but lived in the duties of pastoral care. Their ways might be unfamiliar, but he was ready to learn, and in Christ, whatever our differences, we are members of one family. My mother was more apprehensive about the move to Scotland and adapted less easily, I think because she was not so necessarily and closely involved in the affairs of the local chapels. But I know that, like my father, she came to love the coast and its people and left them with deep regret and great gratitude when they moved south in 1945.

For me, an intermittent visitor, it was the beauty and novelty of the countryside and coast that held most attraction. Here was a great tract of new territory to be explored on foot and cycle, a landscape which combined uniquely (as it seemed to me) a range of beauty in sea, mountain, moor, field, forest and racing peat-brown river – Deveron, Lossie, Avon and the majestic Spey. Much of it was wild, remote, elemental. I remember especially the long slog from Dufftown through Glen Rinnes to Tomintoul (the highest Highland village), with the Ladder Hills on one side, on the other the Hills of Cromdale, and further south the huge granite mass of the Cairngorms as yet totally unspoilt. The nearest hill to Portessie is Cullen Bin, a mere 1000 feet but an easy walk with the reward of vast views from the top. At least thirty times I climbed it, in all weathers and seasons – in purple heather, deep snow, mist and blizzard, in moonlight and starlight, at sunset but never, to my regret, at dawn. And there was the haunting music of the strangely unEnglish names: Tochieneal and Tillynaught, Letterfourie, Farnachty and the Braes of Enzie (pronounced Enggy). I loved it all and revelled in it.

The greatest gift of all that came to me from our move to the north was an introduction to the Highlands. This led to an abiding love-affair with the Scottish mountains. It began in the Cairngorms, which I first visited with a friend in the summer of 1939. We climbed Cairngorm and Ben Macdhui then cycled on to Ben Nevis, whose summit, as so often, we found enwrapped in cloud; thence we biked and trained to Kyle and across the water to Kyleakin. I have never forgotten the magic of that first stay in Skye. Of the island's beauty we saw but little, for the mist never lifted off the hills, and at sea level there was persistent drizzle. But all about us was the whisper of wind and wave and burn, and through the grey, damp murk came drifting the astringent tang of burning peat and the wild cries of curlew and golden plover. It was a world apart, aloof, arcane, inscrutable, brooding over riches withheld from our gaze. Tantalisingly it checked us on the frontier of mystery; we sensed the existence of a promise yet to be revealed – and we vowed to return.

The Cairngorms too were a world of their own and remained so until invaded by the desecration of commercialism. I explored them with my fiancée in August 1945 and again in the two following years. They were used for commando training during the war and for those six years were virtually untrodden except by army boots. Their desolation was brought home to us when, during that first visit, two walkers ahead of us found the wreckage of a bomber which, with its Czech crew of eight, had crashed on Beinn a'Bhuird the previous February and remained undiscovered. In 1947, married now, we camped on the shore of Loch Morlich, which was still a haven of tranquil beauty, and climbed the four main peaks in a day.

It was cloudless and very warm, but the labour of physical exertion was forgotten in that day-long feast of concentrated mountain grandeur unrivalled anywhere in Britain.[1]

Thenceforth mountains became a part of my life, essential as food and drink (though, alas, less easily accessible).They brought me a vast expansion of horizons, both literally and metaphorically. They brought me self-discovery in physical performance and endurance, new skills of compass, ice-axe and tent-craft. They introduced me to new worlds of colour and form – the massive outlines of geological sculpture, pinnacles of erosion and the tortured twist of folded rock, Suilven, Liathach and the Five Sisters of Kintail, Ben Lui, Ben Loyal, Schiehallion and a host of others, at sunset and dawn, in the full brilliance of midsummer, in the crisp clarity of snow against winter-blue sky.

Not least they brought me spiritual enrichment, and this not only by the simple exaltation of walking on the heights in day-long solitude above the rest of the world. For mountain-walking trims one down to size; it induces humility by the dawning of one's total insignificance – a mere speck of conscious matter within the immensities of cosmic time and space. But *conscious*, yes, and aware of those very immensities and sensitive to their mystery. Indeed the mountains present parables of life itself – the long toil to a summit unseen but believed to exist, glimpses of distant landscapes seen fleetingly through the grey curtain of mist, patches of moss campion peeping from the gravel to cheer one's solitariness, and those moments when, as one yields to the embrace of beauty, distinctions of self and other are lost in a climax of ecstasy. Then, quite spontaneously, I have knelt and prayed.

My formal education ended with the examination for Part Two of the English Tripos in May 1939. Then began the prolonged frustration of finding a job. With a double First in Classics I thought it would be easy; but I made some twenty applications and had half a dozen interviews before I was successful. In fact I had more or less given up hope and was cycling home from Perth through the Highlands when a telegram reached me at Killin at the head of Loch Tay; it summoned me to St George's School, Harpenden. I hastened back to Perth, on by rail to Portessie and thence by night train from Aberdeen to London. I arrived at the school in no mood for interview, but to my surprise was appointed to the post of sixth form and Classics master.

[1] In 1952, after repeating the circuit with my daughter, aged 13, I wrote to *The Guardian* claiming a record on her behalf. We were honoured with a brief leader admonishing us for underestimating the perils of mountain walking!

St George's was a private school founded by an Anglican priest named Cecil Grant who, in the one institution, combined a fervent religious purpose with a staunch commitment to coeducation. It began its life at Keswick in 1898; the buildings it now occupied in Harpenden had previously been the home of the United Services College (made famous by Kipling's *Stalky and Co.*). In the forty years of its existence the school had achieved renown as a pioneer in the education of boys and girls together; this, the norm today, was novel and even suspect in the 1930s. Its motto, appropriately for myself, a lover of the hills, was *Levavi oculos [in montes]*.[1]

[1] 'I lifted my eyes to the hills.'

CHAPTER VIII

Appraisal

My departure from Cambridge and appointment to St George's marked the end of my formal education; after seventeen years my role was transformed from recipient to donor. It was not, of course, the end of my education; in one sense it was only a beginning, for education, like growing up, is an ongoing process; while life continues, it has no particular point of termination, but there are stages in the process which offer new directions of development. This seems such a stage and an appropriate point, therefore, for appraisal, a critical assessment after fifty intervening years of the impact on me of my schooling and of my nurture within the manse. 'Critical' is not intended pejoratively, but to suggest a considered judgement from a later position of advantage. For a child is not aware of his growing up nor of the environmental influences which shape him; but retrospect, like an aerial photograph picking out features indiscernible at ground level, can readily distinguish strands which are woven into his making.

It will not be a total, detailed survey of my formal education and upbringing; that would be tedious for the reader and alien to my purpose. Little will be said of Cambridge. Although college and university had a framework of rules and times which required compliance, the education they offered was far less formal, far more self-directed than at school. Compared with what had gone before it was an emancipation, a release from bondage. Moreover, those university years were a mirror reflecting a self already decisively shaped by earlier experience. Appraisal of them would therefore seem impertinent, in the older and the current meanings of the word.

The reader will no doubt have noticed that there is no mention in the previous chapter of religion and its place in my life at Cambridge. This is not because there was no place – far from it; but it seems to belong more appropriately to the next chapter whose central theme is my response to what I have believed to be the call of Christ.

My schooling was of the chalk and talk variety prevalent in the 1920s and 1930s. Moreover, at Magnus and at Kingswood below the sixth form our studies were sliced into 40 minute portions which bore no relation to each other or to the content of individual lessons. Maths, Latin, history, chemistry, scripture followed one after the other in inexplicable sequence; and at the bell's arbitrary command problems were abandoned unresolved, paragraphs suspended in mid-sentence as we scuffled through our desks for the next set of books or scurried off to another classroom. Maybe there is some advantage in being trained to put down and take up a task at will (or another's will), to switch direction at the bidding of a clock; but the effect on me was to create a false impression of knowledge and how the mind works to acquire it; it was a lesson that took much unlearning.

For knowledge is not an assemblage of separate packages, tidily parcelled into different shapes and sizes, neatly insulated each from its neighbour; to fragment it thus is to distort its nature. Knowledge is a whole; its parts are interrelated; one merges into another, and all are brought together in the unity of the experiencing self. Nor does the mind operate in chronometric slices; its activity is continuous, progressive; the problem, not the clock, is the dominant motive in intellectual enquiry.

Further distortion came from the competitive pressures imposed on us by form lists, prizes and examinations. These diverted attention from knowledge itself, the fun of finding out, the acquisition of skills, to secondary objectives whose motivation was outside instead of within the activity of learning. Not interest or curiosity or the urgency of unsolved problems, but the desire to outdo, to pass exams was the goad that drove us to our books. It would be idle to pretend that motives can always be direct instead of derived; even Plato's Guardians needed the inspiration of the Vision of Good. But the danger of persistent indirect motivation is that it may lead to learning by cram – the gulping down and subsequent regurgitation of undigested gobbets of verbiage.[1] Such factual ephemera of the classroom shed themselves like autumn leaves when their brief usefulness is over. It was a danger I did not escape, and this may partly explain why so much of what I supposedly learnt was rapidly and irredeemably lost.

Five years of boarding school also made their impact. At Magnus, though I was scarcely conscious of it at the time, I was part of the wider community of Newark on Trent. Its industries were all around me, evident to eye, nose and ear. The Trent too was part of the town, of its

[1] Superbly mocked by Charles Dickens in the repulsive Bitzer of *Hard Times*.

character as well as its geography; I fished in it, boated on it and sauntered happily along its towpaths. So too was the railway, which gave me days of delight and linked me in imagination with a world of wider destinations. Around the town the countryside offered abundant opportunity of exploration. All these activities I shared with my friends who too were a part, with myself, of the wider local community.

Kingswood cut this short. A boarding school is a self-contained entity, more so then than now when links are formed with local life and other schools. For the next five years I found myself in a world of its own. My friends were with me at school; when, at the end of term, we had departed for our several destinations, I was friendless. At Ilkeston I had an intermittent acquaintance, scarcely friendship, with the two boys at Stanton; at Horncastle I had no friends at all. These were alien worlds; to leave them for Kingswood was a relief, a return to normality, to most of what was meaningful to my adolescence. But it brought estrangement from the local community and left me largely ignorant of the daily life, work and activities of ordinary citizens and the administration of their affairs. This isolation from the real world was aggravated by our sexual segregation; the ways of half the human race were concealed from us, and how we should behave towards them remained obscure. Girls were denizens of a different world; sex was wrapped in mystery and became a source of smut and vulgar snickering. There were, of course, no radio and television to extend our social horizons.

Worst of all, I was increasingly alienated from my parents. For most of the year I lived in a world of which they had no knowledge; apart from the household routine and our common life within the Methodist Church there was little that we could share. I ceased to know them. The loss is obvious and tragic; I never wholly outgrew it.

Prolonged immersion in the introverted life of boarding school was, I believe, the major source of the social illiteracy which restricted my fruition of university life. It left me gauche and ill at ease in company, especially that of the other sex. But the fault lay partly in myself, for I was naturally shy and slow to mature. Partly it lay in my family life: as a son of the manse I was invested with an otherness which raised a barrier between myself and 'ordinary' folk; by them I was seen as different and expected to be different – and I sensed the expectation; this impeded normality of relationship. Moreover my parents' social experience, limited by their frugal lifestyle and their own restricted origins, reflected on to me – though they themselves were not thereby precluded from amiable dealings with a wide variety of people or from exercising Christian pastoral care.

A conspicuous feature of my growing up was a prolonged ignorance of sexual matters and the devious means by which it was only partially remedied. Since I had no sister and almost no contact with girls from leaving Barny to my later years at Cambridge, my natural curiosity remained unsatisfied. The visual aspect of the female anatomy, roughly sketched at Barny by my friend's bald description of copulation and by the jocular crudities of my pals at Magnus and Kingswood was filled in more or less inaccurately by imagination and conjecture. Well into my years at Kingswood the biological relationship of male and female organs and the function of the latter in reproduction remained a mystery; I was equally unaware of sex as a source of affection and tender emotion.

The mystery was deepened by the hush of adult prudery: 'You mustn't ask, dear' was the reply to my questions; curiosity was thought indelicate, ignorance assumed safer. There were, of course, no topless magazines displayed on bookstalls, no *Playboy*, no page three of *The Sun* to pass furtively behind the cover of a desk. Nor was there any official attempt to relieve our ignorance by formal instruction – until, that is, the arrival of a little book from my father which imposed its own distorted account of sex on to my already garbled version.[1] Thus for the most part my sexual information and vocabulary came fortuitously (as at our holiday farm at Beckingham) – a strange route, as I have already remarked, for matter of such fundamental importance.

It is difficult even for those who, like myself, were brought up in the 1920s and 1930s to recapture the atmosphere then prevalent of pretence and prudishness. It was accepted that men and women were different, in physiological as well as social function; but the visual evidence of the former must not be openly displayed – except in classical sculpture and the bosomy deities of Renaissance art. The impropriety of exposure was extended to include the sexual act, which thus attracted to itself the brand of indecency and was curtained off behind a facade of unmentionability. Sex education, where it existed in odd places like Neill's Summerhill or the Russells' school in Sussex, was regarded suspiciously as an aberration from the norm; children, it was thought, were better left to find out for themselves from the crude jokes of their friends or in other devious and dubious ways.

Ludicrous it seems to the 1980s, this refusal to acknowledge the facts of biology, this branding with the taint of shame what is part of normality

---

[1] Later I found for myself and read Leslie Weatherhead's famous book, *The Mastery of Sex*, a misconceived title typical of its time.

and at its best is among the most elevating and enriching of human activities. Meanwhile, of course, behind bedroom doors and in other convenient locations things went on much as they always have and the population continued to increase.

In general the mood of society is now very different. Children have little difficulty in finding access to sexual information and illustration; many schools provide them within the normal curriculum, and where they do not, there is an abundance of books, magazines and cinema posters to provide a similar service. There is a more honest acknowledgement of the facts of life, of human emotions and relationships and of the place of sex within them; there is a more sympathetic view of adolescent enquiry and experiment. Even the BBC exposes the occasional breast without apology. All this is far healthier, far saner than the secrecy and covert probings of fifty years ago; but it is not without problems in teenage pregnancies, broken marriages and the spread of VD and Aids.

It would help, perhaps, if nudity were commoner and more widely accepted. If boys and girls were permitted and encouraged to play and bathe together naked, their natural curiosity would be satisfied and prurience disappear; nakedness (in appropriate circumstances) would be regarded as normal and unremarkable. The differences in our sexual apparatus are not a matter for shame or apology, but facts to be accepted; the human body is a thing of grace and beauty (as well as enormous biological ingenuity); the Greeks certainly found it so and expressed their love of it in sculpture and vase-painting. Sex is not indecent or obscene except to those who make it so by lewdness of fancy or commercial exploitation. It is elevating and uplifting; at its best, intercourse is among the finest things in life, comparable only with the heights of religious or aesthetic ecstasy. It links us with the quickening forces of the universe and (if one believes in God) with the divine joy in creation. The real obscenity is not sex but violence, which divides, embitters and destroys.

If sex is to enrich – as it can and should – and not debase, it must be approached responsibly, and that means with knowledge and with commitment to moral principles. Knowledge is of biological facts but also, and more important, of the role of sex in human life and relationships – a deep source of creative energy, of love and tenderness, which can be directed to its obvious purpose in procreation or sublimated in religious, aesthetic or other activities. It should come primarily from parents in the home, but the school too has an important part to play in the detailed and specialised information which many parents are unable, unwilling or simply too shy to give; and it can provide opportunity for a more objective questioning and discussion than is possible within the average family. The home is also the proper source of the moral principles which are essential for the responsible enjoyment of sex. Foremost among these principles is respect for persons – respect for one's partner in sexual activity, for the possible unborn, and indeed for oneself.

Sexual intercourse is only part of a broader spectrum of relationships in which boys and girls, men and women find friendship, satisfaction and fulfilment. For this larger understanding and association between the sexes coeducation is the most favourable preparation. In the 'hidden curriculum' of daily life the sexes learn from each other in equality of respect and status, with grace and dignity, and without embarrassment. Segregation is an obvious weakness of the single-sex school, more so when combined with boarding. Magnus has now become part of a mixed comprehensive establishment and Kingswood is coeducational.

Common to all human beings are modes of experiencing which belong to the deep roots of our human nature and which education must recognise and seek to satisfy. Sex is one of them. Another is the capacity for a kind of experience which, at the risk of being misunderstood, I call religious – not formal religion, not the beliefs and ceremonies of particular cults, Christian or any other, though some may find expression for it thus. I mean something deeper than doctrine, deeper than creed and liturgy and vestment, something that springs elementally from the dark depths of our being in response to the world and our situation within it.

For the world is full of mystery and our predicament precarious and uncertain. The why and wherefore of the universe are hidden from our enquiry; as we search this way and that we are baffled by the final inexplicability of ultimate fact. 'What would one not give,' wrote the agnostic J. S. Mill, 'for any credible tidings from that mysterious region?' Throughout the ages man's response to this bafflement of unanswerable questioning has been one of awe and reverence mingled with wonder at the intricacy, orderliness and magnitude of the universe as he observes it. Such is the heart of religious awareness, the experience of the 'numinous', the felt presence of a power greater than oneself before which one's 'genius is rebuked'. It is latent in all of us, in some powerfully, in others a merest flicker easily overlooked; and some discover it not so much in mystery as in beauty, the blending of form and colour or of sound and rhythm in a perfect harmony of wholeness that grips and inspires.

This awareness expresses itself in various ways, most obviously in formal religion, the creeds and worship of church and chapel, mosque, synagogue and temple or in the life of religious orders. But these are not necessary to its expression; often they impede it, and many have turned instead to solitariness and contemplation. Others have found it, inside and outside organised religion, in service to their fellows and commitment to the task of human improvement. Artist and craftsman both display it, the former in his striving after ideal perfection through the medium of his particular skill – paint, stone, words, music – the latter in his act of making, by identifying himself however humbly with a cosmic creativity. You and I and the rest of us, whatever our talents or none, can live it out in deeds of love and concern in the daily round of home and work. All these are modes both of expressing religious experience and at the same time of exploring it more deeply; expression is also discovery; doing is learning. Therein lies a message for our schools.

Little of this came through to me in the religious teaching I received at school. Scripture was allotted a single period in the timetable. This made continuity impossible; the content of one weekly lesson was forgotten long before the turn of the next; and the obvious contrast between that one and the four or five for maths or Latin robbed it, in our eyes, of any seriousness of purpose. The teaching itself bypassed utterly the heart of religion, that elemental sense of mystery and wonder that finds expression in reverence and worship, in art, craft and practical service to others. It struck no chord in my own growing awareness of the numinous which came to me in the woods at Barny, the harvest fields at Newark and on the breezy heights of Kelston Round Hill. Chapel we certainly had at Kingswood, day by day and twice on Sundays; this was the outward face of organised religion, presented to us in the unvarying Methodist sandwich of hymns, prayers, lessons and sermon. There was beauty in the building and its setting; there was exaltation of a kind in the surge of congregational singing; but the essence of religion, even of Christianity, escaped my conscious understanding. My eventual commitment to it came in spite of rather than because of my religious education. It came (leaving aside divine intervention) from my upbringing in a Methodist home and later on from the fellowship groups at Cambridge.

But am I being fair? May it not be that those who planned our education at Kingswood relied less on direct teaching than on the gradual infiltration of environmental influence, on the cumulative effect over the years of immersion in a way of life which included Methodist worship and its embracing values as an integral part? I do not know. But there is no doubt that such influences penetrate deeply and sow seeds which germinate unpredictably in later years. I have mentioned the incident in the headmaster's study at Kingswood, when he pointed to the opening chapter of St Mark and asked if there was not something there that I could believe. Another memory from those Kingswood days flashed into illuminating significance in the early months of the war.

It was at Portessie late one night in the autumn of 1940. I was leaning over the garden wall, wondering about the future (which seemed then as dark as the total black-out) and gazing somewhat apathetically at the streamers of the Northern Lights. Away over the sea the reconnaissance planes were flying out from Lossiemouth; their distant droning was the only sound that broke the stillness. To my mood of despair they seemed an epitome of evil, a perversion to destructive ends of man's creative ingenuity. I meant no disrespect, of course, to the men who flew them. It was the planes themselves that oppressed me; they were geared to a vast machinery of death; they were part of a world gone wrong, tortured by evil, the devil's manufacturing. Above in the sky the stars were brilliant; and as I turned and looked at them, there leapt to memory a line from a hymn of Joseph Addison which we had often sung in the school chapel; 'The hand that made *us* is divine' (the emphasis is mine). It spoke to me a message of hope and reassurance, confirming a faith which had been sorely battered by the events of previous weeks. Thus surprisingly can a dormant spark, kindled without conscious intention in the forgotten past, blaze into unsuspected meaning.

Yet direct teaching of religion is necessary too; it must be allowed sufficient time to be effective, and it must be taught both overtly and in the 'hidden curriculum' of classroom and school community. Religion must be presented as a fact of human experience and of history; as a dimension of experience just as authentic as science, technology or politics; as a normal response to the central facts of human existence – birth, death, suffering, love, sex, creativeness, and the mystery of ultimate inexplicability. To be deprived of this is to suffer a permanent impoverishment.

Thus far, despite my earlier disclaimer, this appraisal may indeed seem pejorative, a picking holes in what my schooling did or did not do. That it had deficiencies is undeniable, but these were a product of the times rather than of the schools; things are different today. In fairness, however, I must sketch in the positive contribution of my schooling before turning to the other major aspect of my growing up, namely the enfolding ambience and influence of Methodism.

Among the most precious gifts I received from thirteen years of formal schooling was a love of knowledge. I was encouraged, even compelled, to find out, and in the end I wanted to. Moreover, at Magnus and Kingswood and even in the antiquated Wesleyan School at Barny I caught a glimpse of scholarly ideals of accuracy, precision and unprejudiced pursuit of fact. Embryonic and scarcely realised at the time these were reinforced by university and later experience into unqualified commitment to truth. They also gave me a hint of intellectual horizons far beyond my limited vision but beckoning me on to further exciting exploration. Retrospect can easily exaggerate; and perhaps there was something in my own nature, a sceptical unease, which drove me to question and enquire. But without the prompting of teachers this propensity might well have remained dormant.

Much of the knowledge I acquired in those early years was of Latin and Greek and the classical world. I am deeply grateful for this. To read one's way into the literature of Greece and Rome is a gift beyond price. Some of that literature is pedestrian; but much of it stands at the highest levels of human expression, and to identify with it is to absorb something of its greatness. To me it has given countless hours of enjoyable reading and some moments of rare bliss – Virgil in that last summer term at Kingswood and years later amid the swirling mists of Glencoe; Homer as we sailed delectably along the coast of Ithaca; Herodotus unfolding the saga of the Persian Wars as I sat snug beside a blazing log fire in our moorland cottage.

A classical education also gives access to a major source of almost all European languages; in particular, by disclosing insights of meaning and metaphor it enriches understanding of English.[1] To me it has given a further interest in language itself. This has been of immense value in philosophical studies, which are impossible without close attention to verbal meaning and usage. Further, there are some (and I would incline to be among them) who argue that the world of experience is a structure fabricated by and from the language we use to describe it; the more refined, therefore, one's grasp of language, the more subtly revealing becomes that structure. Finally, exploration of the classical world in its many facets gives a sense of the past, of a present rooted in the past. By thus extending temporal horizons it increases self-knowledge (a major part of wisdom); for we are indeed children of the past and we cannot know ourselves without a knowledge of our ancestry. Of course, I had little conscious awareness of all this while at school or even later at university; and I must admit that for most of my fellow-pupils Latin and Greek were a drudgerous burden, like Pilgrim's packload of sin, to be cast off *quam celerrime*. But hindsight enables me now thankfully to acknowledge the value, for me at least, of a classical education.

Latin and Greek were not the whole of my intellectual world. I am indebted too, brief though it was and incomplete, to my exposure to mathematics and science. The former gave me an ideal of accuracy which assures me that in some problems there is a right and a wrong answer and leaves me restless until the right is found. The latter opened to me a different world of discourse, with language, concepts and values of its own; it led me to respect the authority of a different kind of truth, a truth that accumulates but never to the point of final proof; it helped me to

[1] e.g., companion, scholar, scruple, horizon, helicopter.

discern, no less than in literature and art, the imaginative leap that creates new dimensions of experience. Together they gave me an awareness of intellectual regions which, though I am not equipped to explore them in detail, I know to exist and which cannot be ignored in any serious probing of reality; an awareness too that truth is many-sided and the mind's perspective larger than my own familiar round of linguistic, literary and historical studies. Again, these insights were the dawnings of later years; but it was my schools that made them possible, or at least more readily accessible; for mental vision, once stretched, retains an elasticity which facilitates a later outreach.

There is much that I could add to this catalogue of advantage, but space permits only the briefest mention. I owe to my schooling, and especially to Kingswood, the beginnings of aesthetic awareness. It came in diverse ways: from school plays and concerts, from pictures on the walls and books in the library, from the imposing architecture of Kingswood and the beauty of the Somerset countryside. Whether or not this was deliberately planned, it provided an environment of which beauty was a pervasive element. And however incomplete, it gave me an intimation of desirable destinations inviting further exploration, a hesitant foothold upon a vast untapped store of pleasure and enrichment.

I have written earlier of how, in running and swimming, I discovered my body and the pleasure that comes from its efficient functioning, from physical achievement and endurance pushed to the limit. I mention it again because in later years the pleasure was enlarged to include mountain-walking. This brings its own peculiar joys in vastly extended variety and has been a source of elevated delight for over forty years. The seeds of this were sown in my years of schooling, when Juvenal's *mens sana in corpore sano* was an acknowledged and practised principle of education.

Finally, I gratefully record the countless hours of carefree, spontaneous happiness of those years of growing up both in school and outside. How can one appraise them or by what criteria assess? One can't, of course; but memory can dwell lovingly and thankfully on the exuberance of life, the effervescence of energy that spent itself so profusely in games, walks, cycling, boating and all the other myriad pursuits that boyhood contrives. One recalls the chatter of classroom, dayroom and dormitory, the laughter echoing hilariously down distant corridors, the pranks and frolics conspired without malicious intent against our elders. And there were the friendships we formed in our adolescent years, the companionship of sunshine hours on foot or cycle and the shared bleakness of our winter runs. Ephemeral most of them were, but they were deep-felt at the time and jealously guarded; some were cut short by war; these and others are still treasured in memory and photograph, recapturing a springtime that is lived only once. So whatever the deficiencies, I count myself supremely fortunate in the gift of my growing up.

Growing up takes place in a context which has personal, social, political, geographical, historical and many other aspects. We are what we are partly because we are born into a particular family, at a certain time and place and at a certain point in the development of the country we belong to. The 1920s and 1930s were very different from the 1980s. It is difficult to imagine a world without TV, plastics, jet travel, microchips, nuclear arms and international terrorism, to mention only a few of the items we now take for granted. Something of this contrast must already have been apparent; more will appear in the remaining pages of this chapter. A very special part of the context of my own growing up was the Wesleyan Methodist, and from 1932 simply Methodist, Church.

What was its influence, and what difference did it make in my growing up that I was a child of the manse, 'the minister's son', brought up within the ambient atmosphere of Methodism? Of course, much of that influence was at a subconscious level and unrecognised at the time; but it is possible without undue risk of retrospective distortion to suggest an answer.

The most pervasive and enduring influence has been the Methodist chapel – its architecture, its forms of worship, its hymn-book and the variety of activities that are part of its life. To write thus is not to detract from the impact of a Methodist home and the example of my parents; in practice the two sources of influence were closely interwoven, the former inevitably permeating the life and work of the manse. To the best of memory all my father's chapels were of the same basic design, with a pulpit, not an altar, central to the gaze of the congregation. Behind were the choir and organ; some had galleries right round the buildings, some only at the back. Such is typical of the period when the chapels were built. (The Kingswood chapel is different, and to me at the time unusual, in having a side-pulpit, lateral choir stalls and an altar at the eastern end.) This design impresses, and was intended to impress, the central importance of preaching and of biblical exposition within the total act of worship: the preacher, elevated above the congregation, expounds authoritatively his interpretation of the Word; surrounded and enthused by his captive audience, he can appeal dramatically to their emotions and intensify their response. Hence in part came the success of great popular evangelists like Gypsy Smith and Leslie Weatherhead.

The pulpit's centrality was an inheritance from the days of the Wesleys. Then it was a reaction of protest against the empty formalities of the Church of England; at the same time it opened to mainly illiterate congregations a Bible which they could not read for themselves. In the half empty chapels of today, when sometimes only twos and threes are gathered together, things are different. Even these small numbers are encouraged to participate actively in the conduct of worship by reading lessons and prayers. More recent architecture has adopted the orthodox design of side-pulpit and central altar. The preacher's dominance is diminished.

For me, one effect was to exaggerate the importance of preaching. By focusing attention on the pulpit and its occupant it obscured the reality of a divine presence symbolised in the altar cross. Yet the structure of Methodist chapels also has its symbolism, representing that prophetic tradition which runs so powerfully through Old and New Testaments. God's presence can become very real to a congregation whose attention is focussed on a human interpreter of the Scriptures speaking to them in forceful language plain to understand. In such a situation those who listen are drawn into a closeness of fellowship and shared understanding which itself embodies and reveals the presence of God. To this the homely furnishing of pitch-pine, wooden floors and plain glass windows add their own indefinable contribution. Even in childhood and adolescence I was aware, though dimly, of that Presence and of the sustaining warmth of chapel worship. That is how I remember it; and Christianity has always been for me prophetic and evangelistic rather than liturgical (though these are not, of course, exclusive of one another).

There is a close relationship between the form of a building and the form of worship within it; each to some extent determines the other. Methodist worship is generally non-liturgical. Its Service Book includes (in phrasing of its own) most of the Orders of Worship of the Anglican Prayer Book and the full table of Collects, Lessons and Psalms. But not all of these are regularly used, and even the Communion Service (regrettably) is often pared to its barest essentials. The emphasis in Methodist worship has always been, and continues to be, on scriptural preaching, prayer and the inspiration of congregational singing. And because these are not tied to a set of formulae, they have at their best a vitality and spontaneity which might otherwise be subdued.

I was taken to morning chapel from the age of three; from the age of ten until leaving school I attended twice every Sunday. I was therefore deeply imbued with the form (I hesitate to add the *content*) of Methodist worship. So conditioned was I to its pattern of hymns, prayers, readings and sermon, that the idea of liturgical forms of worship, when I was later introduced to them, was alien and unintelligible. Their appurtenances of incense, candles and robes seemed unnecessary – obstacles rather than aids to the individual's free communication with his God. To me the preacher, who was often lay or 'local', was not a mediator but an interpreter – a man or woman with an urgent scriptural message; when this had been delivered, it was *my* responsibility to come to terms with God and the promptings of my own conscience. There is loss and gain in this; I have since come to appreciate the spiritual worth of ritual, ceremony and an interceding priesthood, and also how much, through mutual understanding, the different forms of denominational worship contribute to the full richness of Christian experience.

Prominent in Methodist worship are its hymns and the practice of extempore prayer; both these became inseparable from my concept of worship. For me the 1933 edition of the Methodist Hymn Book is the best in the English language (I could not say the same of its 1983 successor). Its hymns, especially those of the Wesleys, embody the central theology of Methodism, and their music contributes powerfully to the impact of congregational singing. It is true that some of them are alien to modern linguistic usage and spiritual experience – the world of the Wesleys was very different from ours. It is also true that in singing them it is easy to be carried away thoughtlessly by the emotional surge of tune and harmony. But if they are woven carefully into the whole fabric of worship instead of slotted into a formal sandwich with other constituents, *and* if they are sung with combined attention to words as well as music, they carry a message as meaningful as any scripture reading.

My memory of extempore prayer is not so favourable nor its influence so benign. I recall visions (for I often cheated and peeped through my fingers) of the preacher labouring verbosely over a vast range of seemingly unrelated topics. Extempore prayer is valuable when it springs spontaneously from profound experience; but as part of a normal act of worship it must, paradoxically, be carefully prepared and delivered with concealed artifice. Moreover, Methodism has, I am sure, been impoverished by its neglect of the Collects, many of which are glorious in their theological affirmation and its linguistic expression.

But of course Methodism too has richness of language and a vocabulary which mirrors its theological emphases. The vocabulary became part of me, infused so deeply by constant exposure to hymns, prayers and sermons, that I could never, even had I wanted, escape from its embrace. Essentially it is a vocabulary of liberation expressing a theology of liberation. 'Sin', 'forgiveness', 'salvation' are prominent in it – 'My chains fell off, my heart was free.' That is how it was experienced in the Wesleys' time by those who preached and those who listened; and that is how it is experienced today. The words and the experience of release are not peculiar to any one denomination; but for me, with other words in the same web of experience, they came to express the heart of Methodism.

To this gospel of liberation is due in part the informality of Methodist worship. Release is not only from the burden of sin, but also from the ties of liturgy and ceremonial form; it allows experiment in worship and in the presentation of the Good News. (Regrettably, the typical 'five hymn sandwich' has acquired a kind of liturgical mould of its own, a constricting pattern expected by congregation and accepted by preacher.) The homely, informal atmosphere of chapel worship is among the most cherished memories of my growing up. Again, this is not peculiar to Methodism or even to the Free Churches; but to me it has always seemed a distinctively Methodist contribution to the Christian Church. Oddly, the informality did not, during my growing up, extend to dress: 'Sunday best' was the invariable rule, and the jeans and jerseys common today would have raised many disapproving eyebrows.

For most of his service my father's was an itinerant ministry; three years was the normal stay in any one circuit; a fourth was exceptional. In the third year began the processes of enquiry, invitation and consultation which culminated in transfer. This had many disadvantages: it was costly to the circuits which paid the removal expenses; the minister and his family had scarcely time to adjust to one environment before departing to another; and the system of invitation, though democratic in intention, could prove invidious and a prolonged distraction to all concerned. Even as a child I was conscious of my parents' unease in the months preceding a final decision.

But for myself the balance was almost wholly positive. There was the excitement of exploring new manses, new gardens, new towns; I lost old friends but looked forward to new ones. True, it has left me without a footing in any one part of Britain: when asked, 'What part of the country do you come from?', I have no answer; I belong nowhere, a displaced person. On the other hand it has introduced me to a wide variety of people from all walks of life and thus has given me a non-parochial perspective transcending differences of speech, class and occupation. This is a welcome gift, but there is another and no less valuable: because of it I have come to know many and contrasting areas of Britain, from Cornwall in the south to Banffshire in the north, and in all our circuits, even Ilkeston, the countryside has not been far away.

Several times in earlier pages I have mentioned our straitened circumstances; 'poverty' would be too strong a word, for we were well off compared with many. But our life was frugal and money short. Our holidays came from the generosity of friends and relatives, as did also my clothes. Washing was done at home, manual of course and assisted only by such primitive appliances as coppers, galvanised scrubbers and mangles. Baking too was part of the weekly routine. The bustle and sounds and smells of both these activities were part of my growing up, remembered now in strangely vivid detail as I look back from an age which has revolutionised the domestic chore. Gardening too was a necessity; we grew as much of our vegetables as space allowed. Though imposed by necessity, my father found pleasure and relaxation in it. For me it had little interest, but it involved me in the enjoyable activity, described earlier, of gathering dung from the streets of Newark.

Frugality also required a careful record of personal income and expenditure. Recently I found my father's account book for 1934. Every item is entered in meticulous detail, totted up and balanced. (The amounts, of course, seem absurd: £67 for his quarterly stipend; £4 for a ton of coal.) This scrupulous accounting was more than a necessity imposed by financial straits. In part it was an inheritance from Victorian times, but also and more particularly it was a matter of pride – pride in accurate accounting, in careful husbandry of resources, in rejecting the very notion of debt, in always saving a little against emergencies. What a pity, I thought, as I turned the pages of his financial record, that such virtues are not more widely practised today.

I pondered also on the differences between a minister's life in the earlier and the later decades of the century. Ministers are still poorly paid – but they are not in it for the money. Most have cars; all have telephones; my father had neither throughout his ministry. He walked, he cycled, he bussed, he begged lifts; always he got there. And the distances, especially in the rural counties of Durham and Lincolnshire, were not negligible.

What influence our frugality had on my growing up is difficult to determine; the Second World War imposed a far greater degree of stringency on the whole population and no doubt reinforced whatever influence derived from earlier years. Suffice it to say that I have a reluctance to spend, an antipathy to debt and a propensity to save which my own family have at times found irritating!

I have already commented on two other significant features of our manse life: morning prayers and my father's study. Their importance deserves another mention here. Every morning before breakfast, from as far back as I can remember until I went to university, we came together as a family, listened to my father read from the Bible, knelt while he prayed, and then together said the Lord's Prayer. Morning prayers are an affirmation of commitment and of our human plight. The meaning of this cannot be apparent to childhood; and by me the daily ritual was often unwillingly accepted because of more urgent interest in breakfast or school or play. Nevertheless, to begin the day thus has a value which is psychological and symbolic as well as religious. Built into earliest memories it becomes a part of life's normality which is difficult to discard; long into adult life I continued for myself the practice of scripture reading and prayer as a start to the day. It symbolises a family togetherness, a community of love and activity within a providential embrace; it does so even when its members are separated for long periods, as were we. For me, as childhood grew into adolescence, it underlined and deepened that awareness, which I had already found in nature, of a dimension beckoning from beyond the ordinary.

It is, I believe, a requirement of every Methodist manse that it be large enough to provide a study for the minister, a quiet room for reading, writing, prayer and contemplation. So used it radiates an influence throughout the house, affecting all who live in it. I was aware of this influence from an early age. In every manse the study was a place apart, different from all other rooms; it had an air of sanctity which must not be lightly disturbed; I entered it always with hesitation. Its shelves were filled with books, not only theological but literary too, especially works of criticism and appreciation. Two sets in particular are prominent in memory. There were the black-bound volumes of the *Minutes of Conference*, accumulating one by one through the years and (in my childhood imagination) silently ticking away the interval between each issue. The other was the *Encyclopaedia of Religion and Ethics* – I forget how many of its dark red volumes. These had been a gift, one each Christmas, from Auntie Mabel. I discovered when I inherited them that my father had read right through them, underlining and annotating in pencil as he thought fit. Much of the philosophical writing must have been beyond his understanding, as it was also beyond mine when the volumes first came to me.

I was not greatly given to reading during childhood and adolescence; but the presence of the study in each of our manses and the bookish aura that pervaded it undoubtedly impressed on me the importance of books as a necessary part of life; later I became and have remained an avid reader. How much this was due to propensities within myself and how much to the study I can never know; but I am sure that the latter played its part in inclining me, and no doubt many other children of the manse, towards scholarship and a love of truth. I hope there will always be room for a study in the Methodist manse.

There is an ancient Greek proverb, 'The beginning is everything'. The fact is, men and women are not born human; they are *made* human; what makes them human and – far more important – determines the quality of their humanity is the environment which enfolds their life and growth. The impact of environment is especially important in early years: the child's mind is not a *tabula rasa*, a blank sheet, as some have suggested; but it is uncluttered by the debris of time, so that whatever enters it has a dominance that resists erasure and gives direction to later items of experience.

I have tried in this and earlier chapters to sift out the dominant ingredients of my own growing up. Not all were beneficial; there were debit items which I wish could have been otherwise. But the balance is positive, and outstanding within it is the contribution of a Methodist upbringing. Methodism was woven into the fabric of my childhood – by my father's work which set the pattern of our daily life, by morning prayers and family conversation, and not least by the memories, conscious and unconscious, retained from regular attendance at our various chapels. These last, drawn from the whole spectrum of Methodist worship – pitch pine and hassocks, comforting warmth, reverberating rhetoric, and the gripping tunes and rhythms of majestic hymns – are part of the established furniture of my being.

Through a Glass Darkly

Introduction

GROWING UP DOES NOT END WITH SCHOOL, graduation, or the age of legal majority; it continues throughout life, even after physical decline, until or unless there occurs a collapse of the individual's coherent consciousness. However, the three chapters in this Part II are not a detailed account of my next fifty years telescoped into a few pages. That would have no interest for anyone outside my immediate circle of friends and family; my life has no particular claim to notice; others write of themselves with greater knowledge, insight and authority.

So what is the purpose of the following chapters? My travelling along with Methodism continued. From it I have picked out three areas of importance and, looking back over seventy years with (hopefully) a seasoned reflection, I have tried to summarise in title and content their significance for me. There is nothing special about my Christian experience; I have travelled through territory explored more intimately and charted more expertly by countless others. Nevertheless, it is a journey unique to every individual; through it each of us, under guidance from others (including the divine Presence), must also chart his or her own course. In so doing we may possibly shed a little light for those who follow.

154

The chapter titles, I think, explain themselves; if not, their meaning will emerge as they are read. But the overall title of Part II calls for a brief explanation. 'Through a glass darkly' are the well known words of St Paul. For accuracy of meaning I prefer the New English Bible version, 'puzzling reflections in a mirror'. For in St Paul's day mirrors were not of glass but of polished bronze which could not achieve the clarity of image we expect from a modern mirror; some distortion was inevitable. However, the old translation expresses well enough what I intend. There is a mystery which surrounds and penetrates the existence of humanity and of the whole universe – a final, insuperable question mark beyond which there is no knowing. There are glimpses of meaning – Jesus and his teaching are among them – but no final solution; indeed certainty diminishes and mystery increases as we approach the horizon of questioning. Such is my overriding impression as I reflect on the world and my brief span of life within it. Why, I ask myself, is there anything at all? Why my small spark of consciousness here and now instead of there and then? Why the suffering and the waste that seem inseparable from the world we know?

I shall look at the mystery more closely in chapter 10, whose title (borrowed from Wordsworth) catches for me both the essence of the mystery and the insistent nudging[1] of something both within it and beyond. Chapters 9 and 11 are embraced by the mystery, but they offer some of those glimpses of meaning which enable me to accept it, live with it and hope for future enlightenment.

---

[1] *Oxford English Dictionary:* 'Nudge. To touch or push slightly . . . to attract attention.' The last three words are especially significant.

CHAPTER IX

The Call of Christ

MY PARENTS MADE NO POSITIVE ATTEMPT, so far as I can remember, to make me a Methodist or even a Christian; nor did they enlighten me about other denominations. Of course, I was aware of the Church of England as a building (and there are some notable examples in and around Newark and Horncastle) and as a national institution; but I remained ignorant of its practices and its forms of worship. Nor can I recollect that in those days there was much coming together of the clergy in response to a common concern for the Christian faith and the social problems of the time.

Methodism was my milieu, the mould of Christianity in which I was cast. I was shaped into it both at home and at Kingswood by the habitual routine of morning prayers and chapel attendance. Thus I had accepted it, superficially at least, as a matter of course and conformity, taking it for granted as a scaffolding which gave my growing self a needed structure and support. Officially I was received into full membership of the Methodist Church at the age of seventeen and thenceforth received my quarterly 'class ticket'. But membership and commitment are not the same; sooner or later I must come to terms, by my own independent acceptance, with the Christian religion and the Methodist expression of it in which I had been brought up.

Perhaps this was my father's intention when he suggested that I should conduct worship in one of the small country chapels near Horncastle. For the effort to interpret a text, sorting out its essentials and expressing them intelligibly with appropriate illustration, might indeed assist me towards that end. It was on a fine summer evening in a small red-brick chapel at Mareham-on-the-Hill that I first led a congregation in worship and preached my first sermon. I remember nothing of its theme nor of the occasion except for the hollow nervousness in my stomach as I mounted the pulpit and my deep sense of relief as I left to cycle home.

At Cambridge I continued my habit of church-going by regular attendance at Wesley, the Methodist university chapel, and by occasional visits to the small and beautiful chapel of Wesley House, the Cambridge training college for Methodist clergy. The murals in the latter, symbolising the resurrection and triumph of Jesus, were a source of aesthetic delight and spiritual exaltation; they impressed upon me, as nothing had previously, how much the former can contribute to the latter. I also occasionally attended worship at Great St Mary's in the centre of Cambridge. This was the Anglican equivalent of Wesley as a university church, but in a wider sense. For it was open to all comers and, on Sunday evenings especially, offered a forum for theologians of any denomination and for persons of eminence in other spheres. Of these I can remember only the gaunt figure of Canon C. E. Raven, the brilliant scientist-cum-theologian, whose preaching and writing helped me greatly in resolving what for me at the time seemed an irresoluble conflict between religion and science.

The Methodist manse held open house for undergraduates every Sunday afternoon, providing opportunity for men and women from different colleges to meet and chat over tea and biscuits. This too I attended regularly at first, but the effect on me was to emphasise my social incompetence. Our hosts, the minister and his wife, did their best for me, I am sure, but I had no idea how to initiate or maintain a conversation and little enough to talk about beyond my very limited academic interests. The other sex, of course, was an unknown world which I viewed with distant apprehension. Too often I found myself stuck in a solitary corner silently sipping my tea while all around was a babble of animated conversation and laughter. After a term or two I gave up going.

I derived more benefit from the various 'fellowship groups' to which I belonged during my four years at the university. These consisted of up to a dozen members, undergraduates and others, of both sexes. Under the leadership of an older Methodist they met weekly in college rooms and private houses and discussed all manner of topics from sex and unemployment to the Resurrection of Christ. Many of us had our personal doubts and perplexities as we confronted the mysteries of the Christian faith and grew in awareness of its challenge to a secular world. I have mentioned above the apparent conflict between religion and the confident claims of expanding science; there were also moral problems posed by nature 'red in tooth and claw', by the intrusive spectacle of poverty, by the violence of world events and by the increasing imminence of war. These and many others we were able to air and share and thereby to find comfort and illumination.

There was indeed plenty to talk about; and here, unlike Sunday afternoons at the manse, I felt unconstrained and able to contribute to the interchange of discussion. In part this was due to the nature of the groups, which were small, welcoming and united by the common purpose of exploring the Christian gospel and its practical implementation. Even more it was due to the leadership of Charles Coulson and his wife Eileen. Charles was then a Fellow of Trinity; later he was a Professor of Mathematics at Oxford and a Fellow of the Royal Society. He and Eileen were involved in the organisation of the first of the groups I belonged to and they regularly attended our weekly discussions. As no one else I have known Charles combined intellectual brilliance with passionate commitment to Christianity and a deeply sensitive, practical insight into human problems. He was a leading pacifist before, during, and after the war; despite this (for pacifism was regarded with some distrust by the Methodist Church and even more by society at large) he was elected Vice-President of the Methodist Conference in 1959. His influence on me was twofold and decisive, leading me towards a full Christian commitment and a pacifist interpretation of it.

The groups' activities were not confined to discussion. One of mine undertook visits to a local geriatric ward. I remember vividly my initial shock on entering that forlorn world of groans, decrepitude and the stench of stale urine. We prayed, sang and talked with these social jetsam, many of whom were past caring or comprehension, and hoped that our efforts, meagre but well-meant, had brought some relief to their misery. Among them was a Greek, and as I had recently returned from my tour of Greece, I was able to exchange a few words with him in his own language. His eyes lit up through the shadow of approaching death and with what strength remained he grasped my hand and thanked me. That one incident made the visit eminently worthwhile.

Another group was involved in an experiment in Christian community living. The aim of this, in response to the prevalent poverty and distress of the time, was to give practical expression to the injunction of Jesus to care for one's neighbour. Its members included a school-teacher, a nurse and an unemployed couple and their children; they shared a house and each contributed what they could afford to the rent, running expenses and weekly food bill; thus the better off assisted the poorer. As an undergraduate I could not take part in the experiment, but by association with it I found my conscience jolted and my religious horizons disturbingly expanded from the formalities of worship and theological argument to the urgent realities of social responsibility.

Through this group I was introduced to the Cotswold Bruderhof, a much larger experiment in Christian community whose members owned a corporate farm near Cirencester and aimed to be economically self-supporting. They were Germans of a somewhat evangelical and puritan bent; their clothes were formal and the men all bearded. Having found life impossible under Hitler they had sought refuge in Britain; but in 1939 they were forced to choose between internment and deportation, opted for the latter and re-established themselves in America. Anyone interested could join the community for a week or more and share its life and the work of the farm. I spent a fortnight there in the early summer of 1938 or 1939.

The life was rigorous indeed. Up at 6.00 for breakfast at 6.30, I spent the day in the fields hand-weeding onions and carrots and hoeing other roots. The meals were sparse and vegetarian, consisting mainly of coarse bread thinly spread with a kind of cream cheese, and bowls of mixed salad. They began with prayer and meditation which put an even sharper edge on my already acute pangs of hunger. By the end of my first week these were so overwhelming that I was forced to beg an afternoon off (reluctantly conceded) to cycle into Cirencester and satisfy my appetite. Interesting the experience certainly was; and the June loveliness of the Cotswold countryside amply repaid its rigours. But I was not convinced by this experiment in Christian community; it had an air of urgent austerity which robbed it of joy; and although the men at their farmwork were not uncheerful, the prim garb and demeanour of the women left me with an impression of subjection.

Most of us, as we look back over our lives, can pick out occasions of crisis – in the literal meaning of the Greek word; occasions when judgements, decisions were made, or perhaps forced upon us, which gave a permanent and irreversible direction to events and to our lives within them. I come now to such an occasion in my own life. Without, I hope, seeming pompous or exaggerating its significance, I do indeed see it now, quite simply, as a spiritual Rubicon or, to use a different metaphor, a watershed, the crossing of which made things irrevocably different.

I have indicated earlier that when I went to Cambridge my Christianity was more a passive acceptance than a positive commitment. Every day before breakfast I read from the Bible and prayed; every Sunday I went to chapel at least once; and during university terms I regularly attended the weekly fellowship group. But all this was somehow superficial; there was a missing element – a firm, explicit, *personal* dedication to what I claimed to believe. I had never honestly faced the question: What does Jesus Christ mean for *me*?

There were two principal Christian organisations among under-graduates in the 1930s, the Student Christian Movement and the

Cambridge Inter-Collegiate Christian Union. The former was reputedly conservative and public school, the latter non-class and strongly evangelical (a feature impressed on us by lighthearted reference to its acronym CICCU). Its leader at Queens' was an ardent, bespectacled undergraduate who evidently thought me a suitable target for evangelism. It was in my second year that he came to my room in Friar's Building and, after some initial chat about religion and its place in my life, invited me to pray with him and 'offer myself to Christ'. Which I did; and that is how I became a *committed* member of the Methodist Church. It was not a sudden conversion such as many have experienced. Looking back I see it now as the climax of a process of growth which had many contributory sources and to which my friendship with Charles and Eileen Coulson gave a vital momentum. For long and in ways unrecognised the divine elbow had been nudging me on, and at last I awoke to its reality in the call of Christ.

In the days following that response I felt an unusual sense of peace and liberation. Within the infinity of God's love in Christ all anxieties about the future were dispelled, and the intellectual problems that had been troubling me, though not resolved, now lost their urgency and shrank to unimportance. I understood then, though in a very different context, a little of Charles Wesley's triumphant experience, 'My chains fell off, my heart was free'; and like him I rose to obey the Jesus to whom I had offered myself. Having heard the call and answered, the rest, I naively thought, would be simple – to follow wherever it should lead. The reality, however, was more complicated, as I was later to discover. The problems reasserted themselves; some of them remain unresolved to this day. Although I had pledged my service in answer to the call, I had yet to discover what form that service should take; and this would involve decisions of traumatic significance.

My response to the call, I have said, was the climax of a long process of growth (perhaps it would be nearer the truth to describe it as a high peak in a process of growth which even fifty years later is not yet finished). For most, that is the way it comes, a slow accumulation of pressure, a persistent nudging of the divine elbow that leads irresistibly to a decisive commitment. It may be triggered by an appeal from the pulpit; it may come as a strange warming of the heart, as it did to John Wesley at the meeting in Aldersgate St; it may come, as to me, by the quiet prompting of a friend in the privacy of one's own room; or it may come in solitude as a sudden flash of transforming insight; or in all manner of other ways. Few are called like St Paul in a sudden effulgence of truth that left him temporarily blind; though I suspect that even he had long been brooding over the 'good news', resisting the call of Christ until the deeper levels of his personality burst through and compelled obedience.

However the call comes, it is very personal; Christ calls us as individuals, by name; and the response too is individual, leading each of us along a road which, under divine guidance, we discover for ourselves. The response has also a certain inevitability; it becomes irresistible, like Francis Thompson's Hound of Heaven, pursuing 'with unhurried chase and unperturbed pace', while a voice invites 'to clasp My hand and come'.

An immediate outcome of my response to the call was to accept an invitation to undertake with other undergraduates an evangelical mission to Wolverhampton the following September. Whence the invitation came I cannot remember, whether SCM or CICCU or, more likely, jointly from both. It was interdenominational but organised under the general guidance of an Anglican clergyman in Wolverhampton, in whose house many of us stayed for the week of the mission. This was something which, in the flush of a new enthusiasm, I felt I could not refuse. I recall few of the details: there were meetings in churches and chapels, at factory gates and street corners. My own part was minimal; I was assigned to address a random audience at some pavement corner near the town centre; my subject – the Holy Spirit! Only three or four paused to listen, and these, I suspect more from simple curiosity than any religious interest. I have no recollection of what I said or how they responded; I can hardly think that they were impressed.

The fact is that I was ill-prepared for such a venture, difficult enough for anyone, let alone an immature twenty-year-old just over the threshold of commitment and with very little understanding of a very difficult topic. I tremble now at the sheer effrontery of it. Of course, it was a mistake; but one must be willing to be a fool for Christ's sake; and mistakes are made to learn from if one so chooses. One can never be wholly sure that the direction of one's response is what God is asking. Patiently one must discover how, within the potential of one's self and one's circumstances, one can best serve him. There must always be a probing self-examination and prayer for guidance; and before any practical enterprise, like our mission to Wolverhampton, there must be thorough training and preparation. Enthusiasm is a necessary but not a sufficient condition of discipleship; one cannot serve God as he deserves with tools that are inappropriate or unprimed.

In my fourth year at Cambridge I was confronted with a decision second in significance only to my initial response to the call of Christ. After Munich it was obvious that war was coming; preparation proceeded apace and the only uncertainty was when and where it would start. What should a Christian's attitude be? It is difficult for today's younger generation to appreciate the torment of conscience which this question thrust upon Christians of military age during the build-up to war; the nuclear debate, though not dissimilar, lacks (at present) the same urgency of personal decision. Unhappily, they may find themselves in the same agonising predicament before the century is out. The abomination of Nazism was conspicuous enough, destructive of the basic values both of democracy and of Christianity. There was the claim, too, of social responsibility, of our neighbours towards whom we, as Christians, had a special obligation. How, consistently with that obligation, could one evade the mortal dangers that others must endure? Yet the teaching of Jesus pointed to love as an absolute moral demand and to the Cross as the answer to evil; with such an ethic and such a theology the slaughter of one's fellow human beings seemed wholly incompatible. After many weeks of indecision and many hours of anguished prayer I decided, or rather was impelled by something irresistible within me, to commit myself to non-violence and the rejection of war. One evening, still in the tremulous aftermath of my decision, I walked to Wesley Chapel and there with many others made my pledge. In this too Charles Coulson was a prevailing influence.

Many and many a time I have agonised over that decision and asked myself, 'Was I right?' Can it be that the love of God, manifested on the Cross and embodied in the lives of men and women – can this *really* be the all-conquering power that the Gospel proclaims? Is non-violence a practical policy in a world which rejects that love and is animated by animal instincts of greed and aggression? Can a Christian stand aside from the suffering of others? Does not love call upon us to share, as Jesus did, in the suffering of a world gone wrong, even if that means taking up arms and bringing death to others (which Jesus did not)? Yet surely the way of the Cross is to accept suffering, not inflict it? And so I have argued unendingly with myself and my conscience.

At the time of my decision I had no doubt that I was right; this, as I saw it, was my response to the call; I could do no other. I believed with a passionate conviction that love *can* prevail – naively, I am sure some would say, in the light of what we now know of the horrendous brutalities of Nazism. Nevertheless, I still believe it: love *will* prevail, though when, and whether in this world or another, I do not pretend to know. Meanwhile, in our world as it is, there will be some whose Christian conviction forbids them to kill and destroy; others will interpret their discipleship differently. For both the nuclear threat has transformed the ground of decision. It is for the individual Christian to determine how he or she is called to express in a committed life the invincible love of God. Whatever the choice, suffering and possibly death are consequences that must be willingly accepted for Christ's sake.

In July 1939 I had been appointed to the teaching post at St George's in Harpenden, as described earlier. When war was declared, I was staying with my parents at Portessie. A few days later I made the tedious overnight journey in blacked-out trains to London and thence to the school. For the first months I was too involved in work to give much thought to my situation. But I knew that I must register as a conscientious objector and that eventually I would be summoned before a tribunal to be judged for the integrity of my conviction. The same tribunal would direct me to whatever work or service they thought appropriate. In the event my testimony was accepted and I was ordered to teach. The school, a Christian foundation, respected my pacifism and allowed me to retain my post.

Of course, despite the war children had still to be taught, trained, educated, and the nation's life, such as was possible, must be maintained. And maybe my work as a teacher made some contribution to the nation's good. Nevertheless, looking back I wish now that I had volunteered for, or been directed to, some form of non-combatant service. Thus I could have shared the dangers and the suffering to which others were exposed, whether in the forces or in the blitzed cities of Britain. Not that it was always easy for me in those six years. The white feathers received anonymously through the post I could shrug off without much disquiet. But when I learnt of the deaths of my Kingswood friends and of my sixth form pupils killed while still in their teens, I was overcome with anger, grief and frustration.

It would have been more difficult, indeed impossible, if I had not been convinced that I was called to teach. This had been my intention when I first went to Cambridge – due perhaps to my mother's unconscious influence (she taught for several years before her marriage). There it was brought within my response to the call of Christ and thus confirmed; I had no doubt that education must be my way of witness in daily work.

The teacher's dais is not a pulpit for proclaiming the Christian or any other gospel; although teaching and preaching share certain similarities, they are not identical. The classroom's primary purpose is instruction; it enables teachers to teach and children to learn what the school's curriculum prescribes. With the doubtful exception of religious instruction in denominational schools, this precludes trying to persuade children into accepting religious beliefs. How then can teaching be an expression of Christian witness?

It would need a book to answer that question fully; I must attempt it in a few paragraphs. In a classroom, relationships are of prime importance. These can be divisive and restrictive within a context of assertive authority and mutual suspicion which is negative and miseducative. On the contrary, they can be open, sympathetic, encouraging and communicative, uniting everyone in educative cooperation. Order must be maintained, but it emerges spontaneously from the latter situation; punishment is sometimes necessary, but the manner of it is crucial to the quality of relationships. The Christian teacher's position is clear: fundamental in his faith and no less therefore in his professional practice is respect for persons as persons. By bringing this respect into the classroom, by dealing with his pupils as persons, as children of a loving God, he will be helping to establish a quality of relationship which is truly educative.

His faith also affects his attitude to knowledge and his concept of teaching. The former becomes more than acquisition of fact or even of understanding (both of which, though necessary, are not enough). It is an exploration of the reality and nature of God through increasing cognitive insight into one's self and the world around; it is a revelation, an unveiling of mystery, an expansion of the self into the divine infinity. Within such a concept of knowledge truth assumes a cardinal importance; indeed without truth there *is* no knowledge, only a distorted image. Without truth one lives in an unreal world where objects, persons, situations and relationships are seen as other than they are. Inevitably this impedes personal growth and personal relationships. Ignorance is restraint; truth does, in a very real sense, set one free. The Christian teacher will therefore encourage a critical, even sceptical approach to what is offered as fact by politicians, advertisers, the media and even (dare I say it?) by scientists, historians and theologians. To match this concept of knowledge, teaching becomes an enabling to learn, a facilitating of exploration and discovery by creating an environment which stimulates enquiry and provides the necessary resources. Instead of imparting knowledge from a dais of authority, the teacher stands to one side, yet always part of the community of learning, ready to encourage and assist.

Each curriculum subject offers its peculiar approach to knowledge and to emphases within it. Mine was classics. Here, despite the many inhumanities of the classical world, both pre- and post-Christian, there are honourable ideals – law, justice and ordered government, freedom, beauty, philosophical and scientific enquiry – all of which can be woven critically and constructively into a Christian interpretation of human experience. The children one teaches may be totally unaware of any Christian intention in their teacher; and this, I am sure, is as it should be. Yet all the time there is growing within them a receptive foundation on which ultimately, in the providence of God, a Christian orientation may be built.

I have taught English and religion too. The opportunities here are obvious, but the latter raises problems: should it be Christian instruction? and is it right to use RE to influence children towards Christian commitment? In state schools I believe that RE should be offered as an enquiry into the nature of religious experience and its various expressions; it should not be exclusively or predominantly Christian but should aim to give a genuine understanding of other faiths and their practices. In Christian foundations like St George's the situation is different Here there may be (but I am doubtful) some justification, not for overt proselytising, but for an orientating influence expressed in the selection of material for the syllabus and in the teacher's personal contribution.

What I have said in the last few paragraphs can be summarised under the heading of 'values'. Christian teachers are committed to certain values which derive from their faith and motivate it. Central among these is respect for persons; another word for this is 'love' – which, unfortunately, can be misinterpreted and sentimentalised by those who do not understand the insistent and sacrificial nature of love's demands. From this central value derive others, for instance, an orderly and disciplined freedom, patience, tolerance, impartiality, fairness, truth. To elicit these values from the material they teach, to incorporate them in its presentation and to exhibit them in themselves is a powerful mode of Christian witness.

Education is not confined to the classroom; it spills over into the wider community of the school. The teacher is a member of that community, contributing to a 'hidden curriculum' whose influence on children is more potent and more lasting than curricular instruction. Like it or not, he or she is involved in the whole life of the school, its activities and relationships, and contributes to its ethos.

The Christian teacher has an obligation, therefore, to help in creating a school environment which is supportive of Christian values. This does not mean preaching or proselytising; it does mean carrying Christ with one in one's daily work, but not embroidered on jersey or T-shirt; an unobtrusive witness is far more effective – though occasionally it may be necessary to speak out openly against proposals and policies. Nor does it mean conflict with democratic values; for these overlap Christian values and support them. Both include respect for persons and concern for their welfare; both include a disciplined freedom responsibly exercised, rational discussion and commitment to truth. Beauty too is a value common to both; and its impact is moral as well as aesthetic. Within and sometimes beyond these overlapping values the Christian teacher will find ways of expressing an especially Christian emphasis and motivation of caring within the school and of service to the community outside – shopping for the elderly, assisting the handicapped, fund-raising for charitable causes.

In a religious foundation opportunities for Christian witness are wider. Cecil Grant, the founder of St George's was an Anglican clergyman of inspired vision, a real adventurer for Christ. The school had its own chapel, hymn-book and prayer-book; its ethos was avowedly Christian. I was fortunate in this, for I was able to exercise a Christian witness more overtly than would have been appropriate or possible in a state school. Among my most enjoyable experiences was organising sixth form services in the school chapel. These took the form of discussions, thoroughly prepared and rehearsed, on such topics as the existence of God, the resurrection of Jesus and the problem of evil. As we talked over these issues beforehand and put our thoughts on paper, I often felt that the Spirit was leading us deeply into the mysteries of the Christian faith.

The Christian teacher has obligations beyond the sphere of daily work – to the Church, of course, but beyond that again to society as a whole. Here too he or she has not only obligation but abundant opportunity for a witness which is educative and improving. Our society, any society, is far from perfect; even amid our own affluence here in Britain there are ignorance, poverty, injustice and suffering, much of which is comfortably curtained off and ignored. These are a denial of Christian values. There is a special obligation here for Christian teachers because they have enjoyed privileges of education and training beyond most of their fellow citizens. The call of Christ summons them to dispel ignorance by ferreting out and making known the truth; it summons them to oppose whatever diminishes respect for persons; it summons them to strive for improving conditions of life and work. Is this education? Yes, I believe it is: whatever elevates the human mind, improves the human condition, and thereby expands human potential can be described as educative. I would extend this to include the total human environment, the earth and its resources, which are God's creation, intended by him for our responsible use. These have enormous educative power if they *are* thus used, and the reverse if they are not.

The scope for witness is so vast that an individual can select only one or two particular activities where he or she can best contribute according to interest, opportunity or special knowledge. Road safety has been a close concern of mine, involving me in membership of local Road Safety Committees and countless letters to MPs and the press. Another has been international relations, especially between Britain and the so-called Third World. Later on, as a university lecturer, I had obvious opportunities here, and many have been the enjoyable evenings my wife and I have spent in our home with students from almost every country in Africa – and as so often happens, they have given more to us in numerous ways than we to them.

It may be objected that very little of this portrayal of Christian witness in education can be claimed as exclusively Christian. This is true. Apart from the special circumstances of St George's, what I have written could be taken as a description of any good teacher and, more widely, of any good citizen. A good teacher is dedicated to the values of his or her society – in a democratic society to respect for persons and all that flows from it in classroom and school relationships; dedicated also to the highest professional standards. A good teacher is also committed to the wider task of human improvement both in his or her own society and throughout humankind.

Christian teachers must aim at no less; but what more can they bring to their task? I believe that they can bring to it a sense of vocation, a calling (which is what 'vocation' means), a commitment to a goal which is wider than classroom, school, career, profession or society; and with that vocation comes an added justification and motivation for their work. Because they are linked to the infinite resources of God, they enjoy a sustaining power, a fund of energy and a resilience which keeps them going despite the inevitable setbacks, frustrations and disappointments that tangle a teacher's path. Unless they are teaching RE, they may never utter the words 'God' and 'Christ' in the course of their daily work. But if they respond faithfully to their calling, the divine Presence accompanies them in that work and carries an influence which, though unobtrusive, is both real and unpredictable in its creative outcome. Such is the ideal; I would not pretend to have fulfilled it. Nor could I have articulated it thus when I first embarked on my teaching career.

I left St George's in 1945 for a post at Bristol Grammar School. The contrast was abrupt and disconcerting. It was a boys' school and a day school; in both these respects I felt an impoverishment of the educational environment. Because there were no girls, half of what I had come to regard as a normal school community was missing. And because I had little contact with the boys outside the classroom, there was a discontinuity, so it seemed, of educative endeavour. St George's had about 300 pupils aged from eight upwards; it was small enough to know each one by name, as an individual person; it had a family atmosphere. BGS had over 1000 boys, and I remember my sense of depression when, after four years in the school, I still found myself passing streams of boys in the corridors to whom I could attach no name. It was an epitome of impersonality! Again, although St George's taught to A Level, it was more of a comprehensive than a grammar school; it catered for children of all abilities. BGS was geared to high academic performance; its record here was impressive, rivalling any other school in the country; but an inevitable result was a diversion of attention from the less academically able. For myself, after satisfying as best I could the demands on me of these rigorous standards of scholarship, there was not much of time or energy left for out-of-school activities.

At Harpenden, because of my almost total involvement in the life of the school, I could spare little of myself for the local Methodist Church except for regular preaching appointments within the circuit. At Bristol I continued these and was able also, jointly with a woman leader, to run a weekly mixed youth club. This was hard work and the three hours on Wednesday evenings left us both exhausted. But it was rewarding too, especially in one respect for me. Among the boys who came were a few from an English class at BGS which I was trying to prepare for School Certificate. In school they were among the most troublesome and disruptive pupils I have ever taught; at the club, strangely as it seemed to me, they were model citizens, cooperative and self-disciplined. Perhaps it was the presence of the girls; or perhaps they realised that, if it were otherwise, the club simply could not function. Whatever the reason, they behaved and we were friends!

After four years at BGS I felt I needed a change. I applied for and to my surprise was appointed to a lectureship in the Education Department of what was then the University College of Hull, now a university. I remained there for the rest of my working life. Throughout those years my work was in the theory and philosophy of education and in classics method (how to teach Latin and Greek); for ten years I was also responsible for RE method. This, like school teaching, I regarded as a vocation, different but no less a response to the call of Christ.

The opportunities for Christian witness in the more open, adult life of a university are wider and more challenging than in a school: wider, because one's student-contacts cover the whole world and almost every academic discipline; more challenging, because the very nature of a university demands a clearly thought out intellectual commitment and a close attention to scholarly detail and the logic of argument. The opportunities are also greater in scope, for in a university one has time for research and writing which is not available (though it should be) to school teachers.

University lecturers have four main areas of professional activity: lecturing (including laboratory and field work), tutorials, research and writing. Outside their professional work they can also involve themselves with one or more of the many societies which are part of the normal life of a university. Of these, some are specifically Christian, others are humanitarian without religious affiliation; opportunity for witness exists in both – if only by membership and tacit support. In the professional areas there is no place for preaching or propaganda; occasionally, in order to balance a discussion, it may be acceptable to submit a Christian viewpoint; but in general a lecturer's stance is neutral. This is true even of theology departments, whose task, as I understand it, is not the propagation of the Christian faith but the exposition, duly evidenced and argued, of historical and doctrinal fact.

What room, then, for Christian witness? As in schools, values are paramount. It is in the values he or she is committed to and embodies in daily life and work that a lecturer witnesses to the Christian faith – not overtly, but by introducing students to values which are at the same time democratically acceptable and conducive to, or at least suggestive of, a Christian commitment. Supreme among these are persons and truth. What I have already said about these in the context of the classroom applies equally here; but truth, because of the very nature of university work assumes a greater emphasis than in schools. A resolute commitment to truth is both a basic academic obligation and fundamental to democracy and to Christianity. With it goes a creative scepticism which doubts, not for doubting's sake, but to secure a more reliable structure of knowledge. Part of this commitment is to acknowledge that truth has different forms. Another is to insist on clarity and accuracy in the use of language; there is no greater obstacle to truth than carelessness and imprecision in using words.

Apart from a few articles on the teaching of RE and a school edition of Bede's *Historia Ecclesiastica* none of my writing or research has had any obvious connection with Christianity. I have felt called to expound, mainly through their own writings, the ideas of a few very great men who were deeply committed to education as a means of human improvement; only one of them, John Locke, was a professed Christian. Exposure to greatness or, as one writer has put it, 'the habitual vision of greatness' is a potent means of educating and of communicating values. What I have written myself was written because I felt there was something important to be said or clarified, some falsehood or mistake to be exposed in order to arrive at the truth. I may, of course, have been deluded! My main research has been into the educational thought of J. S. Mill; he was a deeply humanitarian, religiously sensitive agnostic who worked unceasingly for 'the improvement of mankind' (his words). To spend ten years in the company of such a very great man has been a privilege, an elevating experience for which I am profoundly grateful. All my professional work has been a kind of evangelism – not directly for Christianity, but for the kind of education that improves and elevates by incorporating values which overlap and incline to Christianity. How much influence such work has had one can never know. One proceeds in faith and very occasionally a student's chance remark suggests that it has not been entirely in vain.

During my years in Hull I was able to involve myself more fully in the work of my local Methodist church and to serve in its various offices and committees. This is part of the call, any Christian's call; for one is never an individual but always a member of a Christian community which *together* seeks to praise God and to witness to the faith within the area of its church.

I continued preaching, of course, with a little more confidence and, I hope, a little greater clarity of exposition. I have always felt nervous about conducting worship. Often a local preacher is a stranger to the congregation he addresses, and this itself is a source of unease. There is greater cause for diffidence in the immensity of the message which exceeds mental and verbal comprehension; how *can* one contain or convey it? But the greatest things can be said very simply, as Jesus himself showed us. Again, how can one be sure of one's belief, one's commitment? The Moravian, Peter Böhler, advised John Wesley: 'Preach faith till you have it; and then, because you have it, you will preach faith'.[1] There is sound psychological truth in this.

Simplicity of exposition does not come easily to a university lecturer; the temptation is towards complexity of thought dressed up in over-elaborate language. Two or three clear ideas are enough for any sermon; they must be supported by effective illustration preferably taken from everyday life or the preacher's personal experience. Again, one learns from Jesus: stories like the prodigal, the pearl, the Samaritan and the faithful servant stand out with forceful persuasion where subtlety of argument would fail. Gardening and mountain-walking have provided me with numerous illustrations which, I believe, are the more convincing because they come from the heart.

The call of Christ requires a different response, a *personal* response, from each of us. Few are called to spectacular achievement; for most the call of Christ is a summons to the Christ-like doing of the humdrum and the ordinary in daily life and work. For some it means service in obscurity – like the woman I remember so vividly in a BBC Songs of Praise programme. Twenty-one years of her life she had given to the care of a son who was born defective and had never been able to do the simplest thing for himself. How her face shone with the radiance of Christ as she

[1] Wesley's *Journal*, March 4th, 1738.

told of her life! Few are called to such a response of total devotion – and few, perhaps, are capable of it. I felt ashamed that I had had it so easy! Of some the call requires a different response at different stages of life, even a total change of direction, as the Wesleys discovered and many others not so remarkably. One can never be certain that the direction of one's response is what God is asking; patiently and prayerfully sensitive to the divine prompting, one proceeds in faith and hope. And sometimes, looking back over life, one glimpses here and there what seems like a pattern of opportunity and progress within a guiding providence.

In this chapter I have tried to portray the working out of the call of Christ in my own life. The picture is incomplete, for I have said little of my life in the Methodist Church and nothing at all of life in my own home and family. This latter is also an obvious, and at times very demanding, area of response to the call, but it does not belong within the confines of this book. However, I record with affectionate gratitude how I have constantly been aware of my family – Francesca and our four children and their children – as a source of enrichment and support without which my response to Christ, such as it has been, would have been far more restricted and ineffectual.

In what distinctive respect, the reader may again ask, can I be said to have been 'travelling along with Methodism'? Would not any church have served as well if I had grown up within it? Perhaps so, but the fact is that I *have* grown up within the Methodist Church; it is this church of my upbringing that has provided a structure of belief, worship and activity for myself and my family. Here the children have been baptised and one of them married; here we have attended Sunday by Sunday. All of us to some degree have been shaped to the pattern of its history, its theology and its worship. What this has meant for me I shall examine more closely in chapter 11.

CHAPTER X

A Presence that Disturbs

MANY TIMES IN THE PRECEDING PAGES I have mentioned experiences in which I have had a profound and powerful sense of a 'presence'. These experiences have come to me on the Yorkshire Moors and similar moorland areas elsewhere – the Pennines, Rannoch, and the far north. In a different setting there was that summer evening as I cycled through Stapleford woods, enclosed in a symphony of sound, scent and colour, and knew that I was not alone. Or there was the nightingale in the bluebell wood singing its triumphant protest against the insanity of a warring world. Or the lizard in Northumberland which sent me harking back to the dinosaurs and conjured involuntarily as from nothing a poem that crystallised thought and feeling. Kelston Round Hill, my place of repeated adolescent pilgrimage, has never failed to evoke the same experience even in later years. And the mountains! Again and again while walking the tops alone amid their grandeur I have felt compelled to kneel in prayerful adoration of a 'presence' whose reality was as near and unmistakable as my hands and feet. These are but a few instances of many.

It is difficult to describe these experiences – indeed of their very nature they evade description; but some elements common to most of them I can pick out and find words for. Most have come through some aspect of the natural world – moors, mountains, the countryside. They have brought a deep sense of affinity with that world – I a part of it and it of me, as if we were bonded together by some inexplicable alchemy. Not that I felt tied to the present; rather there came with this affinity a sense of transcendence, of a beyondness with 'intimations of immortality', of a reality dimly perceived and inviting exploration.

In all of them there has been the sense of a 'presence', a something or someone to which I am reaching out and which beckons me on. But it is not just a 'presence', a vague sense of ambience like some dimly

172

remembered dream. It is a 'presence' that *disturbs*, that jolts me out of the ordinary into an unfamiliar dimension and brings with it, not so much fear (too strong a word), as a restless unease. Yet with this unease has come a sense of assurance, that somewhere within this wild and uncertain world there are support and solace for the having. In later years, and on the mountains especially and beneath the stars, adoration would be an appropriate word – adoration arising from wonder and humility before the spectacle of a universe so magnificent in beauty, so majestic in the forces that move it, so overwhelming in its infinities of space and time. Above all and throughout life a principal ingredient in all these experiences has been a sense of mystery. In childhood and adolescence this was no more than a vague and distant awareness of something strangely puzzling in the way things are. Later the mystery took shape in intellectual problems whose apparent insolubility permeated all enquiry with a haunting mark of interrogation.

It would be easy to dismiss these experiences as some kind of mental aberration or abnormality, or to attribute them to hormonal imbalance or the emotional adjustment of growing up or even to reading too much poetry. This could be so, indeed such might be the necessary means by which they occur; but if it were, it would not, for myself, detract from their significance or their credibility as arising genuinely from my encounter with the world.

And I am encouraged by the fact that many others have had such experiences; indeed they seem to be not uncommon. Different aspects of them – adoration, assurance, mystery – can be found in the Old Testament psalms and in other religious writings. They occur in European literature from the Greeks to the present day. A notable example is Wordsworth's *Tintern Abbey*, whence the title of this chapter is taken:

> And I have felt
> A presence that disturbs me with the joy
> Of elevated thoughts: a sense sublime
> Of something far more deeply interfused . . .

Richard Jefferies, in *The Story of My Heart*, tells how, during periods of mental and spiritual aridity, he would visit a certain hill with a broad and beautiful view and there commune with earth and sun and air. He was moved to prayer; he 'felt an emotion of soul beyond all definition'; the inexpressible beauty of the scene filled him 'with a rapture, an ecstasy, an inflatus'. These are two particular instances with which I am familiar.[1]

---

[1] See also, e.g., Kenneth Grahame, *The Wind in the Willows* (Methuen, 78th impression, 1944), pp. 161ff.

It may also be objected that I have elevated what were simple occurrences of childhood imagination or adolescent romanticism into something altogether more impressive, adding a gloss of words and a complexity of intellectual content quite alien to the original. Of course, as a child or adolescent I could not have described them as I have here; and it may be that I have read into them more than they contained at the time. But I have tried to be faithful to the text, as it were, reading only what was there to be read. Moreover, the experiences have continued lifelong.

I want now to look more closely at the prominent elements in these experiences; I have mentioned them already, but they call for further exploration. Conspicuous among them is the sense of a 'presence'; this embraces the rest and gives them quality and meaning. I do not know how to describe this – or whether I can, for I am treading here on the verge of the inexpressible. In part it is a feeling of not being alone; 'someone else' is sharing with me the beauty of the country scene, the splendour of the starlit sky, the exhilaration of the mountain tops. But it is more than a simple 'presence' or not-aloneness; it is a 'presence' that calls, communicates, has a message; it is a 'presence' that seeks to make itself known. It is a 'presence', therefore, that has the quality of personality; it is personal or supra-personal.

And so I have never, or only for the briefest of periods, been persuaded that the universe is simply a chance agglomeration of particles which has somehow quickened into life, feeling, consciousness and thought. Quite apart from mathematical calculations of probability, such a notion totally contradicts my awareness of that 'presence' which, on occasion, I have felt to accompany and communicate. It has spoken through natural beauty in flowers and trees and landscape, through the songs and flight of birds, through the teeming abundance of life and energy in creatures great and small – even through the monsters now extinct which have left their fossil signatures in the sedimental rocks. It has spoken through the enormity of cosmic forces which have shaped continents and mountains and carved out glens and valleys. Even the rocks and stones I tread have spoken this message, for every one – schist and granite, chalk and sandstone – is a story book, an epitome of history, of unimaginable aeons of metamorphic time. There is surely more in all these than physical and chemical forces responding blindly to pressure and gravity, heat and light. There is a voice that speaks, a message to be heard, a 'presence' to be known.

Had the word been part of my childhood vocabulary, I would have used 'transcendent' to describe the 'presence'. For in some strange way, though very real to me at the time of the experience, it was outside time, outside the present and its confining limitations. It belonged to past, present and future but was beyond all three of them. It was outside space too; it belonged to a different dimension of being where time and space lose meaning and the word 'dimension' itself is inappropriate because it implies measurement of what is essentially immeasurable. So too is 'being', for the being of the 'presence' is so different in kind and quality from the being of humanity that it needs a different word. Though outside and beyond the familiar universe, the 'presence' uses that universe to express itself and make itself known. But because it belongs to a different kind of being, it cannot be known as we know other things; a different kind of reality requires a different kind of knowing. Essentially it is beyond human understanding, beyond the measures of man's mind; yet we can have an awareness of it by intuition, insight, enlightenment in the quiet of contemplation or in other silent and solitary moments.

Once again I may be thought guilty of exaggeration, enlarging the bare actuality of my experiences by introducing the perspective of later years. Of course, I could not have written the preceding paragraph when I was a child; concepts and language were both lacking. But I am confident that hitherto and in what follows I have done no more than honestly search out and expose what was indeed latent in those childhood and later experiences, neither exaggerating nor embroidering but *interpreting*.

But why 'disturb'? Why the unease that accompanies the 'presence'? The unease itself does not fit readily into words and is better intimated by analogy. It is like the odd feeling you sometimes have on entering a room that, unexpectedly, someone is already there. Perhaps there was a slight sound or some trick of light and shade suggesting a human shape. You don't know who it might be or precisely where; but someone is there; you are sure of it and you feel unsettled, insecure. Sometimes, when walking on the mountains in mist, I have misread the map or misgauged the contours or the orientation and found myself looking down into a glen which shouldn't be there! There comes a momentary feeling of chill anxiety – where am I? Can I get back to where I should be, and how? Then, with the assurance of map and compass now correctly read, I change course and continue in confidence. But unlike the latter experience my awareness of the 'presence' is not a mistake to be corrected; the point of the analogy is my sudden sense of unfamiliarity, of not recognising my whereabouts, and the attendant feelings of disquiet and uncertainty.

But these analogies capture only part of the unease – uncertainty, insecurity, unfamiliarity, loss of bearing; it has other and more important components, and again analogy will help to explain. One of them is a sense of mystery; I have mentioned this briefly above and I shall have much more to say of it later. The 'presence' belongs to a different world, a different mode of experiencing; it speaks an unfamiliar language; it cannot be understood because, inexplicably, it is beyond understanding. It is mysterious, and mystery is always unsettling until its secrets are unveiled, its code broken. But the code of the 'presence' cannot be broken; it remains mysterious. Here is a world in which one is a stranger; one is unsure how to deal with it, how to conduct oneself; yet one is a welcome stranger not a trespasser. Such to me is the world of computers, because I have not been trained to understand and use them; but computers one can master and control, the 'presence' one cannot. When walking the hills in mist one tries unavailingly to peer beyond its restrictive curtain; one knows there are crags on this side or that, but one cannot see them; there is no path and, despite map and compass, the way ahead is unclear. And so one probes beyond the boundaries of sense; but the mist is unrelenting and shrouds the hills in an impenetrable mantle.

Awe and wonder are also part of the unease. For one is in the company of a power vastly greater than oneself which by its sheer magnitude overawes and induces a sense of feebleness and inadequacy. And what other response than wonder could there be when one is confronted with a power that manifests itself at one extreme in the unimaginable reach of stars and galaxies and at the other in the simple beauty of tiny flowers and insects? Simple? – Yes, but only until one looks more deeply into the bewildering complexity of their chemistry and structure. Finally, the 'presence' impresses me with an uneasy sense of my imperfection, my inadequacy, my incompleteness; I feel diminished. Occasionally I have found myself in the presence of a man or woman of such perspicuous goodness that 'my genius is rebuked' (as Macbeth, in very different circumstances, said of Banquo's 'royalty of nature'); I feel ashamed of my moral paucity and impoverishment. So the perfection of the 'presence' heightens into oppressive contrast the darkness of my imperfection and I am 'rebuked'.

Awe and wonder lead to adoration. This is defined in the Shorter Oxford Dictionary as making 'an act of the mind and will in acknowledgement of the infinite perfection of (God)' – presumably one may insert other objects of adoration within the brackets, such as the 'presence'. For me it has not been so much a willed act as an involuntary, irresistible response to the scene about me. Again, though I would agree with 'infinite', adoration acknowledges more than 'perfection', unless that is taken to include all other attributes at their highest degree of possibility. What compels me to fall on my knees and pray on the mountain tops is the grandeur, the majesty, the manifestation of power and beauty, the age-long shaping of crags and corries, the evolution of the cheerful little flowers that sparsely dwell among them – and amidst all this myself, a tiny speck of consciousness abased to insignificance. The psalmists were familiar with this experience; they sang of a Lord who created the heavens, the sun and moon, mountains and ocean depths and all the world's teeming life. They too were compelled to adore.

I have written of 'unease' attending awareness of the 'presence', a sense of uncertainty, insecurity, loss of bearing. It is akin to fear, edging up to it but not quite of it, a kind of nervous thrill. For unlike fear, the unease of the 'presence' brings with it a strange and warming assurance, like a gleam of sun through clouds or a rainbow shining through a shower. Whence it comes or why I cannot say – unless indeed it is that such is the nature of the 'presence' and inseparable from its message. When I have been lost in the mist on the hills, there has come, after the first surge of anxiety, a confidence that map and compass and the strength of my legs will set me right. The assurance of the 'presence' comes not from conscious knowledge but from latent depths within one's undiscovered self. It is the seed of what can later mature into an acknowledged faith in benign purpose within the universe. Such it became for the psalmists: their long experience of the Lord confirmed a faith in his protecting care which they expressed in a variety of persuasive images; the good shepherd of Psalm 23 is the best known among many.

Such then is my experience of the 'presence' – not the whole of it, for there are gaps to be filled and, as we shall see, their filling partly resolves, partly extends and deepens the mystery. What I have called the 'presence' others perhaps would call the 'numinous'. This is the word which Rudolph Otto coined in *The Idea of the Holy* for the object of the kind of experience I have tried to describe – a mysterious, transcendent being of which we have a non-rational, wonder-invoking, uneasy yet comforting awareness. Others might call it simply God, a divine 'presence'; this is my own inclination, and henceforth I shall omit the inverted commas and use a capital P.

Except during periods of adolescent rebellion and once in later life my experience of the Presence has made it easy for me to believe in God as he is traditionally understood. In this I have been very fortunate. Adolescence is commonly a time when adult norms and beliefs are questioned and rejected. So there is nothing specially odd in the defiant scepticism which my headmaster at Kingswood resisted by pointing to the opening words of St Mark. Far more surprising is the sudden wave of unbelief which overcame me when I read chapter six of A. J. Ayer's *Language, Truth and Logic*, 'Critique of Ethics and Theology'; for this was after I had been a committed Christian for over twenty years and a lay preacher for ten or more. Here in half a dozen pages of superficially cogent argument he rejects the reality of God and the possibility of religious knowledge. The existence of God, he argues, is both unnecessary and meaningless, and in attempting to describe him we are inevitably talking nonsense, or at best disclosing the state of our own minds.

His conclusions derive from a particular theory of language and meaning known as logical positivism. There is no point in trying to summarise it here; suffice it to say that, granted his initial premises, his arguments are indeed persuasive; at the time their outcome seemed to me inevitable. However, it did not take me long to recognise that the positivist account of language within the totality of human experience is unduly restricted and its conclusions therefore flawed. I quickly recovered from the shock of my relapse and since then have never doubted the existence of God. Professor Ayer would himself be surprised, I think, if he could know that I was so taken in by the narrow, ebullient dogmatism of his premises. Indeed in the second edition of his book he admits that it was written with a passion unusual in a philosopher and that the questions it deals with are not as simple as he makes them appear!

Although my experience of the Presence has eased the way towards belief in God, nevertheless, like other Christians, I have been attracted by the possibility of proving his existence. From time to time I have read with eager urgency expositions of the traditional 'proofs' in the hope of finding there a certainty which so far had eluded me. I seemed to need this certainty; and if God really *is* there, I thought, it *must* be possible to demonstrate it by rational argument. I believe now that the attempt is futile, and for a number of reasons.

First, I question whether 'the existence of God' can have genuine significance. This is a linguistic problem: the phrase is using human words to express what is essentially beyond the scope of human thought, conception and language. 'Existence' is not, I believe, applicable to God; we use it of him because, being human, we have no alternative; but he does not 'exist' as we exist in a universe of space, time and causal sequence. The being of God is such that we cannot comprehend it within human thought and language; even the word 'being', because it is part of a human fabric of language, misrepresents him. Words cannot express the inexpressible; 'Does God exist?' is not therefore a meaningful question.

Akin to this is a second reason. Not only cannot God be comprehended within human language; he is also greater than rational proof, greater (as I have said of the Presence) than 'the measures of man's mind'. By demanding logical proof of God's existence we are guilty, therefore, both of linguistic fallacy *and* of theological error. If God were the kind of God whose being (whatever that may mean) could be demonstrated by reasoned argument, I could not believe in him; he would be too small a God for me.

Then third, what is this certainty that I have sought, and is it necessary or desirable? Certainty is of different kinds. There is the certainty of logical or mathematical demonstration: if one argues correctly from particular premises, obeying the rules of deduction, one arrives at conclusions which are demonstrably certain. But the certainty is illusory; it depends on the premises from which the conclusions are argued, and these are man-made, contrived; they could be otherwise and are themselves, therefore, flawed by *un*certainty.

It is often supposed that science can provide us with certainty. We demand 'scientific proof' that such or such is the case; in its absence we withhold assent, but if the scientist says so, we are willing to believe. This too is an illusion. Scientific conclusions, or 'facts' as they are popularly described, are no more than probabilities derived from observation and experiment; these probabilities are based on the assumption of a uniformity in nature which ensures that what has been regularly observed in the past is likely, in the same circumstances, to be observed in the future. A scientific 'fact' is an inference or judgement which has not yet been shown to be false but which is in principle falsifiable because past observation does not guarantee what may be observed in the future – like the well-known example of swans, which were assumed only to be white until black swans were observed in Australia. The uniformity of nature which science assumes is no more demonstrable than the conclusions based on it; it is indeed an act of faith.

There are also psychological and emotive certainties. An example of the former is Descartes' *cogito ergo sum* – 'I think, therefore I am'. Spurred on by the quest for certainty, a starting-point for philosophy immune from all doubt, he found it in this seemingly undeniable truth: however hard he tried to think of everything as false, he could not escape the awareness of himself as thinking and therefore as real. From this, to him, indubitable experience of self-awareness Descartes proceeds to argue the existence of God; and in God's perfection of character he finds justification for accepting as genuine our belief in an external world.

We cannot follow him through his various arguments, but what must be said is that his *cogito* lacks the cogency he was seeking. It can be agreed that in this elemental fact of consciousness of ourselves and our environment we come as near as may be to finding a point of certainty in human experience; at the very least it implies that *something* exists or that there *is* existence (though what these expressions can mean is far from obvious). More difficult to defend is his adding to this elemental certainty the particularisation of 'I'; for the nature of self-consciousness and the differentiation of one self from other selves is obscure – indeed it is part of that all-embracing mystery of which I have already written and to which I shall return. Whatever certainty the *cogito* possesses is not logical, as Descartes thought, but psychological; it depends on intuition, a simple act of mental vision which is persuasively self-corroborating.

Psychological certainty, merging often into an emotional assurance, abounds in religious utterance. The Psalms are full of it: 'The Lord is my shepherd; I shall not want'. John Wesley's account of the strange warming of his heart is an eminent example: 'an assurance was given me that He had taken away *my* sins, even *mine*, and saved *me* from the law of sin and death'. Poetry too is full of it: so Keats:

> Beauty is truth, truth beauty – that is all
> Ye know on earth and all ye need to know.

Certainty of this kind can be of enormous value in human life, inducing effort and sacrifice which would otherwise be inconceivable; but it is often superficial and transitory (like knowing one is in love), sometimes even dangerous (like the assurance of an uninformed conscience).

Certainty, whether intellectual or psychological, is not what the Christian should be seeking; indeed the quest for certainty, it seems to me, is self-defeating. For if, supposedly, one finds it, one is thereby putting chains on God and restricting one's understanding of him. God is infinite; he cannot be thus constrained and delimited. Our search for him is an adventure of exploration whose joy and justification are diminished by imposing a terminal certainty. It is like closing a door on abundance of opportunity; it reduces God to the status of a machine – if you press the right button, you get a predictable response; it impairs the delicate, tentative intimacy of our relationship with him. (This is not to say that God is totally unpredictable; we can be assured that he loves and will love us; what we cannot predict, and often find difficult to understand, are the means and manifestation of his loving.)

Not certainty but assurance should be the Christian's objective. I have written earlier of an assurance which has accompanied my uneasy, disturbing awareness of the Presence – a confidence that amid chance and change there are permanence and reliability for the finding, support and comfort for the asking. In childhood and adolescence this assurance, though (I believe) divinely given, was pre- or sub-Christian. There is a deeper assurance which comes from an initial act of faith in and commitment to God's revelation of himself in Christ. From faith and commitment corroborated by experience there grows a profound assurance of God's reality, love and trustworthiness. We do not understand first and then believe (indeed the very nature of God precludes it); we believe in order to understand – Tertullian's *credo ut intellegam.*

Assurance is not certainty; it is a deep, powerful underflow of confidence in the reality and nature of God and his dealings with us. Such confidence, as I have said, is the rich product of faith and experience; it is confirmed and validated by many an intuitive insight when, for a moment, the curtain is drawn and briefly we glimpse into the mystery of the Presence. Such insights come unpredictably – through nature, through events, through people, in prayer and meditation, in Bible reading, in conversation, in the benison of silence and in a host of other ways. Some of mine I have described in earlier pages.

Intellectual 'proof' of God's existence may assist and reinforce the assurance which comes from faith, experience and intuitive insight, but of itself it is not enough to compel belief; it leaves one peering round a door still tantalisingly only ajar. And so, *pace* Aquinas and other great theologians who have sought this way of persuasion, I do not attribute much importance to the traditional arguments and I do not propose to rehearse them here – they can be found in almost any introductory textbook of theology. The most eloquent exposition – and rejection – of them that I know is in Kant's *Critique of Pure Reason.*[1] The idea of a Supreme Being, he concludes, is the crowning perfection of speculative reason:

> it is neither logically absurd nor theoretically empty; and it prepares the ground for an act of faith; but it cannot be proved or disproved by pure reason.

Its only possible foundation, he asserts, is in 'the laws of morality' – a theme which he develops in his *Critique of Practical Reason.*

For me, the most convincing arguments for God's existence have been my experience of the Presence and the fact of Jesus Christ; but these have not been without intellectual support. The universe, in so far as human minds can apprehend it, is not self-explanatory; it poses questions as to its origin and evolution. Now it may be that these questions are illusory; perhaps it is a quirk of our humanity to demand explanation where none is necessary. Nevertheless, the absence of explanation leaves a sense of unease, of dissatisfaction; at the very least there is something puzzling here, an intolerable intellectual hiatus which drives one on to seek a

[1] Transcendental Dialectic Book II, ch. 3, 'The Ideal of Pure Reason' (Everyman ed., pp. 334ff.); the eloquence is unimpaired by translation.

solution. Of course, this is only a starting-point; it has no positive content; but it justifies the search and gives hope of an answer.

Positive support for belief in God comes to me from two sources. The first has some resemblance to the traditional 'argument from design'. This goes back to the Stoics of the ancient world and is offered by Cicero as the most cogent of four arguments for God's existence. In modern times it is often presented *via* William Paley's analogy of watch and watch-maker[1]: a watch exhibits design and purpose; so too does the universe; therefore, just as a watch must have a maker, so must the universe. In Cicero's words[2]:

> When one sees the orderly, disciplined, schematic nature of the universe, one cannot accept that it has no cause; rather, one concludes that there is someone who presides over it and commands its obedience.

My own inclination does not take me as far as this. To attribute *purpose* to the universe as we experience it is to strain the evidence; but *design*, in the sense of orderly pattern or configuration, is among its undeniable features right through the scale of existence from atoms to galaxies. The universe is a cosmos (the Greek word for order, pattern); and this poses a problem. Design in this sense is not self-explanatory; chaos does not automatically organise itself into cosmos; the latter must have some origin, and it is a reasonable assumption that this origin comprises constructive intelligence.

More persuasive than this is the second source – which is not, so far as I know, commonly offered as an argument. It is characteristic of all living things, from the simplest to the most complex, to adapt to their environment. Examples are so numerous that they need hardly be cited: bacteria respond to the use of antibiotics by developing immune strains; human beings respond to climate, geography and other natural phenomena by developing appropriate skills. But men and women are capable of much more than such simple response under pressure of need; they pray and worship, they found religions, they compose theologies; their response is *spiritual* as well as intellectual and practical. How could this be if there were nothing in their universal environment to evoke it? Such response is not self-explanatory. Again there is a problem which leads, like the previous, to a reasonable assumption, that the universe embodies a spiritual Presence.

These are not proofs of a kind that might convince a logician or a scientist (whose proven conclusions fall short, as I have tried to show, of

---

[1] *Natural Theology* (1802).   [2] *De Natura Deorum* II, 13-15.

final certainty). Rather, they are promptings, suggestions, 'intimations' (to borrow again from Wordsworth); they are like guideposts which indicate at least a possibility of access; or like cairns in a mountain mist which give assurance of a goal which, though invisible, nevertheless exists and is achievable. Though inconclusive, they are strongly persuasive; they ease the way to faith and confirm it once attained. What they do *not* do is give more than a partial indication of the nature of the God to whom they point: a constructive, intelligent designer, who evokes in men and women an awareness of his presence accompanied by awe, wonder and a sense of mystery. This takes us far but not far enough; it says nothing of ethical significance or of the relationship of such a God with ourselves. For this we must look to the other of my convincing arguments for his existence, the fact of Jesus Christ. But I shall not enlarge on this now, for I want to consider it within a broader context, that all-embracing mystery to which I have many times referred.

Mystery is an element in the 'disturbance' which has accompanied my awareness of the Presence. But it is not confined to these infrequent encounters; it permeates all experience; it is a fact of life, and the older I become, the more powerfully it impresses me. I ask myself, why is there anything at all? And why am I *this* spark of consciousness here and now instead of someone else, somewhere else, at some other time? And what is this self, this 'I'? What makes it 'I' and not 'he' or 'she' or the cat on the hearthrug? Edwin Muir asks similar questions in his autobiography: 'Our minds are possessed by three mysteries: where we came from, where we are going, and . . . how we should live with one another'. A *Guardian* article also points to the mystery of existence and draws a moral from it: '. . . the sheer oddity of the fact that anything or anyone exists. This goes back to Parmenides, and is important because it makes one suspicious of authoritative pronouncements about the nature of the universe and therefore tolerant before ultimate mystery'. And another article: 'It has always been a mystery how the blind conjunction of random forces has produced a world that appears so coherent and innovative'.[1]

Such questionings and perplexities are the seeds of philosophy. Parmenides was among the most eminent of the Greek thinkers who sought answers to them, and one of many through the history of philosophy who have made the attempt. But the mystery remains. For instance, J. S. Mill in his examination of human consciousness found himself 'face to face with that final inexplicability at which . . . we

---

[1] Edwin Muir, *An Autobiography* (Hogarth Press, 1987 ed., p. 56); David Dulley, 'Face to Faith', *The Guardian*, 14/12/87; *ib.*, 23/10/87, an article based on a book by Professor Paul Davies, *The Cosmic Blueprint* (Heinemann, 1987).

inevitably arrive when we reach ultimate facts'. He does not use the word 'mystery' here, though it is implied; but in his posthumously published essay 'Utility of Religion' he writes thus:

> Human existence is girt round with mystery: the narrow region of our experience is a small island in the midst of a boundless sea, which at once awes our feelings and stimulates our imagination by its vastness and its obscurity.[1]

Mill was a lifelong agnostic of unquestionable integrity, and here we have a frank admission of the baffling inscrutability which frustrates our probing intellects.

There is indeed in human experience a haunting, pervasive mark of interrogation which continually retreats before the advance of our knowledge. At the heart of things is an enigma that thwarts intellectual penetration but lures us tantalisingly towards that ever-receding horizon of 'final inexplicability'. It is both *tremendum* and *fascinans*; it disturbs, yet draws us on – like the fascination that impels one with nerves tingling to peer over the edge of a precipice. There is no escape from this mystery, not even in religion which, in Christianity, as we shall see, presents us with the greatest mystery of all.

Two aspects of the mystery are especially perplexing: the problem of evil, and the fact of death. Their prominence requires for them some consideration, but it must be brief, for there is nothing new and little, I doubt, helpful that I can add to the volumes already written about them. The problem of evil is not peculiar either to Christianity in particular or to religion generally. It is common to humanity, and most mythologies have some form of answer to it – Eve and the apple, Pandora and her box are familiar examples. That mankind is subject to a multitude of afflictions is obvious enough: disease, accident, war, terrorism and natural calamity destroy life and potential, cause unimaginable pain and grief, and interrupt the expected normality of contented activity. Poverty, injustice and man's inhumanity to man increase the toll of suffering until some are driven to self-extinction or to exclaim with Job, 'Why did I not perish at birth and die as I came from the womb?'.

It is sometimes argued that evil in its various forms is all due to human folly and wickedness or to some mythological 'fall of man' whereby the original goodness of human nature was corrupted and inclined towards evil. Much of it is indeed due to the former and could be avoided if we showed greater care for ourselves, for each other and for our environment. But much of it is not. A great deal of suffering is due to

---

[1] *Collected Works* (Toronto University) vol. IX, p. 194; vol. X, p. 418.

forces of nature beyond our control, such as storm, flood, drought and volcanic eruption; we can sometimes mitigate their impact, but only too often they are unpredictable, unavoidable and their consequences disastrous. In all likelihood there will be another Ice Age; alternatively the polar icecaps may melt and raise the level of the sea; in either case there would be a restriction of the earth's habitable area and great potential for conflict. There is no doubt that the earth, the moon and some of their neighbours in the solar system have been struck by large meteors whose impact was awesome and devastating; it could happen again. We live in a universe whose forces are apparently random and careless of living things. How can this be in a world created and presided over, as Christians believe, by a loving God? 'If the maker of the world *can* all he will,' wrote J. S. Mill, 'he wills misery, and there is no escape from the conclusion.'[1]

It is not only that the forces of nature seem random and careless of humanity, whose history is so tiny and seemingly fortuitous an episode in the vast chronicle of the universe; they are also, by human standards, inefficient. The universe as we experience it is characterised by a kind of irrational extravagance. There are thousands of galaxies and millions of stars, including our sun with its nine planets. Apart from the earth none of these countless millions supports life of any kind – so far as we know; most of them we know for certain cannot. During the process of evolution the earth was roamed by dinosaurs for 150 million years. Such small brains in such huge bodies were, to say the least, an uneconomic use of divine ingenuity and resource; but what was God himself doing through all those ages of time? – just watching them play at their savagery until, almost at a stroke and for reasons still obscure, they perished? Again, consider the extravagance of biological nature – the thousands of foxglove seeds of which only a few dozen germinate, or the enormous waste of human sperm in securing a single conception. Life itself cannot be maintained without destroying life; we must kill to eat – even vegetarians, for seeds and plants have life or its potential.

All this suggests an incompetence which, despite the many manifestations of intelligent design, mar the workmanship of the universe; it offends both moral and aesthetic sense and casts doubt on God's wisdom and benevolence. If I were God, I have sometimes irreverently thought, I would have made a better job of it!

What then is the answer to the problem – or problems, for there is more than one? I have none that satisfies the intellect. It is easy to make the trite response that good comes out of evil, that the latter is somehow

---

[1] *Collected Works* (Toronto University) vol. X, p. 388.

instrumental in producing the former, whether in character, invention or advance of knowledge. This is true; but it is no less true that evil and suffering can debase and destroy our humanity. In any case, why might not good be generated by means more kindly, more consistent with a loving God? And why is human suffering so widely disproportionate in its incidence, so that some have an overwhelming burden and others almost none? Moral evil – cruelty, injustice, etc. – is perhaps explicable (if that is the right word) in relation to free will: God gave us this and expects us to use it wisely; without it we would be automata, less than human. But why did he also give us so many proclivities to wrong-doing and so many circumstances in which it might flourish? Why not rational beings innocent of sin and either without passions or with adequate self-control? Such would be a world less interesting than ours perhaps, and lacking in great literature. But this apart, the questions have no answer.

The problem of evil is not the kind of problem that admits of intellectual solution. Its questions have no answers *except* in yielding to its mystery and accepting in faith the world as' God has made it, flawed though it may seem to us. To explain God's ways is beyond our finite understanding; here scientific knowledge exceeds its depth. But faith in what? – in the love and wisdom and power of God. This is indeed an act, or rather a continuing disposition, of faith; and it is not easy. God has made it easier by showing us in Jesus that he identifies with our suffering; incomprehensibly our suffering is his and he is diminished by it. Moral evil he cannot identify with; but this too, incomprehensibly, he takes upon himself and it is lost in the infinity of his purity.

The second aspect of mystery that I find especially puzzling is death. Why especially? – because it seems an unnecessary intrusion into the process of living. Of course, our bodies age and decline; but God could have made them different, and why he did not is a related mystery. As it is, death is built into life; when it comes, it curtails the possibility of our growth as persons; it imposes an incompletion which, like the cruelty and extravagance of nature, is morally and aesthetically distasteful; it is an affront upon the integrity of selfhood, compelling surrender, so it would seem, to a final annihilation. Moreover, death withholds from us tantalisingly the answers to our persistent questionings about the universe – or does it? It might indeed be the door through which we must pass to find them. Here again is mystery – the end of the search or a new beginning? *Know* we cannot, for here again we must abandon knowledge and enter the domain of faith.

For myself, faith persuades that death is not the end, and this for three reasons: God's love, God's justice, and man's *telos* or fulfilment. The love of God forbids the annihilation of persons it embraces; they are eternally a part of him and recognisable as what they are and have been (this is what I understand by the resurrection of the body). God's justice requires that the imbalances of this life – poverty, handicap, suffering, premature death – be redressed in another. It also requires that wickedness in this life be 'punished' hereafter by a remedial purification; for moral evil – evil of any kind – is incompatible with God's nature; it is negative, a non-being, and unacceptable to him; and because God is everything, it must be purged away. Finally, death leaves unachieved the fulfilment of men and women, the *telos* or goal of complete goodness for which they were designed and created; reason itself, let alone God's love, demands a further stage of growth. Moreover, I believe that the grace of God extends to all and that none will ultimately be lost from his presence. Here indeed is mystery, haunting me with wonder, hope and anticipation – like one of Virgil's ghosts with arms outstretched in yearning for that further shore.

It should be no surprise that finite minds cannot comprehend the infinite. The way we see the world, what we see and how much of it, is conditioned and structured by the nature of those minds and of the sense-perception that informs them. Our picture of the world is a product of sensation, reason and imagination; if these were different, our world would be different, and it is restricted by their limitations. If we could break the bounds of our finitude and know what lies beyond,

> who would not desire this more ardently than any other conceivable knowledge, so long as there appeared the slightest hope of attaining it? What would one not give for any credible tidings from that mysterious region, any glimpse into it which might enable us to see the smallest light through its darkness. . . . ?[1]

Despite its yearning for tidiness of explanation, the questing intellect is confronted by ultimate mystery; there is no final certainty. This must disappoint those who, like Mill, seek nothing less; but *un*certainty enhances the excitement of the quest and makes of it an adventure of exploration, a pilgrimage of faith whose direction is clear but not its goal. Moreover, there *is* hope; the mystery is *not* wholly opaque; there do indeed come moments of illumination, of revelation, when the veil of obscurity is partially drawn and one sees briefly, dimly, but with overpowering conviction, into a reality beyond. Such moments are more accessible than is commonly supposed, and they would be more frequent if our attitude were expectant and receptive. When they come, they are compulsive; they bring an intense focusing of inner awareness which

---

[1] J. S. Mill, 'Utility of Religion', *Collected Works* (Toronto University) vol. X, p. 419.

transiently assembles into a unison of meaning the jigsaw of misfits which is our normal experience of the world.

I have mentioned earlier such occasions in my own life, moments of insight and clarification when I have caught a glimpse of the infinite and said to myself, 'Yes, that's what it's all about'. To me the Presence has spoken especially through nature, but its means of disclosure are as various as the diversity of human experience.

It speaks through human goodness – like the woman in Songs of Praise whom I wrote of above, or the Mother Teresas of this world (men and women) who give themselves to others in utter disregard of their own safety and well-being. It speaks through personal relationships wherein occasionally, in mutual joy, grief or understanding, one is aware of a subtle alchemy of inter-feeling which eludes verbal expression and extends one's vision into the beyond. It speaks through sexual intercourse – not the casual fulfilment of urgent desire, but a loving, sensitive merging of life-giving energies which shares momentarily the divine ecstasy in creation. It speaks through beauty, both natural and man-made, in line and colour, form, pattern and design; for God is surely a supreme artist who delights in his artefacts, and this delight is ours too in aesthetic enjoyment. It speaks through craftsmanship; for here, in the making of artefacts, however simple, we hold and are held by the creative hand of God. And so I could go on, for God's self-disclosure is manifold and unpredictable; he manifests himself not least in the commonplace things and events of daily life, transforming them unexpectedly into sacramental expressions of his transcendence.

These occasions of insight, which momentarily sweep aside the limitations of reason and sense-perception, come to most of us spontaneously, not from any conscious effort or expectancy. They seem rather to be a bursting *from the other side* of the barriers of concealment, an effort of communication 'from beyond', an attempt to 'get through' to us. For some they do arise from a deliberate discipline whose practice promotes a conducive state of consciousness. Such is the quest of men and women in religious orders who, by submitting themselves to a routine of worship, prayer and fasting, prepare themselves for a divine influx. And there are those rare individuals whose gift of mystical vision permits a ready interflow of communication with the Presence. To all of us they are accessible, and they would come, and come more often, if we practised a receptive state of relaxation and peace of mind. But faith too is needed, a confidence that there is indeed a Presence that speaks and a message to be heard. For faith, as the Letter to the Hebrews puts it, 'gives substance to our hopes and assures us of realities we do not see'.

My experiences of the Presence and the intellectual arguments from design and response to environment say little of his nature: what kind of Presence is he? What character? Intelligent – yes; constructive – yes; an artist in design and creation – yes; mysterious and awe-invoking – yes; but what else? And so mystery remains. This brings us to the most baffling component of that mystery, which at the same time, paradoxically, offers us the clearest and profoundest penetration of its obscurity.

Christians believe that God, the divine Presence, embodied himself uniquely in Jesus Christ. This is the Incarnation, and it is itself a mystery; as Charles Wesley puts it in his Christmas hymn: 'Our God contracted to a span, *incomprehensibly* made man' (my emphasis). Why should the infinite reduce himself to finite form and cumber himself with the limitations of humanity? We can only grope for an answer. Part of it lies in the familiar words, 'God so loved'; because he loves and cares, he must reach out to us. Moreover, because he is in some strange way personal, he needs persons with whom to share his love – he wants not only to love but to be loved; he must therefore reveal himself in a manner which is personal and accessible to finite human beings. Jesus is thus both a logical and a theological necessity: the nature of the divine Presence is such that it *requires* the Incarnation; without it God would not be the kind of God he is.

The Incarnation of Jesus includes and entails the Crucifixion and Resurrection; all three together give us a picture of God which would have been inaccessible without them. They reveal him essentially as a God who loves and cares. It is part of Christian doctrine that he is also all-knowing and all-powerful – which, as we have seen, raises problems about the abundance of evil and suffering in the world. But central and fundamental to his nature, as Jesus reveals it, is his love. This revelation does not totally dispel the mystery, but it opens a chink in the baffling curtain of otherwise ultimate inexplicability and gives us a glimpse of a reality beyond.

Jesus is one aspect of the Presence – indeed he *is* the Presence in a mode of self-disclosure which speaks simply and clearly in terms that all can understand. Yet, like the Presence, he is mysterious; and, like the Presence, he disturbs. Of the mystery of Christ I have said enough; in the final count it is ineffable; it leaves one speechless. But why and how does he disturb? The Incarnation itself is enough to cause unease, but there is more to be said. The fact is that one cannot live easily with Christ; when he enters life's equation he brings a reversal of values which, together with his own immaculate goodness, makes one profoundly conscious of one's imperfection; he is a moral sensitiser who speaks to us from the other side of evil and shames and challenges us by his example.

Moreover, despite his humanity and his sharing of human limitations and afflictions, despite the comforting intimacy of his companionship for those who seek it, he is nevertheless God 'incomprehensibly made man'. He therefore bears an enigmatic quality of otherness, as coming from an unfamiliar dimension in which we cannot find a bearing (like those rare occasions in the Scottish hills when magnetic rocks make the compass unusable). The disciples were clearly sensitive to this, as were others who knew him closely during his earthly life.

But because Christ is God, the Presence, he not only disturbs but assures. He assures us of a reality whose core is love; a reality which strengthens us to meet his moral challenge; a reality which is utterly trustworthy and which gives us confidence to face life's afflictions and death's apparent ultimatum.

The title of Part II, 'Through a Glass Darkly', and of the present chapter, 'A Presence that Disturbs', are suggestive of mystery. Intentionally so, of course, and I have tried to show that we are involved in a reality whose inscrutability baffles our enquiry. It is breached only by occasional moments of illumination and, more profoundly and lastingly, by the Incarnation and the events which followed. In these latter we are offered a momentous revelation of God's nature; an indeterminate 'presence' becomes a Presence who loves and cares. Yet even they are veiled in mystery – God *incomprehensibly* born, crucified and risen. We cannot escape from 'final inexplicability'.

I have now to ask again how the Methodist ambience of my upbringing and church membership affected my experience of the 'presence', of the Presence, and of the Christ in whom the Presence is disclosed. This will be the principal subject of the next chapter, but I can anticipate briefly here. Whatever church I had been brought up in, or none at all, I would still have enjoyed those rare moments of illumination; they have been part of my make-up, an abnormality perhaps, but welcome and enriching. I have no doubt too that I would have arrived at a firm belief in God, though what kind of God is open to question. The difference has been in my approach to his Presence and to the Jesus who embodies him. For Methodism, though it shares with other denominations a vast area of Christian experience and doctrine, has its own characteristic modes of approach and expression which bestow peculiar and distinctive blessings. These I shall now proceed to explore.

CHAPTER XI

The Peculiar Blessings of Methodism

I HAVE WRITTEN BRIEFLY IN EARLIER CHAPTERS of the impact of Methodism on my growing up; and in chapter 8 I have picked out for particular comment (not all of it wholly favourable) certain aspects of Methodism which have influenced me deeply and some of which, for myself at least, are central to its significance. In the present chapter I want to expand on this and to describe in greater detail the blessings which my growth in Methodism has enjoyed, blessings which, on due and deep reflection, seem to me to be of the essence of the Methodist proclamation of the Gospel. I must emphasise that what follows is a personal statement; others, with a different experience of Methodism, may not agree. It is not a historical statement culled from libraries – though I have sought to confirm and elucidate my experience by reading in the history and theology of Methodism.

Perhaps I should also explain the meaning of 'peculiar' in the chapter's title. It does not, of course, mean 'funny' or 'odd' (though some readers may perhaps choose to understand it so); it means belonging especially and characteristically to Methodism, a distinctive gift or bounty which the Methodist Church offers to those who, like me, grow up within its embrace.

Yet I would not for a moment claim that these blessings are available only and exclusively within Methodism. Some, if not all, are offered by other denominations; and these have peculiar blessings of their own from which Methodists can learn and draw enrichment. But the blessings I shall now describe stand out *for me* as high peaks of meaning and emphasis, focuses of spiritual experience in my journey with Methodism.

Among my most pervasive and persistent impressions of Methodism is the welcoming warmth of its chapels. No doubt memory has graciously erased those occasions when the heating failed in midwinter and we shivered in our overcoats until the final amen. But such were few;

predominantly my impression is of a comfortable warmth enhanced by the pitch-pine of the pews and by the internal structure of the seating which, like a theatre in the round, wove us together from floor to gallery in a single, central focus of attention. (Modern Methodist chapels, with their plastic and metal seats and different internal orientation, have lost in atmosphere what they have gained in mobility and saved in expense.) It was the same in all the many chapels of my father's ministry; their furnishing and structure were more or less identical and in all I found the same atmosphere of receptive warmth. By contrast, my impression of Anglican churches has been, and to some extent remains, one of chill austerity exuding from frigid stone, pillared aisles and distant altar. This I now know to be a distorted image; the typical Anglican church has its own atmosphere of sanctity which contributes no less, but differently, to spiritual elevation.

Warmth literal is not easily disengaged from warmth metaphorical. By the latter I mean the cordial hand of welcome, the spirit of close and friendly fellowship not only in formal worship but in the many weekday activities – bazaars, concerts, class meetings, prayer meetings and the rest which compose the Methodist calendar of events. This too has been the same in different congregations, whether predominantly miners, farmers, fishermen or tradesmen – the same cordiality, the same warmth of welcome. No doubt some of this impression is the product of nostalgic reminiscence, a blending of rosy retrospects which distorts the reality; some of it comes from my habit of snuggling up to my mother and her furs as I sat beside her in the pew, wrapping myself thus in a protective cocoon of warm security. It may even seem trivial, or at best superficial, compared with the deeper experiences of the spiritual life. Moreover, Methodism is not innocent of dissension; there has been bitter disagreement on various issues within my father's congregations. Nevertheless, I hold to my impression and to my conviction that there is in Methodism, both its chapels and its people, a characteristic warmth, cordiality and open-hearted receptiveness which fortifies its spiritual impact and appeal.

I move on now to a blessing which is central to the Methodist tradition and of the deepest spiritual significance, a blessing which no one growing up within Methodism as I have could fail to absorb and to acknowledge with profound gratitude. It is simply this, that I have direct access to God in Jesus Christ and a personal relationship with him. For this I need no intermediary, whether liturgy, priest, robes, candles or any other symbolism. The priest or minister is an essential part of the Methodist as of any other Church; he or she is valuable as guide, comforter, interpreter and mediator; ritual and symbols have value in enlightening the darkness of mystery. But the essence of religion, its very heart and core, is my personal relationship with God incarnate in Jesus Christ, who is presented to us in the Gospels and who still lives and moves among us. The Gospels are the incredible story of God coming near to us in Jesus – incredible not least because this Jesus, who is both human and divine, both man and God, calls *me by name*, speaks to *me*, offers *me* his gifts of forgiveness and a new life through the creative power of his Spirit. And the wonder of it is that these gifts are freely available, on the one and only condition that I have faith in their availability and am willing to accept Jesus as my Saviour and Lord.

Methodism has been dubbed a 'come to Jesus religion' – sometimes with a hint of sarcasm in those who misinterpret its meaning. But there is truth in it, and the truth is this, that Jesus invites each of us as an individual into a direct personal relationship with himself; for each of us it is a personal choice whether to accept or reject the invitation, to enter his Kingdom or remain outside. Thus, it is Jesus the Friend, the Good Shepherd, rather than the Christ of theology or ecclesiastical ritual, who comes to us, speaks to us in home, office, fellowship group, mountain-top or wherever – speaks, calls, invites and offers his priceless, gratis gifts. It is Jesus who makes sense of things and transforms our lives.

Important consequences follow from this centrality of direct relationship with God in Jesus. One has been an emphasis – undue emphasis some might say – on the experience of conversion. This is not, I think, a logical consequence but one which emerges from picturing Jesus as a tangible presence appealing in person to the uncommitted to make their choice – 'Behold, I stand at the door and knock'. Thus conceived, conversion becomes an invitation and a pledge to a decisive reversal of direction from one kind of life to another, darkness to light, falsehood to truth. Sometimes the decision is accompanied by great emotional stress, an enthusiastic[1] impulse of well-nigh irresistible power; as such it is a psychological phenomenon well known to the great evangelistic preachers, who have nurtured it to their advantage with emotive rhetoric and dramatic skill.

But it need not be thus. John Wesley's conversion was a spiritual revolution experienced in the inward quiet of his heart. It was critical, climactic, enthusiastic, compulsive – all of these; and although there was no outward display of emotion, it was nevertheless of momentous consequence for himself and for millions since. It brought a total reorientation of his Christian commitment, a commitment already long established but misconceived as 'what I can do for Christ'; now it was

[1] In the strict meaning of 'god-inspired'.

'what Christ does for me'. It brought him total peace of mind replacing the stressful toil of earlier years, and a new, dynamic motivation; from ecclesiastic he was transformed into evangelist.

I hope I may be forgiven for quoting once again the familiar description of what happened on May 24th, 1738. It illustrates not only the climactic nature of his conversion, the culmination of spiritual non-fulfilment, but also his new and very personal relationship with the Jesus whom he had striven, so earnestly yet so disappointingly, to serve. 'About a quarter before nine while [the reader] was describing the change which God works in the heart through faith in Christ, I felt my heart strangely warmed. I felt I did trust in Christ, Christ alone for salvation; and an assurance was given me that He had taken away *my* sins, even *mine*, and saved *me* from the law of sin and death.' (The emphases, of course, are his.)

I have never experienced conversion myself in this mode of sudden, decisive reorientation; indeed I sometimes wonder whether I *have* been converted! Two occasions stand out in retrospect when I know that Christ touched me through the hand of another; both of them I have described above, at Kingswood in the headmaster's study and in my own room at Cambridge. For me, a sceptic by nature and by training, conversion has been a process of gradual overpowering of mental resistance, a process of rational argument with myself and with others which has led me from possibility to probability and finally to acceptance in faith because I can see no other way: the mystery of final inexplicability yields only, albeit partially, to the incarnate Christ; he alone makes whatever sense of things my human condition permits.

A further consequence of this personal relationship with God in Christ is that religion becomes what in Wesley's time was called 'experimental'; today we would say 'experiential'. This means, first, that religion is deeply and comprehensively *inward*, involving not just intellect or feeling or any other element of our being in isolation, but the *whole* personality. It means, second, that the religious life is one of expanding exploration of the nature and purposes of God. Conversion is only a beginning, a first tentative step into unknown territory; life's vicissitudes are opportunities for deeper penetration and fuller understanding. It means, third, that in experience we have a means of confirming the truths of Scripture and doctrine. In this sense 'experiential' comes close to the modern meaning of 'experimental': theological truth, emerging from Scripture and expressed in doctrine, is proved by the experiment of living it out in practice.

Perhaps the most important consequence of this direct relationship with God in Christ is its emphasis on inward spirituality. For one is forced

XI THE PECULIAR BLESSINGS OF METHODISM 195

to ask of oneself, 'Am I, a sinful and imperfect creature, fit for such a relationship?' The answer is obviously 'no'; but one can strive towards what Wesley called 'scriptural holiness', the goal of which is 'Christian perfection'. Now clearly, perfection is not possible within the limitations of humanity, but by keeping it before one as the ultimate ideal one can at least, however haltingly, progress towards it. And so attention is focused, not so much on the outward manifestations of religion (though these lose none of their importance) as on inwardly preparing oneself, by obedience to Scripture and by methodical discipline, for the companionship of Christ. If not 'perfection', at least 'holiness' (of which there are many degrees and stages) is humanly attainable.

This inward emphasis is less obvious today, but in the early years of Methodism and throughout the 19th century it gave rise to a distinctive form of Methodist piety centred round Wesley's concept of scriptural holiness. Its primary constituents are faith and repentance, so closely fused that neither can be said to precede the other. Faith, wrote Wesley, is 'a sure trust and confidence that Christ died for *my* sins, that he loved *me* and gave himself for *me*' – which clearly implies a state of penitence and forgiven-ness. There follows 'salvation', a purging and redemption of one's sinful nature and a radical transformation of one's whole self, of which the outward aspect is a joyous life of love and devoted service. All of this comes, not of our doing or deserving, but by the grace of God, freely offered and gratefully received. Such, I believe, is still the heart of Methodism; it is the tradition in which, even in the 20th century, I have grown up and to which I remain imperfectly committed. Though its presence is less obvious as we near the end of the century, something of it is preserved in the charismatic and similar movements within the Church; especially is it perpetuated in the annual Covenant Service, which embodies both the essence of Methodist piety and its profoundly personal quality.

Many criticisms have been made of the personal, inward nature of the Methodist experience: it is over-emotional and anti-intellectual; it pays too little attention to theology, the Church and its sacraments; it is individualistic and introverted and ignores the corporate nature of Christianity. When inwardness is practised at the expense of other elements of spiritual life, there is ground for all these strictures; but it need not and should not be so. Conversion, whether it comes as a blinding vision or a strange warming of the heart, involves powerful emotions; how could it be otherwise when what is happening is a total reorientation of personality against the resistance of subconscious forces deep within? But conversion is only a beginning; there must follow a disciplined, methodical exploration and expansion of experience through prayer, fellowship, study and the practice of Christian morality. The convert, if his commitment is genuine, cannot avoid theology – not necessarily academic theology, though this will be the way for some, and there have been many eminent Methodist theologians. The basic truths of Christian doctrine are simple and intelligible to all; they must be known and understood with mind as well as heart. Certainly John Wesley regarded theology with the greatest respect; he preached it continually throughout the fifty years of his itinerant ministry, a theology of particular emphases within a wider doctrinal structure. Nor was he unaware of the dangers of a commitment based only on emotion: 'the question is not concerning the heart, but the life'; mere feeling offers only a foundation of sand.

There is greater justification for the charge that Methodism has been indifferent to the Church beyond itself – the catholic Church – and neglectful of its liturgy. Again, this cannot be said of Wesley himself, who remained a devoted Anglican throughout his life and saw Methodism, not as a separate Church, but as a movement within the Church of England, recalling it to certain theological essentials, derived from Scripture, which had come to be overlooked. I wish that Methodists today were more aware of the universal Church of Christ, of which they are but a small part, and better informed of a history and tradition which has been forged over twenty centuries, often at great cost in sacrifice, suffering and martyrdom. Indeed, I wish that they were more aware of their own origins and history and of the spiritual truths that inspired them. I wish that there were greater observance of the Christian Festivals in addition to Christmas and Easter and of the more notable Saints' Days. I wish that the order of worship for Sunday Service were more regularly used and its memorable language taken to heart (and that a new edition of *The Methodist Service Book* will also include an order for Evensong). But above all I wish that the Eucharist or Holy Communion were more normally included in our worship – and as an integral part, not, as so often, abbreviated and tacked on, like an appendix or afterthought, to the end of a morning or evening service. Here again we should look to John Wesley, who recommended constant attendance at Holy Communion and received it himself sometimes two or three times a week. Yet none of what I wish for should be at the expense of that direct, personal relationship with God in Christ which is Methodism's greatest blessing.

As for the charge that Methodism disposes towards individualistic introversion, this is simply not true. In a few of its members this may indeed be the outcome of inward spirituality and close personal relationship with Christ; but they are exceptional. Christianity, in its Methodist interpretation and practice, is an outgoing religion; it seeks to share the good news with others; and love, which is at the heart of the Gospel, cannot be kept to oneself. From the very beginning of his evangelistic work Wesley encouraged the formation of small groups, each under the guidance of a leader, which would meet regularly for prayer, Bible study and religious discussion. These society classes, as they came to be known, were a powerful means of promoting the spiritual growth of their members in understanding the Gospel and its implications. In their original form and organisation society classes no longer exist; but groups still meet and with much the same purpose; now, as then, they are a valuable means of *mutual* edification, enrichment and support and a safeguard against spiritual isolation. Such fellowship is not restricted to these groups; it permeates Methodism and is among its most conspicuous emphases and peculiar blessings; I shall have more to say of it later.

Another blessing which I owe to my growth within Methodism is an emphasis on the Bible as a source of spiritual and moral guidance. Here, not in creed or catechism, not in liturgy, ceremony or symbolism (important though all these are in their due place) is the authentic well-spring from which flow doctrine and the inspiration to live by it. In the Gospels we meet the living Christ, listen to his teaching, and are assured of his continued presence among us. In the rest of the New Testament we see the early Christians forging a theology from their knowledge, direct and indirect, of Jesus and his vital activity among them. The Bible as a whole is the word of God, a progressive revelation of his being and nature, a means by which his grace is mediated and made effective in human lives. Such was John Wesley's conviction; and, although obscured and undervalued at times, it has remained a permanent possession of the Methodist Church. It was 'scriptural holiness' that Wesley strove for as the basis of 'Christian perfection'; it was to the Scriptures that he turned for confirmation of doctrine. Further confirmation might be found in experience, but the ultimate reference, under the guidance of the Holy Spirit, was to Scripture. 'At any price,' he wrote in the preface to his *Sermons*, 'give me the book of God! I have it: here is knowledge enough for me. Let me be *homo unius libri* [a man of one book]'. In fact he was a man of wide reading and many books, but the Bible was unique among them in its disclosure of Christian truth.

The exposition of Scripture quickly assumed a place of primary importance in Methodist worship. For Wesley himself, a committed Anglican, it was an addendum to the liturgical services of the Church of England; but for most of his fellow evangelists and their congregations preaching from a biblical text was central to their worship. Hence derived the Methodist architecture of the 19th and early 20th centuries which placed the pulpit in a central position and the altar, as if of lesser significance, below it. This emphasis on exposition and its supporting architecture are the more understandable for a period when most of those who listened were illiterate and had no direct access to the Bible; we have since learnt that they obscure other and equally important modes of worship. Accordingly, in modern Methodist churches the pulpit is at the side and the altar has been restored to its rightful place at the focus of visual and mental concentration. We have been slower to modify the structure of our worship (it depends so much on the individual minister); but this too is changing to allow greater prominence to liturgical forms of prayer and response, to music, drama – and even to silence!

There are obvious dangers in a dependence on Scripture as the source of doctrine and authority, and in making its exposition the core and justification of worship. Overemphasised it can induce in congregations a passive credulity which exposes them to rostrum-thumping evangelism of the verbal inspiration, 'Bible says' variety. In the past it has brought resistance to biblical scholarship and the findings of science. 'The Bible,' wrote one 19th-century evangelist, 'has not a single scientific error in it'; and Wesley himself accepted the biblical account of creation as literal truth. We claim to know better now! It is easy to take one's stand on 'the simple Gospel' and evade those major problems with which that not-so-simple Gospel presents us – as, for instance, the mystery of evil within the loving providence of God. Again, what *is* Scripture? How much is authentic and how much has been read into events from a later and very different context – 'memories embroidered and enhanced by excited and devout imagination'? Moreover, Scripture is not all of equal value, theologically or morally. Much of the Old Testament is sublime in both respects, but much of it is not – for instance, the sexual intrigues of King David and his family. In the New Testament there are problems of date, text, authorship and interpretation. We cannot be sure that the Gospels give us the actual words of Jesus – rarely indeed in the language he spoke. Clearly, Scripture must be read sensitively, informedly and selectively if we are to elicit its truths.

With these cautions in mind I gratefully acknowledge and welcome the Methodist emphasis on Scripture. The need for exposition has raised up generation after generation of preachers, ordained and lay, men and women, who have made it their task to interpret the texts they have chosen from the Bible. Through two centuries their influence, both spiritual and in a more widely educative sense, has been immense; among them have been some of the most eminent preachers of their time. In the early days they had little to read but the Bible and the Wesleyan Hymn-book; later they were supported by commentaries which deepened their understanding of what God was saying through them. Now, of course, there is a wealth of scholarship on which to draw.

As for myself, I have twice read the Bible through from beginning to end, marking passages of special significance and possible texts for sermons. This is an exercise that every preacher should undertake once; I am not sure that I would recommend it for twice! For over fifty years I have tried to make a point of reading from it daily; for the New Testament I have normally had a commentary at hand, and my classical education has made available the original Greek – a valuable check on divergent and sometimes eccentric translations! In this I have found a continual source of enrichment and renewal, of encouragement, comfort and guidance. For the Bible, despite its many problems and imperfections (for it is a *human* composition, however divinely inspired), is a treasury of spiritual aspiration unsurpassed in sublimity both of sentiment and also of language. I could not claim to have achieved the 'scriptural holiness' that Wesley sought and preached, but the Bible has pointed the way.

Fellowship is another characteristic of Methodism and among its most important contributions to the doctrines and practice of the Christian Church. By fellowship I mean here the coming together of persons committed to assisting one another towards a deeper understanding of God and a more effective discipleship. But there is more to it than that; for in thus coming together they create between themselves a felt bond of intimacy and mutual concern which itself has value as a means to spiritual growth. Once again, I would not be thought to suggest that fellowship came into existence only with, and belongs only to, the Methodist Church. It has been a part of religious observance throughout the history of religion – a meeting in community of spirit of persons seeking a common purpose in life and experience. It was a feature of the early Christian Church, the *koinonia* or community of believers sharing a common belief within an alien and often hostile world. In John Wesley's time it was revived by the Moravians of Saxony, and it was from them that he learnt much of its value and practice. (Its value has also been recognised and exploited by political parties and a variety of secular cults and sects.)

Wesley was quick to perceive its importance, and the means of fellowship were built into the Methodist Church from the beginning – even before it became a separately identifiable entity. The need for it had been apparent to him before his conversion; he had found it in the Holy Club at Oxford, which his brother Charles had organised with a group of friends seeking a more rigorous and *methodical* pursuit of the Christian life. He had found it too among the Moravians with whom he shared the voyage to Georgia in 1735. When Methodist 'societies' began to be formed, they were divided into 'classes'[1] of about a dozen;

---

[1] The word meant simply 'division', not a means of instruction, which is the dominant meaning today.

membership was open to all who desired 'to flee from the wrath to come' and to seek 'scriptural holiness'. Each had a lay leader who exercised a general supervision over the spiritual welfare of its members, distributed the quarterly tickets of membership and collected a small contribution towards the expenses of the 'society'. They met for prayer, Bible study and religious discussion, including confession of sins and witness to the work of God in individual lives. Members who were sick or too old to attend were regularly visited by the leader or other members. In some 'societies' men and women met separately; there were therefore women leaders, a fact which helped to establish the importance of women within the nascent Methodist Church. In addition to 'society classes' there were also 'bands', a more intimate fellowship group of earnest seekers after holiness, who confessed and discussed 'plain and home' and in confidence their sins and shortcomings and prayed for improvement. How widely these were established within Methodism is uncertain; in time they came to appear superfluous and were absorbed into the 'classes'.

The original organisation and discipline of 'classes' and 'bands' were so precise and detailed as deservedly to attract the name 'methodist'. This is tolerable within religious orders, but ordinary human nature does not readily submit to such regulation; and public confession of sin does not come easily to most of us. Inevitably 'classes' have been modified and adapted during the two centuries since Wesley's death: they are no longer, I think, called 'society classes', nor do we have 'class leaders'; we are no longer issued with quarterly 'class tickets' but with annual 'tickets of membership'; and membership of a class is no longer obligatory. But in one form or another the tradition of the 'class' has persisted: we have prayer meetings, Bible classes, youth groups, men's fellowships, women's fellowships (the sexes are still separate in some churches!), house groups and many other comings together whose purposes are not far different from those of Wesley's day – mutual support in spiritual growth, and the effective implementation in today's world of the teaching of Jesus.

My first experience of this kind of fellowship was in the 'groups' at Cambridge. I have written of these above and told how, in the welcoming atmosphere of a small company brought together by a common purpose, constraint fell away and discussion on all manner of topics was lively and uninhibited. Perhaps they were not scriptural enough for John Wesley's liking, but they were helpful to all of us in expanding our Christian vision in both theological understanding and social conscience. Particularly was this true of the first 'group' I attended, which was privileged (myself especially) to have Charles and Eileen Coulson as its leaders.

In such groups, if wisely led, the ebullient are restrained and the diffident encouraged; and in the interchange of discussion from different personal backgrounds truths emerge which would not have occurred to any individual alone. No doubt there are psychological explanations for this, but I prefer to regard it as evidence of the working of the Holy Spirit. Fellowship groups, whatever name they meet under and wherever, are an invaluable means of support, guidance and spiritual growth for their members. They can also be instrumental in taking the Gospel beyond the confines of the church; for their influence permeates beyond the group itself into the whole society or congregation and beyond that again to the neighbourhood outside, bringing this too, less intimately yet meaningfully, within the encompassing arms of fellowship. A church which makes no provision for them is failing in its responsibility; a church-goer who is not a member of one is missing out on something very precious. Built into Methodism from its beginnings, it is a part of our tradition which we must strive to preserve.

I move now to another feature of Methodism which means a great deal to me, the freedom of its worship and the fact that, apart from the obvious exceptions like the orders of service for Holy Communion, Baptism and Marriage, it is not bound to liturgical forms. In its origins Methodism combines liturgy with spontaneity and freedom in worship. As I have pointed out earlier, the preaching service with its extempore prayer and exuberant singing was an addition to the liturgical worship of the Book of Common Prayer. That was John Wesley's intention; he set an example by his own conscientious observance of the latter, and he enjoined his followers to do the same. So it long remained; it was only in the course of time that 'free worship' acquired a separate identity which led to the formation of a distinct Methodist Church owing no obligation to Anglican orders of worship. There were several reasons for this apart from the aversion to a prescribed liturgy: the influence of the informal 'class' or 'band' permeating the wider 'society' of the whole membership; an evangelical fervour which resisted the bonds (as they were seen) of liturgy; and the growing importance of lay preachers, who had no liturgical training and preferred their own initiative in ordering worship.

We can see now that there is no contradiction or incompatibility between these two kinds of worship; each is enriched by the infusion of the other. Methodism at its best preserves both traditions; it is a 'free church' which welcomes into the freedom of its nonconformity the discipline of a formal liturgy – but not to the extent of dominating the experience of worship. During my lifetime, especially the early part, the tradition of spontaneity has been dominant. Generally, preachers both lay and ordained have adhered to the established Methodist pattern of hymns, readings, prayers and sermon, but have felt free to adapt their conduct of worship to the needs or inspiration of the occasion; prayer has been extempore and readings chosen to suit the theme of worship. The dangers in this have become apparent: the Methodist 'multiple sandwich' of hymn, prayer, hymn, lesson, etc. can become a liturgical form of its own, frozen by habit into a repetitive formula which diminishes the act of worship; it can lead to a casualness or excessive informality in the conduct of worship whose effect is the same. Unthinking acceptance of routine differs vastly from the fervent spontaneity of genuine 'free worship'. Neglect of the liturgy in Sunday worship can lead also to neglect of the sacramental liturgy of Eucharist or Holy Communion. This has happened; I have mentioned it earlier and noted Wesley's advice to attend Communion as often as possible; the Methodist movement which he initiated was both an evangelical *and* a sacramental revival. As for extempore prayer, I have unhappy memories of rambling, incoherent, long-winded mouthings of cliches remote from the realities of worship. It need not be so, of course. As I have suggested earlier, extempore prayer in public worship should bear the semblance of such while in fact carefully prepared and rehearsed beforehand. Genuinely extempore prayer is more appropriate to the privacy of one's own room, where it can be as incoherent and extended as may be – God doesn't care as long as it comes from the heart; or to the close intimacy of a class meeting or house group.

In recent years there has been wider recognition (not yet, I think, wide enough) of the liturgical contribution to the experience of worship. In part this has been due to the influence of a world-wide and interdenominational movement towards 'liturgical renewal', an endeavour to bring alive and make fruitful for modern worshippers the traditional formulae of the Christian Church. A manifestation of this can be seen in *The Book of Common Worship* prepared for the united Church of South India and authorised for use in 1962. Prior to this, in 1958, the Methodist Conference had appointed a Commission to investigate and report on public worship in Methodist churches. Its Report, approved in 1960, recognised the parallel traditions, liturgical and 'free', and its recommendations were aimed at enabling both to play a vitalising role in worship.

Among the welcome consequences of this has been the publication in 1975 of *The Methodist Service Book*, replacing *The Book of Offices* of 1936. The *Service Book*, states its preface, is 'not intended . . . to curb creative freedom, but rather to provide norms for its guidance'. It offers traditional forms in a style and language more suited to the mood of the 20th century; in particular it has abandoned the 'Thou' and 'Thee' of tradition, which has become an archaism distancing the Church from ordinary life. With this wider acceptance of liturgy have also come moves towards liberating 'free worship' from the straitness of the 'multiple sandwich': diversifying the 'sandwich' by changing the order and emphasis of its contents; inviting participation by the whole congregation of worshippers; using song, dance and drama as means of communicating the Gospel. Our new hymn-book, *Hymns and Psalms* (1983), includes hymns in modern idiom of language and music as well as the older well-known hymns of the Wesleys and earlier centuries; it thus links us with past and present, old and new, and brings us closer to our fellow-Christians of other denominations (as its sub-title, 'A Methodist and Ecumenical Hymn Book' hopefully claims).[1]

Methodism's 'free worship' has expressed itself especially in its hymns and its singing. The 1933 Hymn-book asserts categorically that 'Methodism was born in song'. I am not sure that this is historically accurate, but it is a fact that the Wesleys, John and Charles, found in hymns a potent means of theological teaching and spiritual fellowship. Charles is said to have written over 6000 hymns – far too many I dare to suggest; fewer might have been better. But he was capable of great poetry; his themes include every aspect of Christian experience, especially the great fundamental truths of our faith. Many of his hymns have become a treasured possession throughout Christendom, among them the two triumphant paeans of irrepressible praise that we sing at Christmas and Easter: 'Hark! the herald-angels sing' and 'Christ the Lord is risen today'.

It has been said that 'the spirit of early Methodism is discernible more clearly in its hymns than anywhere else'. Not only of early Methodism, however; for the tradition has persisted and wherever Methodists meet today, as likely as not you will find them singing. Here again there are dangers. John Wesley was well aware of them and he advised his Methodists: 'Sing *lustily* and with a good courage . . . Sing *modestly*. Do not bawl . . . Above all sing *spiritually*. Have an eye to God in every word you sing . . . attend strictly to the sense of what you sing, and see that your heart is not carried away with the sound but offered to God continually'.[2] His precepts are difficult to obey; we all know how easy it is to sing with less than half one's mind while the rest is planning tomorrow's

---

[1] Another Report, *Let the People Worship*, was presented to Conference in 1988. It notes significant changes in the intervening years both in society and in the life of the Church; it points also to a widespread disquiet about the condition of Methodist worship and a hunger for something more satisfying. It offers many helpful observations on the nature and conduct of worship.

[2] Quoted in Davies, R. E., *Methodism* (Penguin 1963), p. 114.

shopping or the needs of the garden! Most of the hymns in *Hymns and Psalms* are suitable for private meditation and should be more often so used. In public worship, instead of simply announcing the number of a hymn and reading the first verse, it may be helpful to introduce it briefly, just a sentence drawing attention to its general theme or to particular items of theological or spiritual content. Alternatively, instead of or prior to singing a hymn we might read it through, preacher and congregation together, aloud or silently, and then meditate for a few moments on its message. Certainly, Methodism's hymns and its singing are a great, some would say its *greatest*, contribution to the Christian heritage; it is a blessing we must both preserve and use more deliberately for our spiritual edification.

It must be clear from the preceding paragraphs that I acknowledge the value of liturgy and its contribution to worship: it orders our spiritual experience, giving it form and content; it focuses heart and mind upon the central truths of our faith; it links us with the tradition of the whole Christian Church; its language is often noble and by constant repetition becomes creatively a part of oneself. There is a strong case for regular liturgical worship within Methodism, not every Sunday, but monthly perhaps and conducted by the minister; and also for using prayers of the traditional liturgy, for instance the prayers of preparation and confession and many of the collects. Nevertheless, I could not either as a worshipper or a lay preacher forsake our Methodist tradition of 'free worship'.

As a worshipper I welcome the variety which comes from different preachers conducting worship in their own style and developing a scriptural theme according to their personal vision and interpretation. Liturgy can be constrictive, spiritually claustrophobic; by contrast, *at its best* 'free worship' liberates: the inspiration of the Holy Spirit, channeled through the individual preacher, brings to worship a certain freshness and exuberance. As a lay preacher I welcome the freedom to open myself to that inspiration, whether from within or without, from my own spiritual quest, from the prompting of circumstances, or from the needs of a particular congregation. Moreover, power and persuasion in preaching are more likely, I think, to come from a text that is chosen rather than imposed by a lectionary. There may be a salutary discipline in obedience to the latter; but discipline comes also from prayerful meditation upon a text which has sprung with sudden illumination from the pages of Scripture. In the ordering of worship a lay preacher has only limited opportunity for innovation; he or she is likely to be an infrequent visitor to any particular pulpit, and the reaction of a congregation may be difficult to predict. However, the familiar 'sandwich' can be varied by a re-ordering of its content; and instead of the usual 'solo performance' the preacher can invite his congregation to share the conduct of worship by reading the lessons and in responsive prayer. Methodism was born and grew in a double practice of worship, liturgical and 'free'; I hope this parallel tradition will be preserved and strengthened, but with the greater emphasis on the latter.

A characteristic feature of Methodism throughout its 250 years has been a commitment to evangelism, to spreading the good news (which of course is what 'evangel' means). This commitment is not confined to Methodism; apart from those religious orders which practise silence or solitude, Christianity is an outgoing religion; its news is too good to be kept to oneself. But among the blessings of Methodism I would rank this (for me) among the most important. Evangelism takes many forms; primarily it means preaching the Gospel, the good news of salvation through Jesus Christ; but I would include within it any venture which, under God's guidance, seeks to elevate humanity, whether physically, intellectually, aesthetically or spiritually, and brings it nearer to perfection.

John Wesley claimed the whole world as his parish. In fact, after his 1738 experience his evangelism was confined to the British Isles; but from then on until he was seventy he travelled up to 5000 miles a year, mostly on horseback, preaching four or five times a day to any who were willing to hear 'the glad tidings of salvation'. Others, my father and brother among them, have since carried the good news all over the world; the Wesleyan, later simply Methodist, Missionary Society remains a flourishing Division of the Methodist Church, though there has inevitably and properly been a transfer of responsibility to the local Churches which it has helped to establish. Most of John Wesley's preaching was in the open air: the parish churches were not opened to him – and they could not contain the numbers who thronged to hear him. This has remained a Methodist tradition; few have the gift for it and fewer still have practised it with such dedication, mental agility and persuasive power as Lord Soper. There are dangers, as I have suggested, in placing too much emphasis on conversion; but there is surely a primary obligation upon the Christian to preach, whether by word or deed or manner of life, the Gospel of Jesus Christ. Methodism has always given priority to this.

Home Missions also flourishes; this has been widened to include not only the conversion of those on our own doorstep, but concern for their welfare in social justice and quality of life. In these latter Methodism has again been eminent. Wesley set the example by his constant attention to social problems: 'Do all the good you can', he advised, 'in all the ways you can, as long as you can.' He strove to improve the lot of prisoners, established dispensaries for the poor, attacked slavery, smuggling and political corruption. He prepared and distributed a great number of cheap books and tracts, many written by himself, on a wide range of topics from grammars and dictionaries to pamphlets on medical care; the considerable profits from these were all given to charitable causes. He demonstrated abundantly in his own life a deep concern for the material as well as the spiritual welfare of the under-privileged. He has indeed justifiably been named the greatest social reformer of his age. Methodism has perpetuated his concern in its Department of Temperance and Social Welfare, renamed in 1949 the Department of Christian Citizenship, and now the Division of Social Responsibility.

Wesley was especially convinced of the importance of education. Today the ability to read and write is taken for granted (not that it should be); but not so in the 18th century. The Bible was an open book only to those who could read it; literacy was thus a necessary tool of evangelism; more than that, by enabling them to read and write for themselves it gave men and women a new dignity and self-confidence. His preachers in particular, both ordained and lay, must have access not only to the Bible but also to theological works; they must *know* their faith. His many books and pamphlets were one outcome of Wesley's educational zeal: he deemed it an obligation to inform the uninformed if thereby he might improve their quality of life and also bring them nearer to salvation; he believed also that knowledge – of the right kind – has value as knowledge. Another outcome was Kingswood School, his most lasting educational memorial but not the only school he helped to establish.

After his death education remained a prime concern within Methodism. When universal elementary education became an issue of public demand and policy in the 19th century, the Wesleyan Education Committee vied with Anglicans and Roman Catholics in establishing denominational schools; at their peak there were nearly 1000 Wesleyan Schools, of which mine at Barny was one. Meanwhile more schools after the model of Kingswood had been founded in Britain and overseas by the Wesleyan and other sections of the Methodist Church. Now that education is in the hands of the DES and Local Authorities, Methodism retains its concern. It does so directly in a small number of Methodist primary schools, in its residential schools (of which Kingswood is one), and in its colleges, which provide a Christian content and orientation for graduate studies and the training of teachers. Indirectly its concern is shown in a critical surveillance of government policy and administration. And as the meaning of education has expanded, so too concern has widened to include the environment and its educative influence. Through its Division of Education and Youth education is still seen as an instrument of evangelism – not quite as Wesley saw it, but no less powerful.

Growing up within Methodism I could not escape its evangelical fervour. However, I felt no call to follow my father and brother into the ordained ministry. Instead I came to perceive education as a form of evangelism for which I was better suited; this would be *my* call, *my* life's work; lay preaching would be an important addition. I became fired with an enthusiasm for knowledge, to find it for myself and pass it on to others. This has been the constant motivation of my professional teaching and lecturing and of the books I have written and edited – to know for myself and pass that knowledge on to others, to stimulate thought, to enable understanding, to uncover truth. These are means to freedom and independence; they make us better men and women; they offer a more securely founded faith. As such they are instruments of evangelism. True, they do not necessarily make converts to Christianity (and I am often troubled by the thought how few, if any, have come to Christ through me); but they contribute to J. S. Mill's 'improvement of mankind' and so, I believe, may bring the Kingdom of God a little nearer. I am grateful, therefore, deeply grateful, for this blessing of evangelistic zeal that Methodism has given me and which has found expression in academic work. It has given me a strength, enthusiasm and joyousness of motivation which I doubt could have come from any other source.

Such then are the 'peculiar blessings' which I ascribe to Methodism: its warmth; its offer of direct relationship with God in Christ; its emphasis on Scripture and fellowship; its 'free worship', its singing; its ardour of evangelism. All, as I have suggested, have attendant dangers which require a watchful guard; but such vigilance is an acceptable price for blessings so precious in their potential for spiritual enrichment. Of course, there may be others which I have overlooked and which fellow Methodists would wish to include; of course, too, the whole as always is greater than the sum of its parts and the total richness of Methodism far exceeds this analysis into singular items. Once again I would emphasise that these blessings are not unique to Methodism; I make no such claim. It so happens that Methodism is the mode of Christianity I have grown up in, and I have written here from my own experience.

I look back now over seventy years, but my travelling along with Methodism is not yet finished; it has reached a phase perhaps more suitably called 'growing old with Methodism'. A faith that claims the allegiance of one's living must also be a faith that assists one's dying – and to look beyond death with serene and confident hope. I have no doubt that in this too Methodism's richness of blessing, upheld by the love of God in Christ, will be confirmed.